Educating the Educators

Hispanism and its Institutions

Malcolm K. Read

Newark: University of Delaware Press

Monash Romance Studies

General Editor: Brian Nelson

Monash Romance Studies is a series of refereed scholarly publications devoted to the study of any aspect of French, Italian and Spanish literature, language, culture and civilization. It will publish books and collections of essays on specific themes, and is open to scholars associated with academic institutions other than Monash.

Proposals for the series should be addressed to the general editor, from whom details of volumes previously published in the series are available:

Professor Brian Nelson
School of Languages, Cultures and Linguistics
Building 11
Monash University
Melbourne Vic. 3800
Australia.

Fax (+61 3) 9905 5437
Email: brian.nelson@arts.monash.edu.au

First American edition published 2003

Associated University Presses
2010 Eastpark Blvd
Cranbury, NJ 08512
ISBN 0-87413-840-X

Cataloging-in-Publication Data is on file with the Library of Congress

"How?" cried the Mayor, "d'ye think I'll brook
Being worse treated than a Cook?
Insulted by a lazy ribald
With idle pipe and vesture piebald?
You threaten us, fellow? Do your worst
Blow your pipe there till you burst."

Once more he stept into the street;
And to his lips again
Laid his long pipe of smooth straight cane ...

(The Pied Piper of Hamelin)

Contents

Acknowledgements   i

Preface   ii

Introduction   1

1 Traveling South: Ideology and Hispanism   13

Crisis of a Discipline   13
Imaginary Communities   16
Birth of a Discipline   20
Recent Developments   25
National Literature in a Global Economy   27

2 Allison Peers: For God, King and Country   31

Telling Tales   31
Drabtown versus Oxbridge   35
The Scholarship Boy   38
"A Truly Liberal Education"   40
Manning the Gates   43
The Claims of Specialization   46
University Administration   47
The Academy and the State   49
Marginalized Women, Excluded Proletarians   52
Conclusion   54

3 The Making of a Hispanist   55

4 Writing in the Institution: Malcolm K. Read and Paul Julian Smith   73

Introduction   73
In the Prison-House of Empiricism   74
Hegel without Hegel   76
Postmodern Beginnings   78
A Star is Born   81
The Matter of Freud   83
Inscriptions of Desire   84

The Ideological Unconscious   86
Bodies, Bodies and More Bodies   88
Transitional Discourses   92
Freedom to be Exploited   96

5 Who walked a Crooked Mile   **99**

6 In the Meantime: British Hispanism and the Rise of
Cultural Studies   **115**

Realist Social Theory   117
Some Problems and Re-definitions   120
Constraining Contradiction: the Parkerian Tradition   123
The Unconscious Empiricism of Parkerianism   125
Empiricism and Class Conflict   127
Concomitant Compatibilities   129
The Emergence of Competitive Contradiction: the Case of Psychoanalysis 133
Conflictual Ideologies   135
After the Break   137
The Moment of Competitive Contradiction   139
Contingent Complementarity   142
The Advent of Cultural Studies   146
Conclusion   148

7 Placing Changes   **151**

Bibliography   165
About the author   171

Acknowledgements

"Traveling South: Ideology and Hispanism," first appeared in the *Journal of Hispanic Philology*, 15 (1991), 193-207. I am grateful to the editors and publishers in question for permission to use this material in the present book. "In the Meantime: British Hispanism and the Rise of Cultural Studies" was accepted for publication by *Hispanic Cultural Studies* but subject to changes so far reaching as to reconfigure radically the article's design and critical scope. Consequently, it was withheld from publication by its author and incorporated into the present text. Successive versions of *Educating the Educators* were submitted to Liverpool University Press, and held by it for several years, before being rejected on the grounds that the Press suddenly found itself "over-committed."

Preface

It is not uncommon these days to discover in the middle-class press complaints about the continuing educational failure of working-class youth. Linda Grant's "Lessons to be learnt," which appeared in *The Guardian Weekly,* is typical of the genre. It points to a social situation in which, in Britain, girls and ethnic minorities, otherwise the "new technological proletariat," are taking advantage of "greater educational equality" to the detriment of boys. The latter, pressed down to the level of a lumpen underclass, are in danger of becoming recruitment fodder for neo-fascism.

There is a predictability about the journalistic response to what is undeniably a very real problem. The boys are blamed for their inadequate "strategies" and "over-confidence," and for "drifting along in a world that has no bearing on reality." Fifteen year-old Gavin Morgan, of Tony Upper School, Bradford, who thinks that exams are "crap," is singled out as a case in point. Ms Grant struggles to contain her contempt for this pupil and for the parents who condone his attitude. Not for a second does she pause to consider whether the ultimate determination of such social behavior lies not in individual motivation or lack of it, but in the dictates of a capitalist business cycle; whether it is an economic system, rather than "attitudes," that produces failure as a source of unskilled labor; and whether, in a world in which qualifications ensure neither good pay nor even steady work, it could be Gavin Morgan, rather than the high-brow press, who has the most objective grasp of the exchange value of education.

However, if I pause to consider Ms Grant's article in more detail than I normally would, it is not for her blindness to structural causality but for her evocation of a postwar period that many people view retrospectively with growing nostalgia. Laudably, Ms Grant insists on its very real defects: "When parents argue now for the return of selection, they usually forget that when it existed the majority of children did not go to grammar schools, and the child who should have passed the 11-plus, but didn't, would need all his or her wits to find a way to acquire any qualifications at all, let alone enter higher education." The exam to which she refers was indeed a fateful event, not least for those who fell on the wrong side of the binary cut. I recall particularly the manner in which the results were conveyed to myself and fellow classmates. The headmaster and his smiling, self-satisfied deputy lined us up one gray, windswept afternoon. The playground, they informed us, was untidy and part of the class was to be detailed to collect the litter. Silently, almost dramatically, the headmaster walked down the line, like a sergeant major reviewing his troops. And as he proceeded, he tapped on the chest those of us whose lot in life it was to labor manually, beginning that very afternoon. The remaining pupils were led inside, and within a few minutes, the school exploded to their distant, joyful cries. We stood and listened outside, as the significance of the occasion gradually dawned. "Me mam 'n dad'll kill me," blubbered one. (Inside the cheers continued.) "There goes me brand new bike," mused another. A few affected not to give a damn. But for all of them it was a long walk home through the streets that day.

Ms Grant is right. This is a scenario that now many usually forget. The only stories that were ever told were those of the successful, notably of the "scholarship boy," who *did* make it into higher education. But even he, notoriously and for his own good reasons, only ever wanted to forget. As for the majority of children, who failed, their voices have remained silent: history, after all, is written by the likes of Ms Grant, and she, as we have seen, blames these failures for perversely refusing to see "qualifications" as the gateway to the "good life." If only they had a different attitude! True, there were odd rejects that did "have their wits about them" and so were able to give the system the slip. Whatever became of them? Perhaps they could have been mined for case studies, through which to furnish models worthy of emulation by their comrades? Ms Grant is welcome to mine. Hi lads, remember me?

Briefly, every imaginable obstacle was placed in my path to make sure that my exclusion at eleven would stick. At each step of the way, I was made to feel cheap and common, denigrated for my squat working class body, my accent, spelling, table manners, in short, for my whole "culture." On more than one occasion, when attempting to defend proletarian values, I was told quite openly that I had no right being in the academy and invited to return to the gutter from which I had so presumptuously crawled. Subjected to all kinds of unbearable pressures, isolated and alone, I sometimes teetered on the edge of breakdown and despair. For my own reasons, I also only ever wanted to forget.

But that was in times gone by. Things change, not least of all in politics, where memories are particularly short. As Ms Grant reminds us, attempts are currently being made to resurrect selection, notably by Blair's New Labour, whose program is to be "education, education, education." The "old" parades as the "new," to the extent that it is suddenly necessary to remind people how it really was. My aim is not simply, or primarily, to haunt the living, although I have sometimes dreamed of vengeance, but rather to explore and *dramatize* the workings of ideology, and the ways in which human beings, in order to operate as social agents, identify with, internalize and, sometimes, resist the existing world.

*   *   *

Of all the intellectual projects that I have undertaken throughout what now qualifies as a long academic career, none has been more bedeviled by fate and circumstance than the present one. In its original form my manuscript consisted of a number of disparate articles, published and unpublished, on British and North-American Hispanism, that were held together simply by a common, thematic concern with institutional issues and by certain autobiographical threads, which loosely attached the theoretical articles to one autobiographical chapter ("The Making of a Hispanist"). At this stage, Mike Sprinker, whose opinion as a reader I valued above anyone's, was significantly guarded in his response. In its current form, he felt, the manuscript's structure left something to be desired, in that some of the occasional pieces and book reviews made little sense when detached from the ongoing debates out of which they originally grew; there was a notable omission of any discussion of more recent developments in Latin Americanism within North America; and the autobiographical chapter, although in itself well written and often moving, was of doubtful relevance to a volume on Hispanism. At the same time, Mike did concede that if my story had been continued, through university and postgraduate studies, some connections and continuities might have become apparent. In response, I argued that, while Mike's first two points were undoubtedly valid, I strongly disagreed with him about the autobiographical chapter, which was, in my view, the crux of the whole project. To which Mike responded in an equally forthright manner: yes, the autobiographical chapter was certainly basic to the others, but it "ought to remain buried, viz., [...] should inform your work without having to tell the tale itself." He also argued that the autobiographical asides in my other pieces, while interesting in themselves, could prove distracting to my main line of argument.

Our correspondence broke off at that point – we agreed to continue our discussion on my return to Stony Brook from sabbatical leave in New Zealand. My intention was to press the claim that, rather than moments of personal indulgence, the autobiographical asides were nervous anticipations of a broader project, relating to issues of structure and agency, which was struggling to emerge, however imperfectly, in *Educating the Educators*. More specifically, while I accepted the existence of social structures that totally transcended individual awareness, I objected strongly to the Althusserian tendency to see individuals as "mere supports," instead of complex structures in their own right, through which, in the last instance, social structures were necessarily mediated. The implication was that my autobiographical component actually needed to be enlarged and woven more closely into the texture of the work. But our anticipated discussion – Mike's and mine – never took place: tragically, Mike died that summer, physically devastated by cancer. And so my project temporarily lay in limbo.

Some time later, I resuscitated the manuscript with a couple of chapters on more recent developments in North-American Hispanism, while eliminating the more incidental pieces, along the lines of Mike's suggestions. However, true to my own original conception, I also added a second autobiographical chapter ("Who Walked a Crooked Mile"), on my early academic career. The response of colleagues, to whom I submitted the final result for comments, was not encouraging. Several obviously felt that I had gone over the top in terms of political rhetoric and ad hominem criticism. More painfully, others failed to respond at all, as if embarrassed by the whole enterprise. So again *Educating the Educators* stalled and I was side-tracked by other, less problematic projects and by my involvement with translating and promoting the work of Juan Carlos Rodríguez.

But it was to be the ongoing attempt to master the Spaniard's theoretical concepts that, paradoxically, sent me back to my own, earlier ruminations on structure and agency. I had long been interested in the personal relevance of the Althusserian concept of the "ideological unconscious," and indeed had arrived at an understanding of it through the light that it shed upon my own intellectual development, even while acknowledging that this application flew in the face of Rodríguez's own emphasis upon the social structures as opposed to individual "psychology." My preoccupation with issues of agency found support in Rodríguez's own increasing attentiveness, in his more recent work, to the mediations exercised by individualities, particularly when it came to theorizing the poetic production of a number of contemporary Granadine poets. How could a poet be totally constrained by an ideological unconscious, Rodríguez speculated, and yet "know" that s/he was so constrained? How could one write bilingually, from within and outside a language? etc. One seminal comment caught my attention: a reference to contradictions "que la filosofía siempre había intentado *representar* y *suturar* y la literatura siempre había intentado *presentar* y *disolver* en sus textos" (Rodríguez 1999: 261). In some strange kind of way, I decided, "suturing" (explaining theoretically?) and "presenting" (enacting imaginatively?) was precisely what I had been attempting to do in *Educating the Educators*. And so again

I took out the manuscript and, with renewed enthusiasm, began to rework it, in a final attempt to arrive at a dialectical balance.

The result is here, in what follows, for the reader to judge. My focus is now upon British Hispanism – there is a new chapter on the rise of Cultural Studies –at the expense of the chapters upon North-American Hispanism. A third autobiographical chapter has been added, better to foreground the dialectic between theory and lived experience that constituted the intuitive core of my original design. And the chapter on the trajectory of Paul Julian Smith has been expanded, to include a comparison with my own. I hope, thereby, to restore a sense of the social stratification that has governed the development of the discipline, while refusing to relinquish attention to "lived" experience within the academy, at the level of individual trajectories. The goal has been to recharge the "work of thought" with some of its primal meaning, and also with a sense of what it means to labor against prejudice and self-delusion. My ultimate purpose is to cultivate a kind of discourse which is *concrete* but not *empirical*, which allows me to step back and survey the conditions of my own possibility, as an object of thought, along with those of Hispanism in general.

My conviction is that the inner secret of the work now stands revealed: a stratified or "emergentist" Marxism – I take the term from the burgeoning tradition of Critical Realism – that holds in focus, conjointly, the irreducible levels of person, practices and structures. As such, *Educating the Educators* flies in the face of currently conceived post-structuralist wisdom within the literary academy. More specifically, it refuses to treat as interchangeable personal and social identities, on the grounds that the former, among other things, explains the capacity of individuals to resist the latter. It is personal identity, I believe, that explains the sense of abiding unity and continuity in the life of an individual, that provides him or her with the internal resources to resist interminably the situational logics into which s/he was born.

A final point. I have often been asked why I chose to work within a relatively marginalized discourse, namely Hispanism, within a larger discursive practice, namely literary criticism, which is itself scarcely of central importance to revolutionary practice. The short answer is that I "chose" nothing of the kind, as hopefully will become apparent during the course of this work. The contingency of one's beginnings simply has to be taken as a given. It comes with the ideological world into which we are born and in which we begin to think. The longer answer is that since everything within a social formation ultimately relates to everything else, Hispanic studies, where I happened to find myself, seemed as good a place as any from which to begin. Practically, I would concede that Marxists can survive only when they draw sustenance from and are affiliated to working-class groups, particularly during a period of revolutionary downturn. Disengaged from political activity, they inevitably become vulnerable to academic colleagues who, troubled by residual humanistic pangs of conscience, seek to implicate others in their cynicism and thereby in their individualistic, opportunistic, frequently vicious scramble for professional status and prestige. In such circumstances, enlightenment can lead not to a sense of liberation and revolutionary potential, but to despair.

And a comment. *Strangers in Paradise: Academics from the Working Class* came to my attention relatively late, when my own project was nearing completion. While the community of interest between both works should be obvious, there are a number of significant differences . Firstly, Ryan and Sackrey deal with the career paths of working-class academics in North America. My experience in a British society fettered by feudal traditions was different in important respects. Secondly, whereas Ryan and Sackrey's work encompasses the whole academy, my focus of attention is on the development of a single discipline. Finally, and most importantly, unlike the scholars whose testimonies are recorded in *Strangers in Paradise*, I am concerned to play off my personal experience and circumstance against my intellectual development, and to understand this in turn within broader disciplinary trends. The final effect is an ongoing dialectic between subjective and objective levels that is different in kind from anything that Ryan and Sackrey, or their contributors, undertake.

Introduction

"Traveling South: Ideology and Hispanism," my opening essay, first appeared in the early 1990s. Written in response to a bewildered, nostalgic assessment of the current state of American Hispanism by Michael McGaha, in an article entitled "Whatever Happened to Hispanism?," it displaced the center of attention towards the (for me) more familiar terrain of British Hispanism. Its principal goal, on the basis of evidence drawn largely from past numbers of the *Bulletin of Spanish Studies* (subsequently *Hispanic Studies*), was to develop a sequence of disciplinary paradigms with which to plot the evolution of modern Hispanism and to explain the State's encroachment upon the autonomy of the University.

As a modern university discipline, British Hispanism was constituted after the First World War, against the backdrop of an imperialistic, competitive capitalism, organized along increasingly monopolistic lines. Its programmatic aim was to re-assert the values of a pre-capitalist culture that, while largely surpassed in the heartland of Europe by the end of the 18th century, still survived in Spain. Ideologically, it exhibited a profound ambivalence towards commerce and trade, whose materialism it despised but whose existence underpinned its own cultural enterprises. It is its anti-materialism that largely explains the discipline's early aversion towards things Latin American and the canonically privileged position it accorded to the literature of Romanticism and the mystical tradition of the Golden Age.

While still staunchly attached to traditional, neo-Catholic values, Hispanism after the Second World War became more professional in its attitudes, in the service of a more intense capitalist accumulation. This is the period of Fordism, when Western societies were reorganized along consumer lines. It fell to the humanities, within a rapidly expanding tertiary system of education, to facilitate this reorganization by producing a new breed of professional manager. Hispanism during the boom period of the 1960s embraced the thematic structuralism of Alexander Parker, as it was applied to the theater of the Golden Age. This orthodoxy began to collapse in the mid-1970s, when universities in Britain were subjected to a painful process of reconfiguration, in accordance with the requirements of a multi-national mode of production. Ideologically, we witness the displacement of Golden Age studies from the center of Hispanism, leading to the kind of fragmentation lamented by McGaha. This displacement, along with the rise of Latin-American studies, was symptomatic of the relative collapse, within the global context, of the distinction between the imperial center and the colonial periphery.

The neo-liberal restructuring of Hispanism – and of the University in general – continued apace throughout the 1980s. What had once been a semi-autonomous state apparatus, in which residual pockets of pre-capitalist ideologies survived relatively intact, increasingly assumed the form of a corporate body, organized by a recharged bureaucracy along profit-and-loss lines. In America, where the market mentality and a rampant individualism were already firmly entrenched, the process was taken to the extreme. McGaha could muster all kinds of evidence to the effect that the consensus within Hispanism had collapsed and that the discipline was hemorrhaging badly in terms of student numbers. His response was to try and recreate what he perceived to be an earlier sense of community, but even as he spoke the eternal verities to which he appealed were being dismantled and replaced by agreed-upon language games. Even in British Hispanism and its off-shoots in Australasia, a new spirit of vocationalism saw the discipline brought into line with a private, deregulated economy, as Business Spanish began to appear alongside traditional courses. Hispanism quickly became a negative image of its early 20th-century configuration. Such was the developmental path that I set out to theorize.

For all those students familiar with the disciplinary nature of British Hispanism, the latter's response to "Traveling South" assumed a largely predictable form: the charge of "scholarly" inadequacy – the specific point at issue was an error in the transcription of a quotation – was used to deduce my general intellectual incompetence and so disqualify me as the source of critique (see Round). It was a tactic of condescension and infantilization habitually employed against any student who dared to critique basic, sacrosanct principles. Round failed to address the substance of my argument, which concerned paradigmatic developments within British Hispanism and the extent to which individual career patterns were structurally conditioned. One charge, however, merited respectful scrutiny, namely that Professor Allison Peers' work deserved more detailed consideration, including the books on tertiary education that he wrote under the pseudonym of "Bruce Truscot." Without conceding anything to Round's polemic, it is certainly true that Peers exercised an enormous influence over modern British Hispanism for several decades. That it was Peers who masqueraded under the pseudonym of Bruce Truscot has of course been known for some time (see Mountford). My aim in my second essay, "For God, King and Country," is to consider, through a review of Truscot's ideas, the problems of adjustment faced by the academy, in a climate of working-class militancy, at the end of the Second World War.

British education until this moment had been subject to the relatively mild supervision of the night-watchman state of classical liberalism. The latter limited its interventions to reproducing the general conditions for a competitive capitalism. Typical in this respect was the Education Act of 1870 (1872 in Scotland) which required the state to supplement the provision of voluntary schools. Neither the labor movement nor the landed or professional classes had been overly concerned to promote a national educational system, the former being preoccupied with the provision of a "ladder" for the gifted working-class child and the latter with the cost of reproducing a disciplined work force. Even in the 1920s, labor ideologues such as R. H. Tawny were only advocating the need for three types of school: grammar, for the middle classes; technical, for the elite fraction of the working class; and secondary, for the vast majority. This was a suggestion eagerly taken up by the Spens Commission of 1938, and reinforced by the 1943 Norwood Commission, and was embodied in the Education Act of 1944.

This, then, was the historical conjuncture which, mediated through the circumstances of Peers' own upbringing, determined his views on education. Peers was himself the typical scholarship boy of lower-middle class provenance, who passed through Cambridge on his way, finally, after a period of school teaching, to a Chair in the provinces, at Liverpool. The ideological parameters corresponding with such an emplacement can be plotted fairly precisely: Peers was perfectly poised between the more conservative, aristocratic strain of liberalism, as fostered by England's "ancient universities," and its more commercially dynamic, North-American counterpart. More specifically, he embraces the ideology of the professions, distinguished by the importance that it attributes both to social responsibility and organic solidarity and to individual efficiency and competence. The organic component, dominant in the combination, is in essence a secularized version of the feudal model of noblesse oblige, otherwise the view that the privileges of high rank presuppose the recognition of certain duties, including the obligation to protect the socially inferior. The concomitant aversion to commercial interests is tempered, within the professions, by recognition of the market and of the need to adjust one's activity to its requirements.

Transcribed into pedagogical terms, the notion of universal service encouraged Peers to envisage the teacher as the custodian of society's spiritual and moral values, a bulwark, as it were, against the forces of modern materialism. In practical terms, his program consisted of blending the more positive elements from both the old ruling class and the working class, whilst eliminating their more negative counterparts. It is clear exactly what Peers objected to about the aristocracy: he is contemptuous of its idleness and wastefulness, epitomized by the degenerate behavior of the sons of the nobility, as he encountered them at Cambridge. At the same time, he was envious of, and felt compelled to emulate, the aristocracy's refined social graces. A similar ambivalence characterized his attitude to the working class, so that while he admired the diligence and application of the scholarship boy, he disparaged his social shortcomings, and saw as part of his own professorial mission the severing of ties that bound the scholarship boy to his "home" community.

Predictably, Peers carried over the principle of compromise into the sphere of educational policy, at the national level. Predictably, in that, as a member of the aspiring class of professionals, he depended upon the State both (a) initially to open up the academy, otherwise the academic market, to members of the middle class and (b) subsequently to defend the latter's professional, monopoly status against further expansion of the principle of free competition. Hence, while Peers supported grants for the scholarship boy, the London external degree, and the creation of "redbrick" universities, he strongly criticized the State's "interference" with university "autonomy." Unfortunately, in key respects the "lower professions" were more vulnerable to such encroachment than were their "higher" counterparts, notably medicine and the law, in that, whereas the latter presupposed direct payment by client-patients for services rendered, the former were financed out of state revenue. State supervision, then, was the price that Peers was forced to pay if, that is, universities were to avoid the kind of dependence upon private finance that, he believed, would fatally compromise intellectual "freedom." From Peers' perspective, everything depended in the last instance upon a wager, to the effect that state bureaucrats could be more easily intimidated than their private counterparts into minding their own business.

In sum, at the heart of the relation between the State and the University, as Peers envisaged it, lay a contradiction, which was destined to make this relation tense and even precarious. It consisted of an opposition between the need for professional independence, on the one hand, and the academy's moorings within a corporate structure, on the other. At first blush, it is true, the nature of the opposition is not immediately apparent. Indeed, professional autonomy would seem to have been conditional upon the corporate connection, without which academics would have been vulnerable to the pressure of private finance in the way that Peers most dreaded. Corporatism, it would appear, allowed Peers and his fellow academics to insulate themselves against the "outside world," otherwise the market, and, by the same token, to live within ideologies of their own making (mysticism, etc.). Unfortunately, however, there was a catch to this otherwise convenient arrangement: the principle that allowed experts to select at will the inputs they received from the laity (in the form of inspectors, etc.) could only be effectively justified and defended by those professionals oriented towards the market. In other words, market exposure (attenuated, it is true, by their own control over their profession) was the price of professional autonomy. But of course, it was precisely this kind of commercialization that, in Peers' view, compromised the "disinterested pursuit of Truth," etc, and that he hoped to avoid through his reliance upon the State. And so to the wager.

There was nothing privately obsessional or idiosyncratic about Peers' ruminations or the attention that he paid to issues of state. On the contrary, state intervention was a widespread feature of national policies from the 1930s to the 1960s, as evinced by the New Deal in the USA, National Socialism in Germany, and the Labour Government in Britain. Moreover, it was by no means a tendency restricted to capitalist countries, as the phenomenon of Stalinism indicates.[1] Truscot appealed for and received government assistance for the simple reason that national States during this period were increasingly inclined to participate in the production process, as opposed to simply providing conditions for it to take place. Such policies were conducive to an imperialist rivalry that was to produce two world wars.

My third essay, "The Making of a Hispanist," is of an autobiographical nature, and records the experience of a working-class boy, brought up in an English industrial town in the North Midlands, in the gray years immediately after the Second World War. My world, needless to say, was not Peers' world, although he walked through my world every day, on his way to the University: "The air is heavy with the perfume of fried fish," wrote Truscot (Peers 1996, 265). Well, not exactly my world, but its equivalent in Liverpool: "The houses were mean, filthy, blackened with age – some of them, homes of the poorest type; others, tumbledown shops and dingy 'publics' [public houses]". And though Peers never met the women folk of my family or their children, like me, there can be no doubting what he would have thought of us: "Women, with tousled hair, and wearing men's caps on their heads, sat on the unwashed steps of their houses, exchanging raucous arguments or screaming to half-naked children about the pavements – their only playground" (272-73). Literature and libraries, Peers always implied, were to be isolated from such communities, whose role in life was simply to produce the wealth that

---

1.   For some scholars, of course, Stalinism is itself a form of state capitalism (see Callinicos 1991). Trotskyists have insisted on seeing Stalinist Russia as a degenerate workers' State (see Morris).

allowed him the time and space to indulge in his mystic and cultural pursuits.

The chapter's central theme is my negotiation of an educational system that in no small way Bruce Truscot had helped to determine. As we have seen, British society in the post-war period still exhibited the 19th-century division between those possessing landed wealth or professional prestige, and those possessing neither. The infamous 11-plus examination in effect reproduced within education this basic class structure. So resilient did it prove to be that, despite the climate of working-class militancy between 1945 and 1950, little was achieved in education (in contrast, it has to be said, to the national health service). It was only in 1950 that the Labor movement pressed the Party to promote "comprehensive" schools and to oppose the 11-plus, although the politicians continued to drag their feet. Even when it was returned to office in 1964, with plans to abolish the 11-plus, the Labour Party had still not come up with any well-thought-out comprehensive scheme.

In any case, the developments of the 1960s came too late to influence my own academic career. Labeled a "failure" at 11, I was dispatched to a "secondary modern" school, there to be processed and prepared for appropriate forms of labor. For a while my destiny seemed set, particularly after another battery of intelligence tests at the age of 13 confirmed my allegedly congenital inadequacies. But while the forces of Authority proved overwhelming, gradually I began to devise (what I now perceive to be) strategies of resistance, with which to undermine its diktats, not in a confrontational kind of way, but through burrowing quietly and stubbornly. It is this "experience" which I wish to off-set against exaggerated estimates, common among Althusserians, of the prevalence of the dominant ideology. Intellectuals are only too willing to see ordinary people as the dupes of ideology. The realities of interpellation and, which is the same thing, of the "class struggle," are far more complex and contradictory. Agents are emphatically not mere supports or effects of a system but composite structures in their own right. True, the social structures that affect individual behavior can, and generally do, transcend the subject's conscious and unconscious levels of awareness, to the extent that we are often condemned to reproducing, as opposed to changing, the social system. But what Althusserians never "knew" and therefore never began to theorize (except belatedly) were the ways in which the proletarian subject could "understand" without yielding to interpellation. What may have seemed like a dumb unresponsiveness was in reality a posture of watchfulness or aloofness, in the face of an Authority that possessed an impressive capacity for repression and violence.

What my experience suggests is that the socially mobile working-class individual refined a theoretical practice with which to negotiate a system that was specifically designed to thwart his or her advancement. This practice consisted of a blend of elements drawn from working-class culture, with its dominantly socialist bias, and from "official" knowledge. The conflict of discourses enabled one to separate out from the contingency of one's origins, so as to be able to conceive the possibility of alternative ways of being. I venture to suggest that, from the standpoint of pedagogical methodology, it constitutes a technique of self-education that deserves respectful consideration, always bearing in mind that, in essence, it served the purposes of evasion, survival and advancement within a disciplinary apparatus. The trick was never to become an openly defiant or "bad" subject. Bad subjects were severely dealt with, and in any case were inevitably complicit, through a curious process of inversion, with the very system that they confronted. Even relatively sophisticated counter-ideologies were in their own way vulnerable to accommodation by the dominant ruling ideology. In particular, the ethic of personal achievement and the new sociology of aspirations proved seductive in the extreme. But total absorption was never entirely possible, as I try to show, to the extent that the past still had the capacity to reclaim its own, even after years of virtual co-option.

My fourth essay compares the respective career developments of myself and Paul Julian Smith. The aim, as regards my own work, is to treat it as objectively as possible, a task facilitated by the existence of a series of "breaks" at key points within my trajectory. It is the existence of such breaks that led me, qua theoretician, to distance myself from "Read," addressed insistently in the third person. The tactic, which some may judge to be ponderous, is consistent with my overall aim to enact the slippage between disparate, contradictory and emergent levels of subjectivity, without succumbing to the fashionable reduction of subjectivity to random states of flux. I begin by tracing Read's struggle to escape the grip of a native empiricism, which took him, in the early stages of his career, through a broadly based Hegelian approach, and finally into psychoanalysis. Subsequently, I describe how he embraced a form of Althusserianism that was largely inspired by the work of the Spanish Marxist, Juan Carlos Rodríguez. The suggestion is that Read knew precisely what Rodríguez meant by the "ideological unconscious" for the simple reason that he had spent a life-time struggling to liberate himself from its clutches. Contradictions at the level of everyday experience made him keenly aware of being inserted involuntarily into structured and enduring relations that shaped his actions in determinate ways.

However, this sudden enthusiasm for the Althusserians' notion of a "process without a subject" brought with it problems of its own, as far as Read's personal trajectory was concerned. "Experience," in Althusserian terms, is the preferred terrain of ideology; indeed, it is in itself an ideological concept through and through. From this perspective, the strength, say, of the bourgeoisie in the 16th century is determined not by the number of individuals who can be classified as "bourgeois," but by the objective existence of a certain set of social relations. One effect of this emphasis upon transcendent social structures is to minimize the role of individual will. Positions within these relations can be, and were, occupied by individuals of all kinds – ennobled bankers, warring knights, nobles, and even the occasional bishop. The result is an ontological gulf, at the analytical level, between the social and individual dimensions of human existence.

Even more troubling, from Read's standpoint, was the Althusserians' antipathy, shared by the post-structuralists, towards any concept of "human nature." While it was wholly laudable to insist, as Rodríguez did, upon the need to historicize the ideological category of the subject, it was another thing entirely to restrict one's attention to "social being," or so at least Read argued. An historicization that went all the way down left the Marxist with no basis upon which to defend his or her own abiding sense of individual identity, not to mention the powerful moral claims that constitute the core of the classical Marxist program. The only way round this problem, Read proceeded to argue, was to construct an emergentist, Critical Realist model of Marxism, which allows for a distinction between different layers or strata. Minimally, it is important to distinguish "species being," consisting of a determinate range of biologically based human needs and capacities; an "interactional order," connecting individuals with structural properties of social systems; and the social systems themselves, operating at the macro-level. What remains to be debated is whether this critical realist move, on Read's part, masks a covert reversion to a fundamentally Kantian preoccupation with levels of being, the ultimate effect of which is to neutralize the force of Rodríguez's indisputably seminal concept of the ideological unconscious.

Similarly, Read has come to believe increasingly that Althusserians failed sufficiently to defend, in ontological terms, the existential status of the structural relations that they proposed. As a result, he argues, they eventually succumbed to an epistemological relativism that, while it may have suited the numerous post-structuralisms that blossomed in the aftermath of 1968, raised insuperable problems for any kind of Marxism, and indeed facilitated the passage of a generation of Marxists into the various post-Marxisms. Althusserians, the claim is – and here the contribution of Critical Realism is again crucial – were insufficiently *realist*.

As will quickly become apparent, my aim in this fourth chapter is to interweave the narrative of my own development with that of Paul Julian Smith, as in a kind of counterpoint. Smith, I will argue, also worked to distance himself progressively from orthodox critical practice, although in his case strictly within the parameters of reformism. Indeed, at the start of his career, Smith was positively welcomed by the more enlightened of the older scholars who, traumatized by recent events, looked to a rising star to eke out their discipline's meager intellectual reserves. Within a short while, however, Smith had abandoned his historical focus upon baroque reading habits to advance towards a full-blooded post-structuralism, which argued that if everything, including reality, class allegiance, subject positions, is ultimately constructed in discourse, then we could only be deluded in thinking that one theoretical model was preferable to another or had a better claim to justice or truth. Soon, Smith was taking on board a postmodern "hyper-reality" that carried him even further from his moorings within a traditionally conceived Hispanism. Gradually, the political consequences of this paradigmatic shift became apparent and, seemingly, they were of a kind congenial to conservatism. Social conflict and imperialism were remodeled by Smith on the basis of "difference" and the "other," in ways that deprived "exploitation" and "oppression" of all specifically historical or experiential content. Of course, Smith could not avoid shocking the more stubbornly entrenched elements within British Hispanism, but by the time his queer theory was out in the open, he had passed beyond their professional reach. In any case, Smith had little to fear in the new market, in which "pink" symbolic capital ultimately wielded as much power as most others, and a good deal more than its old-fashioned humanistic counterpart.

What made Smith's work so singularly difficult to locate, ideologically speaking, was the illusion of radicalism that characterized it. Although undoubtedly enhanced by the disciplinary background of Catholic reaction from which it had emerged and against which it was inevitably projected, this illusion was not peculiar to Smith, or to Hispanism, but to postmodernism in general. As Paul Resch suggests, the dissident postmodernism of the 1970s "functioned as the loyal opposition during the birth pangs of multinational capitalism and in this respect has been simply the ideological obverse of the New Right" (Resch 8). Smith's anti-Marxist tendencies surfaced clearly in his third work, *The Body Hispanic*, in which he dismissed the working class as a potential revolutionary agent (just a few years after the miners had engaged in one of the bitterest and most prolonged battles in British labor history). It is impossible to miss the emotional investment in his repeated denigration of a "po-faced" socialism that refuses to collude with his postmodern *jouissance*. (Capitalism, by way of contrast, figures within Smith's texts only parenthetically, and in the most blandly accommodating manner.) Equally visible from very early on was the elitism of his pluralist tendencies, not to mention the dissolution of the distinction between critique and affirmation. In his work on the postmodernist Spanish film director, Almodóvar, non-conformism evaporates in a celebration of commodification and consumerism. Under the cover of his defense of homosexuals, Smith has more recently crossed over from postmodern subversion into neo-liberal respectability, as a result of which the young Turk now finds himself no longer driven into the margins of British Hispanism but, on the contrary, firmly lodged at its very center. A future of postmodernist accommodation seems assured.

"Who Walked a Crooked Mile," my fifth essay, resumes autobiographical themes. Its main objective is to give a further twist to the dialectical interplay between structure and agency. In particular, I am concerned to describe how techniques honed in earlier encounters continued to be deployed at a higher level, and in particular to confirm the extent to which the "success" of the socially mobile proletarian lay in his or her ability to negotiate the double functioning of interpellation. The existence of (at least) two conflictual discourses finds the subject to some degree unhoused ideologically, and therefore with a capacity to defamiliarize more habitual or taken-for-granted attitudes and beliefs. The individual raises his/her subjectivity to a high point, by a process that involves what I can only describe as thinking with the body, even when, as in my own case, "official" wisdom sometimes gains or is stabilized at the expense of its informally acquired, plebeian counterpart.

There are, I realize, hidden dangers in emphasizing the extraordinary effort it took to dissipate the dense ideological fog by which I was engulfed. Inevitably, it will be objected, my account begins to assume all the trappings of a Lukacsian grand narrative, in which the heroic individual struggles towards self-consciousness, dogged by feelings of guilt and class betrayal. I certainly do not intend to deny the obvious, and willingly concede that there runs throughout this essay a strong sense of transition from alienation to enlightenment, and that, indeed, it clearly posits the existence of a theoretical *break* in my development, a point at which *experience* of exclusion was transformed into a *theory* of exclusion. At the same time, it would be unfortunate if the experiential bias distracted attention from my implicit contrast between the plebeian experience of struggle and the more familiar bourgeois attempts to reduce life's options to "rational choices" (Rational Marxism) or ongoing conversations of mankind (Pragmatism). Equally implicit is the opposition between a multi-accentual, polyphonic ideology, given prominence in the present essay, and the deceptively similar postmodernist preoccupation with different "phrase regimes" or, for that matter, the eclecticism and pluralism beloved of liberal humanism.

My sixth essay theorizes the changes that have taken place in post-war British Hispanism and that lead directly to the rise of a distinctively Hispanic version of Cultural Studies. During this period, the discipline has developed through a series of cultural configurations, whose inner situational logics I set out to theorize, through the deployment of a number of conceptual categories taken from the work of the Critical Realist, Margaret Archer. Throughout the 1940s and 50s, Hispanism was dominated by the logic of *constraining contradiction*, otherwise the compulsion to reconcile opposing positions. This logic was gradually superseded in the 1960s and 70s, by that of *concomitant compatibility*, a logic through which supposedly seminal insights were systematically extended to other areas. During these decades, the dynamics of the Cultural System or systemic level of the social formation prevailed over those of Social-Cultural relations (between agents and individuals) whilst being finally mediated through them. The 1980s and 90s were characterized by a growing disorder, at the S-C level, dictated by two kinds of situational logic. The first, *competitive contradiction*, in which irreconcilable elements fight it out, dominated during a relatively brief period, from the end of the 1980s through the early 90s, whereas the second, *contingent complementarity*, which permits different positions to co-exist, in a state of flux, imposed itself thereafter, during a period when British Hispanism was being actively reconfigured as a cultural studies program. The progressive sequence of cultural dynamics, it is argued, is determined by the development of social relations under capitalism, at the level of the social formation. Constraining contradiction helped to stabilize these relations during the post-war crisis; concomitant compatibility produces and is produced by the buoyant optimism of the 1960s; competitive contradiction corresponds to the global crisis that began in the 1970s, but which only culminated in the late 80s; and contingent complementarity parallels the political opportunism of Blair's New Labour, whose ideological needs it serves.

The final essay, which also functions as a kind of epilogue, brings my autobiographical trajectory up to date, in a somewhat partial and schematic manner, it has to be said, and with my focus decidedly upon the interface between theory and practice. The essay confirms, if confirmation is needed, that my aim throughout has been less to write a book in the currently fashionable academic genre of memoir writing than to uncover the political and ideological presuppositions of Hispanism, as these were filtered through my own life experiences.

1
Traveling South: Ideology and Hispanism

Crisis of a Discipline

While it is true that academics in general have done little to theorize the nature of their work and their role in society, Hispanists have been particularly reluctant to engage in any form of critical self-scrutiny. Inevitably, therefore, they were ill-prepared to meet the crisis of the humanities which, taking shape throughout the 1970s and 1980s, suddenly took a qualitatively different hold in the early 1990s. Illustrative of Hispanism's backwardness in this respect was the appearance in 1990 of Michael McGaha's "Whatever Happened to Hispanism?" The piece was notable for its sense of professional outrage but not for the depth of its analysis:

A year ago, as we entered the last decade of the twentieth century, I celebrated the twentieth anniversary of completing my Ph.D. As I enter the second half of my career, I can't help being astonished by the changes that have occurred in my profession in two brief decades. I feel extremely privileged to be a Hispanist. The sheer joy I find in studying and teaching Spanish language and literature has only increased with the passage of time. Nevertheless, I have often had occasion to doubt the wisdom of my career choice. (McGaha 225)

To be sure, Professor McGaha proceeded to address disciplinary problems that were very real and that pressed for attention. Comparing the MLA convention of 1970 with that of 1989, he was able to highlight the progressive fragmentation of Hispanism as a reading community. Whereas in 1970 it had been possible to attend all the individual sessions and to become acquainted with all the major participants, in 1989 an emphasis on specialization had reached the point of virtual solipsism. What we are now witnessing is "the fragmentation, if not atomization, of the profession, and the loss of any sense of one's field as a community of scholars" (229). In other words, Hispanism exhibits all the symptoms of anomie and dehumanization that afflict industrial society in general. The way out of this crisis, in McGaha's view, lay in a sense of community rediscovered:

"When we attack each other, pitting women against men, natives against non-natives, Spaniards against Latin Americans, we are diminished and further marginalized. If our profession is to survive and prosper in the twenty-first century, we must come to our senses and rebuild the community of American Hispanism, acknowledging that our common bonds are far greater than the differences that divide us" (230).

The transnational nature of their discipline is such that most Hispanists will readily recognize, although they may not actually identify with, McGaha's self-portrait. Even those who distance themselves intellectually from it are more likely than not to find that they are implicated institutionally: we do not work in isolation, and the current reality of our disciplinary status – or lack of status – affects us all. Left high and dry by the receding cultural tide, we cut tragic (some would say pathetic) figures: "Several times I had to cancel my seminar on *Don Quijote* – the love of my life – because no more than two students had enroled in it, and instead teach an additional language class" (226). Of course, as we shall see later, minority culture has long been fighting a losing battle against its commercially sponsored counterpart. What has changed is that recently the latter has threatened to overrun the former totally: "Things fall apart; the center cannot hold" (229). The golden age of Hispanism (McGaha continues) is over, its practitioners subjected to the brutal imperatives of the division of labor. A brief respite in the 1980s and the benefits that accrued from a certain governmental panic about the "disastrous condition" of American education, especially as regards the teaching of modern languages, have been off-set by other "storm clouds" (226). Few things look certain about the future, except that the liberal arts are set to continue their slow decline. Again, we have long been familiar with the myth of the loss of innocence: what is new in McGaha is the depth of his cultural pessimism.

How are we to understand the pervasive nostalgia that is now afflicting the minority arts? The first step must be to draw back, so as to encompass within our range of vision, and consequently within our analysis, those very material, institutional conditions in which Hispanism perforce operates. Seen within this context, academic specialization emerges as an extension of capitalist division of labor in general. Also thrown into relief is Hispanism's ideological role in the (re)production of the whole social order. There can be no question, in the light of such functional links, of simply salvaging the past, within an autonomous discipline. Capitalism, under pressure to compete internationally, has entered a more abrasive, aggressive phase. Faced with the current crisis in the world economy, it can no longer tolerate independent cultural positions of the traditional minority type. Hispanism is now more or less directly exposed to major market forces: "The year I entered the job market, hiring of foreign language faculty declined 26.7%. I was fortunate enough to get a tenure-track job at a respectable liberal arts college" (225).

But even the old elitist universities offer only a degree of protection. Plummeting labor values, and therefore real pay levels, threaten professional security, not to mention advancement. Hispanists survive only to the extent that they can successfully "instrumentalize" their discipline, in accordance with market demands, and sell themselves as language teachers, or alternatively serve as ideologues of the capitalist system – hence their promotion of literary organicism. Even so, suddenly, they are confronted by the kind of behavior formerly reserved for the shop floor. Thus, when challenged over arbitrary procedures of renewal and promotion, their dean of arts advised McGaha and similarly dissatisfied colleagues to "keep [their] mouths shut" (225) or face replacement by a cheaper, readily available (because unemployed) labor force.

At the root of their misery was a decline in demand: "During the 1970s I also experienced a steady erosion in the quality of my students in general, and a drastic decline in the number and quality of Spanish majors" (225-26). Where did the more talented students go? Presumably to more (economically) rewarding areas. For the academic nurtured within the idealist enclave of a Golden Age (of Literature), protectively distanced from the debased realm of history and society, redundancy came as a shock: "In a difficult economic climate Spanish literature seemed to be a luxury that bright, talented students could no longer afford" (226). Like the academic him/herself, literature could survive in market conditions only to the extent that it lent itself to commodification: hence the much vaunted magic realism of modern literature. Lacking any exchange value, minority literature was deemed worthless.

"Whatever happened to Hispanism?": those at all familiar with the state of the art will capture the nuances of the question, the subtle combination of perplexity and indignation. Is not *Don Quijote* manifestly important?! How dare they scorn the classics!? Equally obvious is its purely rhetorical status. McGaha can describe what is happening, but, lacking any appropriate model, he cannot explain it. His overriding concern is, pragmatically, to surrender as little ground as possible. The transition from a Peninsular to a Latin-American emphasis is conceded, though one suspects grudgingly. In contrast, the predilection on the part of research students for modern as opposed to pre-modern literature is received with overt anxiety: "This suggests that departments will have increasing difficulty in staffing courses in medieval and Golden Age Spanish literature and colonial and 19th-century Latin-American Literature" (227).

But what can McGaha say to those around him (and they are increasingly numerous) who would reply "So what?" Of course, common sense suggests to McGaha that he is defending a serious, important body of literature. But it is precisely this "common sense" that is no longer common currency. (Here, again, the center will not hold.) A "new vocationalism" feels uncomfortable with, when it does not reject outright, those disciplines or activities that do not contribute directly to the Gross National Product, in accordance with which a new breed of entrepreneurial Hispanist promotes the instrumentalist equation of "learning" with "training" for employment within a social system which s/he accepts as given. To such collusion, McGaha replies with simple moral indignation, only to discover that his moral values are no longer as universally accepted as they were. One sympathizes with him. Obviously, no student of the humanities can really believe that education lends itself to "marketing." We all know that our work cannot be qualified and quantified in terms of "exchange values." At the same time, it is also regrettably true that the role of education as preparation for a whole way of life, for active participation in a genuine democracy, can no longer be assumed, but needs to be explicitly argued for and vigorously defended. It is at this point that McGaha's limitations are so painfully obvious. And what is most worrying is that they are not primarily *his* limitations, but those of Hispanism, that curiously conservative, intellectually closed community of which McGaha proudly proclaims himself to be a member.

Imaginary Communities

We suggested above that McGaha lacks any contextual understanding of the function of Hispanism. This is unfair to the extent that he also presupposes, and quite crucially so, a homology between the loss of unity within Hispanism and the breakdown of society in general. Fragmentation "is in fact endemic to American society and threatens our very survival as a nation" (230). Identity, nation, community, bonds, culture – these are the foundations upon which he builds his case. Unfortunately, however – and this is the nub of our disagreement – these are all "key words" (see R. Williams 1983 [i]) and rather less secure and unambiguous than McGaha believes. In particular, they need to be carefully scrutinized for their ideological content if untold damage is not to be done. As it stands, McGaha's shallow, rather desperate rhetoric, which derives from the combined deployment of such terms, ignores the origins of state-building in the crises of feudal relations of production, the unadulterated violence that attended the imposition of national, high culture on localized, low cultures, not to mention the "invention of tradition" in the period 1870-1914, as imperialist powers struggled for mastery. In a word, it fails to recognize the extent to which the construction of inclusive national identities is a modern phenomenon that demands explanation (see Callinicos 1987: 157 ff.).

What McGaha fails to understand is that the development of the nation is a response to the social-psychological need to bind together communities ravaged by the disruptive transition to capitalism. The nation state redefines notions of time and space, "realizing the 'historical' unity of individuals by the very act of separating them from their very real history – older identifications with family, village, religion, and so forth, which are modified and destroyed" (Resch 340). These very real historical processes are, of course, re-enacted within the Hispanic academic community. Non-Hispanic Hispanists share one characteristic: by definition, they operate at one remove from those local communities in which most people learn their mother tongue. McGaha himself implies as much when he concedes that Hispanics offer students an "insider's perspective" on their literature and culture in ways that non-natives cannot (McGaha 227-28). Beyond this basic homogeneity, however, these same Hispanists are liable to have originated in rather different circumstances. What has also become clear is that ambulant, petty-bourgeois intellectuals are more responsive to the appeal of citizenship defined at a national level. Their model in this regard is an American society struggling to integrate culturally disparate elements. In the words of Arthur Schlesinger, quoted approvingly by McGaha: "If we repudiate the quite marvelous inheritance that history has bestowed on us, we invite the fragmentation of our own culture into a quarrelsome spatter of enclaves, ghettos, and tribes. The bonds of cohesion in our society are sufficiently fragile, or so it seems to me, that it makes no sense to strain them by encouraging and exalting cultural and linguistic apartheid" (230).

"Cultural and linguistic apartheid." Quite so! We have all borne witness to the kind of prejudice that McGaha observes in the U.S.A.: "each subgroup seems determined to fight the others for its 'piece of the pie'" (230). But at the same time, it is perilously easy to miss the equally ideological form of the liberal response. We are all British, all New Zealanders, all Americans, are we not? Liberalism rightly recognizes no distinctions before the law. But it is a grave mistake to believe that formal definitions of class, color and creed exhaust the debate on social identity. As Raymond Williams explains: "To reduce social identity to formal legal definitions, at the level of the state, is to collude with the alienated superficialities of 'the nation' which are the limited functional terms of the modern ruling class" (R. Williams 1983 [ii]: 195). Of course, it is the (partly unconscious) strength of conservative liberal discourse that it is blind to its own "nationalism." It speaks persuasively in the tone of innocence: "we must come to our senses and rebuild the community of American Hispanism, acknowledging that our common bonds are far greater than the differences that divide us" (McGaha 230). There can be no question, it is true, of counter-balancing this with some more restricted version of organicism and of the slow formation of cultures. "But it should be equally obvious that this long and unfinished process cannot reasonably be repressed by versions of a national history and a patriotic heritage which deliberately exclude its complexities and in doing so reject its many surviving and diverse identities" (Williams 194).

Appeals to the "unity of mankind" have never been a prerogative of the Right, and, at a time when the forces of international capitalism are mounting an unprecedented assault upon the working class, it is important for the Left to sustain and extend its internationalism. At the same time, we must decline McGaha's treacherously appealing invitation "to put aside ancestral quarrels and grudges in a proud celebration of the rich heritage shared by the Spanish-speaking people of the world" (230). For as things stand, exactly who shares this heritage? And if McGaha feels "extremely privileged to be a Hispanist" (McGaha 225), does this imply any social privilege? Can anyone become a Hispanist in the States? And on a point of information (for somebody who has never been there), is the distinction between the "premier liberal arts colleges on the West Coast" (226) and the "state colleges" a social distinction in the differential sense? Such questions, I know, will seem irksome, but McGaha must realize that in a systematically and radically unequal society, his calls to "pull together" will remain unheeded by some. Impatiently, he wishes to move, not forwards, which could only be towards the loss of his privileges, but backwards, to larger, more centralized identities. While ideologically these identities facilitate the impersonal operations of modern industry, their artificiality cannot but prove uncongenial at lower levels. When state nationalists perceive that their enthusiasms are not shared, they readily resort to abuse ("Left-handed Lesbian Latinas"). This in itself is symptomatic of a loss of hope: thus, the quincentennial celebrations "will be the occasion for bitter quarrels and recriminations that will make the former tensions seem like sweet harmony" (230). But so they should. The working class has every reason to be distrustful: to have imagined itself to be part of a nation – as in Zimbabwe and Poland, to take two recent examples – has proved consistently disabling, sometimes fatally so (see Callinicos 1987: 205, 207). Social Democracy in the 20th century has taken many forms, but it has been consistent in one respect, namely in its capacity, at moments of revolutionary crisis, to betray the proletariat that supported it (see Callinicos 1991: 14-15, 93-96, 132-33).

Why, some may finally ask, do we still need ideologues such as McGaha to promote the virtues of patriotism and loyalty? Clearly, they are far less in demand than formerly – hence the precarious state of Hispanism. Literature has now been replaced by ideologically much more effective electronic media such as television and film. But why, given the realities of multinational companies, do we need Hispanists at all? Are not "nations" in the process of being superseded on all levels that matter? Yes and no. No, to the extent that the human need to identify with others, in a common culture, to cope with the realities of suffering and death, survives, even (or especially) in the nightmare of modern civilization; and Hispanism continues to address this need. Moreover, Hispanism gives expression to those instincts marginalized by capitalism: "The sheer joy I find in studying and teaching Spanish language and literature" (McGaha 225), "the love of my life" (226). Life indeed would be pretty bleak, not to say unbearable, without literary consolations. By deduction, capitalism needs to be absorbed through those aesthetic qualities which otherwise lack currency. Faced by symptoms of imminent social breakdown – most apparent in the inner city – authorities rely on images of organic community to control the desperate (when not drugged), unpredictable monads of the modern cosmopolis. Hispanism generates such images, and at minimum cost: on both accounts, McGaha gives eloquent testimony.

Something of Hispanism's limitations can be appreciated if we consider the response to comparable crises elsewhere in the humanities in recent years. In English studies, for example, scholars have not only arrived at detailed historical perspectives on the history of their discipline (e.g., Lentricchia, Baldick, Fekete, Mulhern), but also speculated in depth upon its contemporary situation, not to mention its future prospects (e.g., Brooker, Widdowson, Humm). Comparable attempts in Hispanism have been by contrast either relatively schematic (e.g., Mariscal 1990) or brash exercises in self-promotion of an intellectually non-serious nature (Boland and Kenwood). In the light of such work, we suggest the need to reformulate and elaborate McGaha's titular question. Thus: why was modern Hispanism created in the first place? What ideological, institutional roles did it perform? How and why have these changed? What social developments account for Hispanism's loss of currency?

Birth of a Discipline

Nobody can read the early editions of the *Bulletin of Spanish Studies* (later *BHS*) without becoming aware of the extraordinary importance attached to traveling. Article after article attests to the fact that the Hispanist is a "northerner," a pilgrim journeying southwards, both to Spain and within Spain. "Literary Pilgrimages in Spain," with which Allison Peers launched the *Bulletin*, is a perfect example of the genre. In this article, Peers describes his escape from Madrid into the "Earthly Paradise" of Seville. It is at once a journey into Literature (in quest of a volume of the Romantic writer Angel de Saavedra, the Duke of Rivas) and into Religion ("But when all is said, the attraction of Sevilla is her cathedral" [1923: 13]). But perhaps above all it is a journey into the (m)other – note the stylized feminization of "Seville" – or into the Self. After a show of coyness – his apologies for his article's "playful mood," its "subjectiveness," its "too personal a nature" – Peers proceeds to lead us to that inner sanctum of the Individual ("In the mystical sense which is truth, he is ALONE" [14]).

The ideological role of this privatized subject is apparent even from the restricted context of Peers' article. Most obviously, its interiority is a minority attribute – the inhabitants of the poorest, most crowded quarter of Seville (in the immediate vicinity of the Library), in particular of the "malodorous market," are massified and subjectless. In other words, this subject is a natural member of an elite, a ruler. It was the irony of this isolated Romantic subject, however, that it longed to surrender the aloneness it so diligently cultivated. Thus, perversely, by traveling southwards, Peers enters an organic, pre-individual, pre-capitalist community, comparable to the "merrie England" of contemporary English critics such as F. R. Leavis, but in the case of Spain, refreshingly real, surviving, that is, into the 20th century. What "never fails to thrill a traveller from the north," in the words of William Atkinson, one of Peers' academic colleagues, is "this disregard of logic which despises time, money" (Atkinson 74, 75). In Spain we find "a truer sense of eternal values than in the harried atmosphere beyond the Pyrenees" (75). The quality of life it preserves is conspicuously absent from capitalist society – "magic names," the "charm of the people," the "glory of its literature." Above all, as another leading Hispanist, J. W. Rees, observed in the second volume of the *Bulletin*, in a review of a work by Peers: "In an age of materialism like the present, to write a book on mysticism is in the nature of an adventure" (Rees 95). To analyze in further detail the tensions and contradictions of the Romantic subject, however, let us turn to that prototypical British Hispanist of those early decades, Aubrey F. G. Bell.

Like so many of his generation, Bell was something of a vagabond or, to be more precise, a pilgrim, traveling south: "The whole of this road is a garden of Eden, and the scenery opening from it is a succession of marvels" (1926: 172). But even as he draws back from modernity, and takes refuge in mythopoeic consciousness, Bell fetishizes the immediate. He leaves unchallenged the forms of bourgeois class domination, even as he criticizes some of its results: "Near Alajar a frail little old man of nearly eighty was tottering along on his staff, much like a three-legged stool, a great sack over his shoulder. Fortunately, just as one was about to offer him an alms, he explained that he was returning from 'mis tierras'" (172). Far from being a momentary slip, an incidental aberration, this reference to capitalist relations alerts us to what is repressed from Bell's work, to what is a veritable textual unconscious. In his stillness, Bell is able at times to engage in a sensitive critique of aspects of capitalist alienation. But his negation is of an abstract and therefore reactionary kind, which mystifies human relationships by not directing its analysis at the social structures themselves: "man has always been a wolf to his fellow-man" (1933: 165). And so the possibility of an alternative future barely arises: "It is the fatal weakness of modern theorists to persuade themselves that they are going to create [an age of gold on earth]" (165).

In many respects, Bell is a successor to that 19th-century radicalism which consists in breaking away from one's own class (see R. Williams 1963: 175-81). The would-be radical finds a cause – the "genius of Spain" – and identifies with it, passionately so, in a mood of rebellion. "The emotional, intellectual, aesthetic and ethical elements are combined and harmonized [in Spain], sometimes imperfectly, in a living whole" (Bell 1936: 4). But Bell never faced the true crisis of the outcast who opts for socialism, since as an Englishman living abroad, he was doubly exiled and able to keep the Spanish peasant at a distance. He was thus saved the painful discovery that the "people" only appear to be a mass, that many are as ugly as the capitalist bosses that exploit them. (Not news, as Raymond Williams notes, to anyone who has actually lived amongst them.) His writings on Spain do not register an objective reality: their immediate reference is his own personal drama. Whilst his distance was maintained, Bell achieved that rare paradox of being at home in exile. This situation ended at a point when, during the early thirties, the real social relations within Spanish society reached such a point of revolutionary turmoil that even the likes of Bell were obliged to take some stock of reality as opposed to their fantasies and illusions.

Already, in Bell's early work, the contradictions begin to multiply as the realities of social division clash with the "eternal values" beloved of liberalism. Spain, the argument runs, is an "imperfect" organic community, typified by the "hunger-ridden Paradise of Las Hurdes" (Peers 1924: 54). The outcome is a species of crude invective against "modern liberty," as embodied in the attempt by "small minorities" to set themselves above "God, King and the Nation." Mobile, free-floating intellectuals, as we have seen, readily take exception to what they perceive to be spurious, imagined identities: "Not, one infers, the true, genuinely Spanish Spain" (Bell 1933: 175). National communities, it seems, transcend such fabrications.

Resistance to the collapse of the illusory center was tenacious, and had to be, at a time when the reality of fragmentation was extreme. In his "Cartas de Madrid," L**** the *Bulletin*'s Spanish correspondent sustained the key values of the organic community: "España representa en el mundo nada más que una fuerza espiritual y es difícil imponerse en esa forma en los tiempos en que grandes naciones como los Estados Unidos parecen no entender otra cosa que las columnas llenas de números de un libro de cuentas" (L**** 1926: 177) ("Spain represents a real spiritual force in the world, and finds it difficult to impose itself in an age when great nations such as the United States seem to understand nothing more than endless columns of numbers in a ledger book"). The willed blindness reaches bizarre proportions. At a point when the violence that preceded the Civil War was already underway, L**** was still protesting: "La situación general no es alarmante, ni ocurre nada realmente .... Es lo cierto que una vez más podemos decir satisfactoriamente: 'Aquí no pasa nada'" (1930: 181) ("The general situation is not alarming, nor is anything really happening .... In fact, once more we can say in all confidence: 'Nothing is going on here'"). Suddenly, he finds himself holding at bay not only the actual course of events but alternative views that the *Bulletin*, as any good liberal journal, felt obliged to publish in the interests of "objectivity." Not surprisingly, our Madrid correspondent suddenly disappears from the *Bulletin*'s pages, leaving an embarrassed editor, Allison Peers, to explain his silence.

This displacement of "patriotism" to certain key symbols – the monarchy, the heritage, the armed forces, the flag – betrays a profound collusion with the forces of capitalism, beneath an apparent disparagement of commerce (e.g., Atkinson's "though commerce were dead and Latin America a back number, what need we any further incentives?" [75]). Indeed, the mystical individual, in his aloneness, is the very image of that mobile, isolated monad of modern industrial society. It is no surprise that, at this time, a former British minister and Ambassador of the Crown, Sir Malcolm Robertson, appeared in the *Bulletin* to stress the role of Literature and Culture, the twin columns of the organic community, in the business of buying and selling. The supporter, at one moment, of traditional organic values of community and loyalty, the Minister can be found, at the next, advocating economic policies with respect to Argentina that involved the dispossession of the pampas by agribusiness and the massive displacement of their inhabitants to the shantytowns of Buenos Aires. The classics of literature thus find themselves in juxtaposition with considerations of cost-effectiveness, profit and advantageous production. "If the Argentine will only stick to the soil and leave manufacture alone for which he has neither the aptitude nor the fuel nor the raw material, he will continue to flourish as one of the main food producers of the whole world. That is his real job in life" (Robertson 79).

The ex-Minister is clearly troubled by the low standard of living in the Third World, and feels "uneasy" in the face of that "ugly word "Imperialism" (84). But he is reassured by the thought that the Argentinean peons "are happy and would scoff at our ideas of a high standard of living" (79), and also by the fact that the superpower which is the USA, not the poor little Yookay, is now the recipient of anti-imperialist ire. And, of course, we British have wisely used Literature and Culture to smooth over potentially difficult, conflictual relationships. To trade successfully, one needs a knowledge of the history, institutions and culture of the nation with which one is dealing. Familiarity with Spain's "wholly wonderful literature" is a "very definite commercial asset" (88). The implication is that if you can talk to an individual about his classics, you can sell him anything. In the same spirit of confidentiality, Sir Malcolm is not afraid to show *us* his hand: "Of course I do not deny for one moment that self-interest has a considerable deal to say to it" (85).

Before we dismiss such articles as the unhappy intrusion of a material world into the otherwise spiritual, other-worldly domain of Hispanism, we would do well to ponder the textual evidence, which suggests that our early predecessors were far from averse to a bit of flag-waving. The Empire figured prominently, for example, in the thoughts of William Entwistle: "It has remained by consent intact: consent of its members that the association is the most humane they can know, and consent of other nations to a substantial good. And this being true of the empire, it is also true of all human intercourse" (quoted by Morley 188). And thus does one of Hispanism's premier linguists construct a model of human discourse upon an imperialist model of exchange which totally represses the actual inequalities of power that characterize real conversation.

If, as we have seen, it proves impossible to sustain, even in the case of Spain, the notion of a present-day organic community, there is a certain inevitability about the turn to bygone ages. The journey to the South becomes a journey into the past. At this point a consideration of Bell again proves instructive. Unable to contemplate any genuinely alternative social system, he came to believe that there was nothing to be won but the past. And since it is one of the most notable features of the Golden Age that it is always elsewhere, Bell was inevitably constrained to replay those battles already fought over modern Spain. His tone is more frenetic but his position equally, if not more, vulnerable. The defense of traditional values, he was bound to concede at the outset, in the light of Américo Castro's argument for a "conflictive age," is a lost cause. The Golden Age was hard and cruel, and rampantly elitist: "culture has [n]ever been more than the privilege of a handful in a barbarous age" (1933: 164). Sixteenth-century society, by any reckoning, was desperately divided: "The Reformation of Luther had cast a shadow similar to that cast by Bolshevism four centuries later" (167).

The mention of Bolshevism is interesting. It reminds us of the extent to which Bell was the mirror image of his natural enemy, the Marxist intellectual of a period when the Revolution seemed to have failed, high-jacked by the Stalinists. Both, while seeming to deal in factual observation, project a "mass" onto actual working people. They then proceed in opposite directions, Bell presenting them (in their peasant form) as the model of the good life, the Marxist writing them off as incapable of consciousness and therefore of revolutionary action. Both in fact are merely registering the pressures of feeling exiled.

If, however, Bell saved himself from the pessimism of his Marxist equivalent, it was only because in reality he had already accepted the finality of defeat: "loving traditional Spain to the exclusion of the Spain of the twentieth century" (165). Ironically, he could only arrive at such a view by projecting the modern sense of citizenship and nationhood back into the past and thus misrecognizing the still embryonic Absolutist State as one in which the individual "[was] more inclined than now to identify himself with the service of God, King and Country" (172). When confronted by people less eager than he was to indulge their fantasies, Bell's response was to raise still further the level of rhetoric. Thus, in the 16th-century, "the individual felt himself a part of the greater whole" (173), and voluntarily restrained his criticism of society, or so at least Bell alleges. Clearly, such views could be sustained only on the basis of historical and cultural ignorance and delusion, and by an emotional investment that sometimes borders on the hysterical: "it was an age not of puling, creeping hypocrisy [like the present] but of a grand enthusiasm" (179).

On these terms, history assumes the form of a meta-narrative of the loss of innocence. This loss, we have seen, begins already in the Golden Age, "the more insidious dangers of the Reformation and Protestantism bringing the shadow of the coming chaos, anarchy, dissension and particularism in their train" (Bell 1944: 78). The devolutionary fall from unity is prolonged by the Enlightenment: "For three centuries Spain lived in her enemies' day, in the day of a civilization which ran counter to all her high ideals" (79). There is no way forward: only retreat, into the organic community: "The question now before the world is whether civilization will return to a saner, more natural ideal" (79). Accordingly, Bell denounces compulsory education as a "cruel outrage" and defends the virtues of poverty and illiteracy (1946: 284).

Recent Developments

Later developments in Hispanism did lead to some revision. The Golden Age remains the standard, but there is a shift from aesthetics to morality. The Romantic subject came to be seen as a dangerously rebellious model to place before the new classes gaining access to higher education. The organic community had to be bound more closely, through morality. For Alexander Parker the unity of the text reflects that of society: "The key to this unity is to be found in the moral conceptions governing the presentation of the theme – so common in the Spanish literature of the later Golden Age – of the rebellion of the individual against the social order. Treason and rape are dramatically unified in *Fuenteovejuna* because they are morally akin – aspects of an individual will to social disorder" (Parker 1953: 145-46). In order to achieve this unity, "theory" and "method," inherently dangerous, were rejected in favor of an empiricist idealism in which reaction against speculative idealism was tempered by subjective overtones: "No one has a keener eye for thematic unity and strict relevance in every detail of a play than Calderón" (150). The result was a denial and underestimation of history, symptomatic of which is the recurrent appeal to universal or atemporal characteristics of the human spirit.

Parker constantly re-deploys the same critical strategy. What is most striking about his analysis of *Don Quijote*, for example, is the extent to which he actively reproduces the text, while claiming to release its concealed meaning, in such a manner that what others might see as a sprawling, uneven work, fractured by the pressures of a carnivalesque discourse, is reduced thematically to a "clear and ordered design of plot, a kind of circular pattern" (1956: 9). The hermeneutic circle serves to re-contain the Romantic subject, to burden characters with a sense of responsibility for their actions and their effect upon others. *Don Quijote*, on these terms, is a tale of simple moral development (16), whose classic status lends it a certain intimidating presence, a cultural capital which, we suggest, "is denied to subordinate classes and which has the double function of exclusion, and of legitimation of the social order " (Frow 228). In other words, Hispanism under Parker and the epigoni of "thematic structuralism" becomes firmly implicated in a "culture of control," a culture sorely needed in the reconstruction of Britain in the aftermath of World War II.

While Parkerians continued to dominate British Hispanism into the mid 1970s and even beyond, they were becoming a visibly residual feature within the academy. The real danger was emerging from elsewhere, in an ideological landscape rapidly being transformed by the New Right. And it was this New Right which, by the time the Conservative government was driven from power in Britain, in the mid 1970s, was overshadowing the elitist and more moderate centers within Toryism. The Labour government of Callaghan actually facilitated the swing towards neo-liberalism, as social democracy found itself powerless to resist the demands of monopoly capital. The reality was that state power, by definition national, was finding itself increasingly at odds with multinational capitalism. By the mid 1980s, Thatcherism was dominant, and set on opposing an emphasis on equality which, in its view, had encouraged too many to want to go too far in society. As a senior Civil servant said at the time: "When young people cannot find work at all ... or work which meets their abilities or expectations ... then we are only creating frustration with perhaps disturbing social consequences ... people must be educated once more to know their place" (Quoted by Benn and Chitty 13). Sweeping educational reforms were begun both at the primary and secondary levels, where attempts were made to break up the comprehensive system, and at the tertiary level.

The consequences of these developments were particularly grave for the traditional liberal fraction. In generational terms, many of its academics were products of the 1960s, whose permissiveness was widely held by the New Right to be responsible for the dire economic straits in which the nation found itself. They accordingly became the target for a populist pogrom initiated by the New Right. Having said which, permissiveness was scarcely a charge that could be leveled against the quietly conservative, marginal discipline of Hispanism. What changes had been made in the 1970s had been largely cosmetic and constituted relatively minor acts of accommodation to innovatory forces. Not without reason, many leading Hispanists could not understand the animosity that was suddenly being directed against them. Their solution was to take the easy option – one by one, they drifted into early retirement, leaving behind them a discipline in total disarray. For while a state of intellectual retardation was nothing new in Hispanism, quite suddenly decades of mediocrity seemed to catch up with it, leaving a gap between itself and its sister disciplines. The latter were more internally diverse, and therefore possessed the resources to respond more positively to the crisis. What was needed was an ideology capable of revitalizing the humanities but in ways that would placate or at least not offend a resurgent neo-liberalism. The need was accepted to abandon any thought of criticizing social injustice from the standpoint of class solidarity. A nominalist (or textualist) stance denied any possible basis of appeal to the realities of oppression as known and experienced by members of the relevant class or community. Theory was reconstituted as a play-off between multiple competing "discourses" or "subject-positions," devoid of any ontological grounding. This was the moment of postmodernism, and its impact on British Hispanism was heralded by the dizzy ascent of the postmodern hispanist.

National Literature in a Global Economy

In analyzing the implosion within Hispanism, occasioned largely by the relative eclipse of Golden Age studies, it is only too easy to simplify. On the level at which teaching and lecturing actually occur, practice is complex and contradictory in the extreme. Indeed, one of the most astounding characteristics of younger, career-minded Hispanists is their untroubled ability to span radically conflicting discourses, to commodify even those analytic models which seek to expose and thereby resist reification. It is precisely this syncretistic capacity, however, which forces us, with a renewed sense of urgency, to return to the recent history of Hispanism, and to reconsider liberal humanism's vulnerability to New Right vocationalism. Almost overnight it seems – whatever happened to Hispanism? – hegemonic forms have been challenged, their legitimacy contested, and their credibility undercut. How, ideologically, do we account for all of this?

One line of argument could run as follows: the control of the content of Golden Age courses served the purposes of a conservative elite, anxious to defend the prevailing relations of production, just as surely as the superannuation of these same courses is related to the need to expand the forces of production. Its virtues are considerable: it would explain, to begin with, why moralism, of the kind inculcated by Parkerian criticism, gives way to the production of desire, an indispensable ingredient of consumerism, and to the technicism of the commercial translator and interpreter. But intriguing as such suggestions are, their inadequacy becomes apparent as soon as we seek to clarify what precisely we object to about the new vocationalism. Not the very necessary task of reskilling the workforce; not even the glibness with which otherwise upmarket theoreticians talk of student "wants" (a term significantly left undeconstructed). What is fundamentally at issue is the creation through vocationalism of an alternative conservative ideology. Youth unemployment, the labor market, and the labor process are only indirectly implicated. (Does anyone seriously imagine there are jobs for hundreds of Spanish students?) "More specifically, in considering the relationship of occupationalist educational ideology to production it is necessary to keep in mind its extreme abstraction. Despite its rhetoric of 'realism' – the 'needs of industry,' employability, skills for the new technologies, etc. – it is in reality almost entirely a construct of ideology and theory, of free market utopianism and behaviorist psychology. Its scientism is as spurious as its economics" (Moore 232-33). In the same vein, the realism promoted by the entrepreneurial Hispanist is every bit as mythological as that of his/her predecessor.

In such circumstances, it is not hard to see why McGaha finds himself no longer needed. He shares the Romantic's distaste for the 18th- and 19th-century laissez-faire utilitarianism that the new vocationalism confessedly revamps. Let us recall again the aversion of Peers' Hispanism for commercialism: a Spanish Committee of the Modern Language Association (1935), reporting on the teaching of Spanish in secondary schools, concluded that "in the past some have unduly stressed the alleged utility of Spanish, and that attention has been frequently diverted from its value as an element in a liberal education" ([Peers] 1936: 73). Of course, in practice, as we have seen, the traditional Hispanist, by cultivating the subjective sensibilities of a minority (who ran the Empire), served the middle class in its capitalist exploitation of Third World Countries. In contrast, the new vocationalism serves that section of the middle class based in industry and commerce. As Robert Moore has explained, the key factor in all of this is the autonomy of the educational system: "Hence, 'the new vocationalism' is an *ideology of production regulating education*, rather than an *educationalist ideology servicing production*" (Moore 241). Necessarily, there have been casualties in the transition: Hispanism, in its traditional guise, was one. The only continuities there can be are ideological: thus, to take but one example, the images of Spain promoted (by foreigners) through Expo 92, which was held in Spain, were none other than the inventions of our Romanticist predecessors, recycled in the interest of profit margins. (Spaniards themselves are significantly more anxious to stress their country's technological arrival.) This not-so-strange irony can only confirm McGaha's suspicions – and here, for once, he was absolutely right – that Hispanism was not a good career choice.

One small comfort that McGaha can take from the advent of multinational capitalism is that it has by no means entailed the eclipse of the nation-state, as the most significant unit of monopoly capital, for the simple reasons that "economic and ideological functions cannot be delegated to a supranational or super-state apparatus without destroying the illusion of representative government which sanctions and legitimizes the entire process" (Resch 359). It is also important not to misconstrue the neo-conservative reaction against "big government" during the 1980s, or be deceived by the Reagan-Thatcher effort to "roll back the State." As we indicated above, such rhetoric belies the increasingly interventionist activity of the State, not least of all in matters of education. This is not to deny the reality of privatization and deregulation. The claim is simply that they are the converse of undiminished government intervention, in the service of international capital.

While it can be no part of our extended discussion, it is worth considering, by way of conclusion, to what extent the current disciplinary emphasis upon modern Latin-American literature constitutes a logical, adaptive extension of the relatively overt nostalgia that has long pervaded Hispanism. After all, where is the substantial difference between Bell's picturesque portraits of the poverty-stricken peasants of Spain and the more recent visions of primitivism that evoke the exoticism of an imperial colonial past and present? Moreover, just as Bell's contemplative stance is the product of the consumerism that he condemns, so also is the promotion of magic realism by a commercial sector itself notably short on magic. True, there are observable differences: the erstwhile lament on the "decline of the West" – in other words, on the petty-bourgeois fall in social status – has been transformed into a pseudo-radical commitment to women's issues and to conveniently distant revolutions in Central America. But there lingers, beneath the thin veneer of change, an ideological program to re-contain what would otherwise be unbearable divisions within the community, a program which is, at the same time, a covert rejection of any genuinely alternative social and cultural order.

2
Allison Peers: For God, King and Country

"We ought to regard with suspicion the demand that the university should continually be thinking of 'society,' teaching citizenship, stimulating the social consciousness, mingling with people of all classes and occupations, supplying experts to local industries, taking part in local activities, and the like."
(Bruce Truscot)

Telling Tales

Until recently, it was necessary to guess at the personal life history of Allison Peers. He came, one assumed, from a family of middling status, one high enough for him to mix with the aristocracy at Cambridge, without feeling too uncomfortable, but low enough to know what it was to study in the cold of one's bedroom. One might have even gone so far as to suggest that his family was from the "sunken" middle class, a location that would have bred in Peers his characteristic loathing for the working class, whose environs he was forced to share, and his equally characteristic contempt for the aristocracy, whose circles he longed to join.

The recent publication of Peers' autobiography, together with his academic novel, *The Autobiography of "Bruce Truscot,"* has relieved us of the need to speculate, at the same time that it has gratifyingly confirmed our original hunches. Peers' family, it transpires, had a servant, "in what was otherwise a predominantly working class area" (Peers 1996: 62-63). His father was an officer in the Customs and Excise, with little money but a "business instinct" (71); he was also a man with some pretense to education, being widely read in English literature, who was distinguished above all by his "moral energy" (74), from which we may infer that Peers' family belonged to that declining faction of the petty bourgeoisie which was in the ideological pay of an antiquated ruling class. Of this faction, Bourdieu writes: "To have their revenge, they only have to place themselves on their favourite terrain, that of morality, to make a virtue of *their* necessity, elevate their particular morality into a universal morality" (Bourdieu 1984: 353). Peers would continue his father's interest in theology, and probably, like Bruce Truscot, would have gravitated towards the Church of England (as opposed to Methodism). "These groups," Bourdieu concludes, "not only have the morality of their interests, as everyone does; they have an interest in morality" (353). Indeed, Peers' spirituality extended to publishing a number of works of a devotional nature, in which he compared his vocation, as university lecturer, to "the cure of souls" (1966: 255 n96). Equally revealing is the reference to the "cold bedroom" at home, where Truscot worked (210) and whither, presumably, Peers retreated to escape the communal chaos of the kitchen.

For those who shared their ideological bias, the two major works on university education written by Allison Peers, alias Bruce Truscot, at the end of the Second World War, "exerted an influence for the good wherever English is understood" (Mountford 11).[2] They exhibited, so it was argued, the same "broad humanity" that allegedly characterized Peers' more specialized, professional work in Hispanism, a discipline whose modern development he did so much to determine. Few would now be prepared to endorse with the same enthusiasm the cultural ideal that Peers' many books and articles, taken as a whole, embody. Intellectuals from the same mold, it is true, still survive in the academy, but in such reduced numbers as to border on extinction.[3] Their sympathetic dramatization in several recent films – notably *The Browning Version* and *Dead Poets' Society* – has not been without its confusions and contradictions. Symptomatically, the preferred filmic setting has been that of the American private or British "public" school that, despite its elitism, has not remained immune to the brash, aggressive technicism of a hegemonic neo-liberalism. The dominant tone is one of nostalgia. We are given to understand that, lamentably, something is passing never to return.

What is passing, we would argue, is an intellectual of a traditional kind, who flourished under the *ancien régime*. Objectively considered, his defining characteristics are fairly clear. His ideology is shaped by spiritual values that ostensibly transcend the mundane turmoil of civil society. The university is "a corporation or society which devotes itself to a search after knowledge for the sake of its intrinsic value" (Truscot 1951: 65). His

---

2.   Truscot plays mischievously with the question of his own identity (Truscot 1951: 14-15). Anonymity, he explains, ensured, firstly, that his ideas, as opposed to his personality, would be discussed, and, secondly, that he could legitimately indulge in a certain amount of bias, through which to startle the over-complacent Redbrickian. Anonymity, one might argue, also protected Peers from possible retaliation by his superiors on the University Council, an institutional body that he criticized in the severest terms.

3.   Predictably, they include the editors of Peers' recently published *Redbrick University Revisited: The Autobiography of "Bruce Truscot,"* who believe, somewhat remarkably, that Peers recorded "personally yet objectively" the academic history of his times. Likewise, his ideas on the University "still strike us as bold, relevant and, strangely, modern" (Peers 1996: 19, 405).

civilizing mission, so at least he boasts, is to spread a knowledge "hitherto available only to one class, community or language group, for the benefit of others" (71). In reality, he is dependent upon a centralized monarchical power, whose interests he finally serves. As far as Britain was concerned, these interests extended to an Empire, for which reason it was difficult to say what appalled Truscot more, the Student Union support in 1940 of "the right of Indian people to immediate and complete independence" (222) or the attitude of those Oxford students who later, in a Union debate, "declined to fight for their King and country" (223).

King, Country and, crucially, God. For religion, with its other-worldly themes, is profoundly important to this traditional intellectual. Indeed, in an earlier age, in addition to being a man of letters, he would also have been a cleric, the relics of whose discourse abound in Peers. For example, the disinterested search for knowledge is a "basic article of faith" (68), in a very literal sense; the university is a place in which to retire "from the life of the world" (69); truth is pursued by "laying down and voluntarily embracing such discipline as is necessary" (69); academics may cease to do research but "can no more regard their vocation as having ceased than can an aged monk, or a retired priest" (72); and the people who attend public lectures by professors "will remain to pray" (246). Indeed, one of the aspects of the contemporary university that most disturbed Truscot was the neglect of religion (228). England, he insists, is a Christian country, with age-long Christian traditions and an Established Church, facts which ought to be manifest in the everyday life of the university community. Correspondingly, pressure is brought to bear on the freshman student to become involved in religious groups: "you can never rest in agnosticism – and deep down within your personality you know it" (Truscot 1946: 105). Peers, we recall, specialized professionally in Spanish mysticism.

Needless to say, far more is at issue than a certain verbal residue and the observance of simple daily ritual. The very lifestyle of the university, in Truscot's view, should be contemplative in the religious sense, and far removed from earthly, political concerns. He observed with dismay the way that undergraduates at the redbrick university "would stream daily into the busy city from all four points of the compass" (1951: 27). The religious ideal, as Truscot envisaged it, required that the university be separated from this urban turmoil and the teeming masses that pullulated in it: "… more than one of our modern universities stands in the midst of the humblest dwellings – not far removed, to put it bluntly, from slums" (27). Not for a second did he pause to consider that the industrial areas of Liverpool generated the social surplus off which the intellectual lived and which made possible his life of ease. At this point, the ethos of the High

Church converges with that of a genteel aristocracy: "One has only to contrast the present Redbrick University, situated in (or very near to) the slums, with a Redbrick University City of the future, lying well outside the municipal boundaries, with its Great Hall, its playing fields, and, above all, its Greengates, its White Gables and its Goldcrest, each creating traditions of its own" (59). In his vision of the new post-war university, let us note parenthetically, Truscot was something of a prophet, for it would indeed be built, in most cases, on a private estate or campus outside the urban centre. Idealism, in this sense, would be built into its physical location.

The problem for the traditional intellectual, as should be obvious, was that protection from market forces and bureaucratic structures, afforded by an earlier, pre-capitalist social formation, was rapidly being eroded. Symptomatic of the change was the newly arrived Department of Commerce, which Truscot viewed with barely disguised abhorrence. Not without reason, he associated it with the instrumental modes of discourse that were beginning to challenge the metaphysical world view which traditional intellectuals such as himself promoted. In such circumstances, the very roar and surge of city life sufficed to remind him of the vocational topics promoted by the Student Union. Factory visits and association with local leaders of industry had little to do with education as he understood it (77). Students, he was painfully aware, were only too willing to surrender their hearts (not to mention their souls) to the vocationalists, "who henceforward can lead them hither and thither at their will" (77).

Yet there is a paradox implicit in Truscot's work that should be made more explicit, in which respect we need to press a little further the parallel between the university and the Church of England. The latter, as Truscot reminds us, is an *established* church, whose operations, while largely restricted to the private sphere, are also tied to the State. Likewise, the modern university, whose autonomy was also "sacred" (299), was funded largely and increasingly by the State. Far from deploring its economic dependence, Truscot actively promoted it. Indeed, his major works on the university constituted in essence a plea for increased public spending on tertiary education. Their logic would have been difficult to fault, had the liberal pursuit of Truth been as ideologically neutral as Truscot claimed it to be. But it was not, any more than was the government upon whose funding universities had come to depend. And it was here that so many things started to go wrong for Truscot.

Traditional intellectuals, however modest their ideological claims, have always contributed decisively to the reproduction of prevailing class and power relations. Moreover, recent changes have fully integrated higher education into a corporate, state network tied to and serving capitalist interests. This is a process that Truscot in part bemoans and resists, but that he also encouraged. True, he never went so far as to break with traditional elites, in contrast with some of his more radicalized and secularized colleagues. But as we shall see, he was crucially concerned to promote the social status of the professional stratum to which he belonged, to make maximum use of its monopoly of knowledge, and to exert any bureaucratic leverage that it possessed to the full. To this extent, his work has to be understood within the context of the modern growth of vast monopolies of bureaucratic control, of which the expansion of modern universities is simply a part.

Drabtown versus Oxbridge

It is possible to progress a good way into *Red Brick University* (1951 [1943]) without being able to see beyond the repugnance its author evinces for the provincial university's grimy gray walls or hideous, "grinning" red brick, not to mention the ugly blue and yellow tiles of its interior. "And what is true of the buildings is equally applicable to the personnel" (28). Such statements exude a class hatred so pure and distilled that one cannot imagine them as emanating from anyone other than a traditional intellectual who identifies totally with the class outlook of the aristocracy. Truscot was clearly pained to his aesthetic core by a provincial institution that was "unmellowed by tradition and attended by men who actually live with their families and probably have only the faintest idea of the respective significance of a dinner jacket and a white waistcoat" (31).

Yet read with an appropriate attention to detail, *Red Brick University* gives clear evidence of its ideological ambiguities. Take, for example, the question of the scholarship system at Oxbridge. Truscot attributes this system's existence to attacks by adherents of "that troublesome institution known as the Labour Party" (51). While such sentiments unambiguously originate in the author, who never passes up an opportunity to inveigh against socialism, they are also overdetermined by an irony that slightly distances him from them. Even more ambivalent are the ensuing remarks concerning Puddlewick Grammar, the Drabtown Municipal Secondary School, which is described as "quite too impossibly 'bad'" (52). The inverted commas signal an intradiscursive dimension that serves a dis-identifying function. Likewise, the references to "good" schools and to "nice girls" (50) reverberate with the sense of belonging elsewhere. But exactly where? To an aristocratic elite, perhaps, but one with which Truscot does *not* identify. It is difficult not to conclude that, at some level,

Truscot wished to hold aloof from the upper classes whose values he otherwise embraced and trumpeted.

Of course, the ambiguities more frequently work in the other direction, that is to say, to complicate Truscot's commitment to an ostensibly democratic principle. Consider, for example his attitude towards the external degree system of the University of London. This system Truscot agrees, had brought the university degree within reach of thousands who previously lacked the necessary "advantages." But it is not altogther clear whether this is to be considered a vice or virtue, when viewed alongside the allegedly negative effects of an "over-inclusive" American system of tertiary education. Overall, our final impression is one of ideological uncertainty and equivocation.

Redbrick and These Vital Days (1945) throws further light on the nature and extent of Truscot's contradictions, particularly over the respective merits and demerits of the British public school. This institution was currently being subjected to measured demands, in terms of access and funding, by left-wing intellectuals, such as R. H. Tawney. In a climate of increasing working-class militancy, conservative intellectuals like Truscot were forced to define their positions more precisely. By instinct they remained evasive and defensive of aristocratic privilege. Thus, for example, Truscot refrains from considering in detail the "great many reasons" why public schools should not be abolished, on the grounds that "most people would think it a waste of time" (1945: 156). Briefly, he insists that disendowment would look uncomfortably like "legalized robbery" (156), that the well-taxed rich have a right to freedom, and that "the granting of a fuller life to one class should not involve a restricting of life for another" (156). Needless to say, it escaped his attention that the capitalist extraction of surplus value from workers involves a form of legalized robbery, that the freedom of these workers is constantly infringed by cut-throat managers, and that dominant classes have, throughout history, enjoyed a fuller life at the expense of those who serve them.

The depths of Truscot's ideological blindness have yet to be reached. Incredibly, he cannot think that the statistical proof that the nation's leaders are largely recruited from public schools "proves very much" (166), for the simple reason that, as he proceeds to explain, while the kinds of people on which this evidence is based – bishops, deans, judges, magistrates, leading civil servants, bank directors and the like – certainly occupy positions of power and influence, they cannot be said to be the nation's *leaders*. The divorce, on this basis, between politics and the real centers of social power, and the consequences for British democracy, does not trouble Truscot in the slightest. And for obvious reasons: three generations of Truscot's family, it subsequently transpires, have attended public schools. Some readers will be disinclined to continue, and not without reason.

Granted the existence of such obvious prejudices and blindspots, the exact nature of Truscot's ideological location may seem beyond dispute. Yet, as we have been at pains to insist from the beginning, the traditional intellectual exhibits unsuspected complexities and contradictions, and Truscot is no exception. In the present context, is important to weigh his aristocratic bias against his more critical appraisal of the public school and "the deplorable *ancien régime*" (167). For while confessing the very real advantages, in social and material terms, of public school education, Truscot does not flinch from condemning its rampant bullying, its perverted sexual practices, and, in short, its total artificiality as a way of life. Notwithstanding its successes, he elaborates, public school education proves to be a personally damaging experience for many of its less able pupils. It is wrong to dismiss such comments as a mere subterfuge, on the part of someone simply anxious to neutralize Tawney's demand for greater proletarian access. While no working-class intellectual, Truscot argues convincingly that token gestures affecting a few individuals (a) do little to benefit the vast majority that are excluded, (b) deprive Drabtown of its most talented natural leaders, and (c) fail to take into account the personal anguish and suffering of those "bursary boys" who actually gain entry. Equally difficult to fault is his conclusion that, short of a more radical transformation, working-class children stood to benefit most from improvements to state education.

Of course, the charge against Truscot's biases remains and needs to be re-affirmed in the face of reassurances as to his own neutrality ("unbiased by prejudice" [112]). After all, a keen concern to safeguard an established order is constantly in evidence throughout these texts, most strikingly in the prospect of "schisms," "open clashes," and "civil war" that proletarian access to the public school would, allegedly, bring in tow. The point is simply that Truscot's illusions of impartiality need to be understood as materially based, to the extent that they depend upon his location *between* two other contending classes. Only from such a position could he know, really know, what it meant to be a "simply frightful backyarder" with a Northern English accent and a nervous or hesitating manner (200). True, he had not been personally subjected to the "old style arm-twisting," traditionally meted out to working-class boys, but he was familiar enough with the phenomenon from his school days, "where I met it in reverse, circumstances obliging me to go daily from a cultured home to a poor type of Elementary school" (201).

Symptomatic of Truscot's sense of dual class-belonging is, as always, his linguistic instability. Particularly striking in *Redbrick and these Vital Days* is the confusion generated by the very term "public school." Truscot cannot confront directly the outrage of this misnomer, but must have recourse instead to makeshift terms, such as "independent public schools" and "public boarding schools," as opposed to "Secondary schools." On one occasion he refers to the "genuinely 'public' school'" as opposed to "the private one" (190). Such stylistic quirks and contortions are the hallmark of a reformist discourse, of the kind practised by the traditional intellectual. They betray his allegiance, sometimes his antagonism, both towards the working classes, whose Drabtown he despised, and towards the high bourgeoisie and aristocracy, whose idleness and decadence he found equally contemptible. In an important sense, I am saying, Truscot did not belong entirely to either Drabtown or Oxbridge. Rather he explores in his work what it was like to travel *between* them, in the metaphorical sense. And it was for this reason that his attention turned to the "scholarship boy."

The Scholarship Boy

The classic portrait of the scholarship boy remains that contained in Richard Hoggart's *The Uses of Literacy*. Hoggart is perfectly positioned – not too close, not too distant – to capture his essential features: the isolation of someone who is emotionally uprooted from his class, has an intelligence above the average, and an unusual self-consciousness and tendency to self-dramatization (Hoggart 291-304). But what makes Hoggart's account a *classic* portrait is the note of ambivalence that he discerns: the longing to remain within, as opposed to break with, the gregarious working-class family group, if, that is, the individual is to "get on." Memorable too are the nuances: the trouble with accents, the length of time spent amidst the women folk, a father who is still at work or drinking with his mates, a constitutional tenseness, the awkwardness in middle-class society, and the grubby finger-nails.

The anecdotal evidence mentioned earlier, regarding his downward mobility, suggests that Truscot himself was no scholarship boy, at least of the working-class variety. Nor, in other respects, did he betray any residual features of having been one. Of course, it is the habit of such people to cover their tracks remarkably well. As Gramsci always insisted, the scholarship boy is not a stage in the evolution of the organic intellectual. On the contrary, he invariably becomes a faithful servant of the class that he joins. Typically, he will be more aggressive towards the working class than his bourgeois masters are. What makes for detection as regards particular individuals is that the process of total transformation is very rarely complete, given the endurance, or whatever it takes, to change a whole bodily habitus. Tell-tale traces normally remain to remind the scholarship boy, and others, of what he once was.

But if Truscot was not himself a scholarship boy, how did he come to know so well what it was to be one, including what it took to re-adapt constantly to changing environments (Truscot 1951: 36)? Truscot himself alerts us to the key, namely the experience he gained at Oxbridge and at Redbrick: "And I well know what strain can be caused even to a sensitive undergraduate by living for several hours of each day, or months of each year, in a humble, perhaps a desperately poor, home, and for the rest of the time in a cultural and well-educated community" (1945: 201). One surmises that Truscot's journey to Oxbridge from his sunken middle-class world required adjustments that overlapped with those of his socially inferior brethren. More likely still, Truscot learned something from traveling a similar route to the scholarship boy, between Oxbridge and Redbrick, after his appointment to a provincial university. (The shortcomings of professorial life in the provinces was to become one of his pet subjects.) Finally, Truscot would have been able to glean much about the trials of the scholarship boy from direct contact with him, on a daily basis, within the provincial university. He certainly spoke knowingly about the fears and anxieties that plagued comparatively mature, by no means hypersensitive, young students from a poor background.

It was doubtless this daily contact that encouraged Truscot to see the scholarship boy as a *problem*, something, that is, to be resolved and overcome as much as understood empathetically. The carrot that he held before his protégé was the privacy of a room of his own in Oxbridge. "Instead of going home everyday at tea-time," he elaborates, "to listen to Dad on the political situation and Mum on the current market prices or the iniquities of the neighbours" (1951: 32). These are telling images, which reveal the depth of Truscot's insight and understanding, not to mention his personal experience. And there was more where they came from. As we indicated earlier, he also knew about the promiscuity of the working-class kitchen or living room, that made it a difficult place in which to work, and about the cold, damp bedroom into which the scholarship boy sometimes fled in search of peace and quiet. Even more persuasive is the reference to the "dad and mum obligato" about how much they'd all scraped and saved for their son's benefit, with the commands to make the most of it. One might be fooled into thinking that, at some point, Truscot had been the proverbial fly on the wall within the working-class home.

At the same time, Truscot's sympathies also had their limits. While he spoke warmly about home life in relation to public schools, when it came to the university, he could not see beyond the benefits to be accrued from learning to sign on and off in letters and from reading the *Manchester Guardian* and *The Times* as opposed to the tabloid press. It counted for nothing that the scholarship boy was, in effect, being asked to turn his back on the shared joy, the humor, love, solidarity and security that was also part of working-class life. "The more often he can be put into evening dress and made to behave formally, the better" (212). Hence Truscot's sheer impatience with the student who quietly avoids the formal occasions. The fear or horror of being "shown up" socially was simply not part of his own class experience. What made such behavior particularly exasperating was the damage it caused others, such as the younger pupil who desperately needed a role model, the Head Master whose career stood to be boosted by the success of his star pupil, and even the lazy Etonian who stood to gain from increased competition.

But despite his frustrations, Truscot refused to be daunted. For when all was said and done, the scholarship boy had very real attractions for the liberal pedagogue in his battle with the moribund forces of feudalism. Not only was he both earnest and industrious but also obedient and deferential. More importantly, he was a subject or "character" in the making, in a way that set him apart from the "pleasant scoundrel" of public school extraction. Once weaned of his instinctive pragmatism and vocational bias, there was no telling what feats he would perform. Truscot aimed to recruit him in limited, if sufficient, numbers, and in order to do so, was prepared to devise a kind of education perfectly suited to his needs.

"A Truly Liberal Education"

One of the most arresting facts about the university, as an institution, is its longevity. Its basic structural components are already in place in the Middle Ages, including a body of teachers, otherwise salaried officials, that derived its authority from the institution and, functionally, served to sustain the hegemony of the aristocracy and its social apparatuses. This feudal system was able to survive relatively intact into and beyond the 19th century because the development of the bourgeoisie and of the forces aligned with the capitalist mode of production was effected, to a great extent, behind the back of the universities (see Lerena 120, 138).

Truscot, needless to say, has a different, more idealistic story to tell: "[The universities] originated, during the Middle Ages, in groups of learned, single-minded and enthusiastic men who wanted to live apart from the ordinary material business of the world, and throw off its cares, so that they could devote their whole lives to finding out things not previously known" (1946: 9). In order to achieve their aims, so this version runs, these recluses pooled their own resources, financial and otherwise. Their monasticism survives in the residual "seclusion" of the modern university, or so at least, from his own ideological standpoint, Truscot was anxious to argue. Imagined in these terms, as a society in miniature, the university is defined by its "corporate spirit" (8) and the "selfless devotion" (10) of organic, pre-capitalist communities.

Such continuities notwithstanding, readjustments had to be made, not least of all in the domain of ideology. Like the feudal aristocracy, the bourgeoisie aimed to secure a basically unequal social order, which was both natural and just. However, its biologistic logic was differently nuanced, in favor of "stock," as opposed to "blood." Truscot, given his contradictory class location, struggles to blend both ideologies. "Only the minority of its undergraduates come from the Little Back Streets and the Drabtowns," writes Truscot of Oxbridge, "Most have had the advantage of tradition and breeding, a cultured home, a public-school education, foreign travel in vacations and so on" (Truscot 1951: 44). Here, as whenever he refers to aristocratic institutions, one cannot be entirely certain that his words are, in the strictest ideological sense, his own. "Breeding" and "tradition," one suspects, were not entirely congenial to him. He is happier talking about different kinds of family background and educational institutions, which raise problems not of genetics but of socio-economic handicap. The latter concept is liberalism's own way of naturalizing, and thereby preserving, social relations (see Lerena 322-32). Truscot perfectly captures the ambiguities involved: "For character has very little relation to birth and none at all to the means of one's parents; and it is developed, not created, by education" (Truscot 1945: 168).

Needless to say, Truscot himself had little notion of the dynamics of ideological conflict and change, and none whatsoever of an ideological unconscious. For him, as for any liberal, a social or academic formation can be traced back to some primordial agreement or contract. Contracts, the liberal further assumed, can only be signed by "free" subjects, who, by implication, *precede* the particular formation. These subjects include the employer and employee, the doctor and patient, the husband and wife, and, last but not least, the teacher and pupil. The concept of a contract masks the violence that characterizes what are, in the last instance, relationships of inequality in exchange. Thus, to limit ourselves to the educational process, we witness the formation of character "*both in socii and discipuli*" (1951: 70-71, my italics). Truscot means by this not only that professors themselves learn in the process of teaching others, but that, as officials of a benign and neutral State, their task is simply to provide conditions in which mutually beneficial exchanges can take place. Let us elaborate.

Liberal education consists basically of a theory of extraction. Appropriate aptitudes are assumed to be already present in the individual, to the extent that teachers are encouraged to seek out "like-minded" individuals among the young (69). All that needs to be done is to provide an environment conducive to their unfolding. This is the task of the educational institution. Society itself may be bad, but education is neutral, and is able to negate society's worst effects. Individuals are given a chance or "opportunity," through scholarships, to "prove themselves." The teacher, also neutral, needs only to assist the student in a process of self-recognition: "... without knowing it, one grows in honesty, generosity and love of truth – or fails as a scholar" (71). Study and research permit a space in which natural talents and ability can develop. Tests and exams establish individuals' aptitudes and help chart their progress.

According to the liberal theory of education, let us reiterate, it is possible to arrive at specifically human qualities that are independent of particular social relations. Liberal pedagogy is, in other words, a species of philosophical essentialism, in which all human contact is reduced to interpersonal, inter-psychological relations. This stress on communication is crucial to the way liberalism imposes relations of domination. Unlike other systems, which brainwash in a hatefully repressive manner, liberalism prefers to be humane. Students are taught to work *with*, not *for*, their lecturer, whose manner will be correspondingly tentative and hesitating (1946:16). The essence of academic success, Truscot warned them, is to have a lively mind, "to be ready to question, examine, investigate and discover at every turn" (1951: 191). The difference between this and more repressive systems is significant in practical terms, but not theoretically. Through being non-directive, liberalism hides its relations of domination and consequently minimizes the possibility of resistance.

Within what is a basically Kantian universe, a strict division is drawn between factual knowledge and morality or, to use Truscot's term, "critical" knowledge. At the university, so the freshman is reassured, he will never be marked wrong for critical judgements that are well argued (1946: 17). For example, he well may believe that Byron was a better poet than Wordsworth, and has every right to believe so. For this reason, it is advisable never to read a book about a book until one has read the book itself and formed one's own impressions. Moreover, when exposed to criticism, the student should continue to exercise his critical judgement (75-76). After all, the purpose of literary criticism, or so Truscot implies, is not to impose value judgements on others but to facilitate a direct encounter between reader and author.

In practice, needless to say, the illusion of spontaneity and freedom was constantly betrayed by the covert violence at the heart of the liberal system. Significantly, Truscot is quick to point out that no mature critic would value Byron above Wordsworth, and that any student who disagrees will come, with more experience, to realize the error of his ways (75). But it is not simply as a critic that the student must learn to know his place. While the freshman was encouraged to call upon and speak personally with the Professor, he was also reminded that "you are a very junior learner and he is a very senior one" (23). Likewise, although the lecturer is the student's collaborator, it should not be forgotten that he is "in a considerably higher class" (1951: 191). The qualification is significant: it betrays the domination that Truscot would otherwise deny, as does the comment that good ideas in a lecturer, irrespective of his style of delivery, will hold students "at the feet of a man" (192). Even the critical attitude towards books that Truscot hoped to foster in his overly credulous students was somehow transfigured into "a refusal to dogmatize or to accept dogmatic judgements" (189). The truth was that liberalism needed to curtail the critical faculty far more urgently than it needed to develop it. Its hidden priorities are registered in the passivity of the students' response. *They* knew, and accordingly simply regurgitated material.

Manning the Gates

What was particularly striking about the British system propounded by Truscot was the emphasis it placed upon the exclusionary role of education. The basic cut took place at the age of eleven, when pupils were divided into two groups, one of which fed into secondary-modern schools and, ultimately, into blue-collar labor, the other into the grammar school and white-collar work (see 1945: 134-35). Truscot welcomed the creation and expansion, through government funding, of new kinds of institutions – polytechnics, technical institutions, schools of domestic science, etc. – on the strict understanding that they were to serve as a buffer zone between secondary and tertiary education (1951: 270). The implication is that they would allow the universities to contain their own expansion within (by Truscot's definition) reasonable limits and thereby preserve their elite status in what was obviously going to be a turbulent post-war period. In the event, as we know, these same universities were about to experience a historically unprecedented growth. The enormity of Truscot's miscalculation calls for comment and explanation.

Particularly instructive, in this regard, is the contrast between the binary system preferred by Britain, and an American system that extends the process of exclusion through a variety of variously graded institutions and institutionalized dead ends, up to and including university education. The basic difference is that between one country (Britain) in which feudalism exercises a residual influence and another (America) in which democratic institutions appeared *before* the entrenchment of industrial capitalism.[4] The ideological consequences were marked, notably in the relative importance attached to utilitarian as opposed to cultural values. Truscot was appalled by that mentality "which (to quote an equation which I have actually seen in print) puts the cultural value of modern language study on a level with that of typewriting" (67-68). Unfortunately, America appeared to be setting the trend: even in Britain the modern university not only *looked* like but increasingly behaved "like a glorified technical school" (27). It was a trend to be resisted: vocational training should be introduced into the university curriculum only on condition that it was recognized as an addition to the university's essential work and not claimed as a part of it. "A technical school, a secretarial or domestic science school, a cramming institution," Truscot protested, "are all quite distinct from a university" (68).

But if university education is not about "useful" knowledge, what is it about? Obviously, from Truscot's liberal standpoint, about the disinterested search for truth. What precisely was the value of this search? Truscot did not ask this question, for the simple reason that it could not be articulated within his own liberal framework. Indeed, it marks the limits of liberal ideology, of the classical kind. All that was left for Truscot to do was to draw a number of nice distinctions through which to defend his beleaguered social distinction. Thus: university work requires cramming, but "education in a much broader and humaner sense must be the chief and ever-present aim" (68); both research and teaching are important, but the former is more important than the latter, which cannot, even in its refined forms, escape its vocational nature; method, mental retentiveness, quickness of apprehension, and skill in argument are, in the last instance,

---

4.   As David Hogan explains: "Due to the peculiarities of America's non-feudal past, the revolution of 1776, and the nature of its politics in the early nineteenth century, much of the nineteenth-century working-class politics was essentially *defensive*, protecting the earlier achievement of republican democracy against what it perceived to be its chief enemies: monopolists, aristocratic forces, Catholic foreigners and, later, socialists" (42). For further comparison between the British and American systems, see Holly. For the blocking of the dual school system in the States, see Bowles and Gintis 1977: 216.

technical skills, and so "of less moment than selflessness, humility, sincerity and balance of judgement" (70-71).

Truscot's depreciation of merely mechanical skills extended to the amassing of facts for parrot-like regurgitation in examinations. A truly liberal educator, he believed, should encourage students to scrutinize received information critically, prior to deploying it creatively. The passive collation of facts, damagingly equated by some with research *per se*, was for him an inferior kind of intellectual activity, permissible only if carried out "in an eager and questing spirit" (71). It is, we would add, the hall-mark of the petty-bourgeoisie, and otherwise not far removed from the instrumental instincts of the working-class family.

Here we approach the ideological core of the kind of education that Truscot promoted. Its essential purpose was to create subjects able to occupy professional positions within the burgeoning state apparatuses. These subjects were expected to combine qualities such as leadership, a sense of responsibility, initiative, in other words, "qualities of character" (1945: 126), to be exercised upon their inferiors, with a willingness to obey the orders of their superiors. Accordingly, Truscot made every effort to cultivate alongside his students' sense of "increased power," a "keener sense of their own weakness" (1951: 72). By the same token, he expected of his *discipuli* who chose to go "out into the world" that they should feel "fuller, yet emptier" than when they entered university (72). Such sentiments, and the ideological accoutrements that went with them, were indispensable for anyone hoping to survive and flourish in the middle strata of society.

Or at least, they had previously been indispensable: "The position developed quite naturally. England, at a point in her history when she was rapidly growing in prosperity, needed a large number of leaders" (1945: 167). It bears consideration to what extent the traditional liberal subject was less serviceable in the climate of post-war Britain, at a time when this country had ceased to be a major imperial power. The association between education and character was beginning to sound "priggish" even to Truscot, though of course "only because it is unfashionable to write of such things in a natural way" (1951: 78). In reality, what was involved was less a change of fashion than the onset of a process of proletarianization within the professions, the most visible symptom of which was the routinization of precisely those medial positions which had formerly been filled by men of "character." Since the 1970s, this crisis of the professions has deepened to the extent that it is now threatening to destabilize the whole capitalist system (see Gorz; Callinicos and Harman 13-51).

The Claims of Specialization

As the gates were breached and the university flooded with undesirable people of all kinds, the need arose to erect various internal barriers, through which to reassert the necessary social divisions. Hence the appearance of different kinds of degrees to match the more varied student body. This rearguard operation was made more difficult by the pressure to specialize, which, Truscot was the first to recognize, originated outside the academy and was rooted ultimately in the increased mechanization of daily life. Part of Truscot, it goes without saying, was deeply hostile to such developments. As a traditional intellectual, he advanced the concerns of the "generalist," within the sphere of cultural studies. If excessive specialization was the result of social demands, the reply was simple: "societies must be induced to demand more" (1951: 287). At the same time, there were significant nuances to his argument. For while in certain respects Truscot was retrospective and nostalgic, he also took care to distance himself from the generalizing dilettantism of the gentleman scholar. The bourgeois industriousness and initiative that he valued was conducive to a certain professionalization of his discipline, which in turn required at least a modicum of specialization. Warnings to this effect are delivered to freshmen (74).

Specialization, as should be obvious, was a complex issue fraught with all kinds of difficulties. Broadly, it is important to distinguish between the creation of new specializations within the common trunk of a profession, and the skill differentiation occasioned by the fragmentation of the labor process. One could characterize Truscot's position by saying that while he approved of the former, he was vigorously opposed to the latter and, by implication, to the social changes that, historically, had followed in its wake, namely de-skilling, the loss of artesanal status, de-professionalization and proletarianization. Ideally, the distinction between these two kinds of specialization should mark the boundary between technical training and university education, or so at least Truscot argued. Hence, his ongoing struggle to exclude vocational courses from the University, which he associated, not unreasonably, with the broadened concept of "calling" that prevailed in North American universities and which served to dignify a greater number of technical and specialized pursuits.

But in this, as in other respects, Truscot was nothing if not a realist and therefore disposed to compromise. And one way of compromising, when it came to specialization in tertiary education, was to redefine the concept of "general education," so as to allow for appropriate discriminations, such as that between the Pass Degree and the Honours Degree. The former,

Truscot explains, is suitable for a second-class mind, by virtue of its generality, whereas the latter requires the "higher qualities of mind" necessary for specialization. Specialization, however, was to be understood in "the broad way" (287), an important nuance that helped distinguish it from the narrow focus associated with vocationalism. What Truscot had in mind was interdisciplinary work of various kinds, such as that in which, for example, the study of English literature shades into philosophy. The final result was to extend the exclusionary principle operative at the university entrance level into the degree system itself. Open access was a danger to be guarded against throughout the system.

In sum, then, Truscot had no difficulty coming to terms with the demand for an increased specialization, "a bogy that has haunted educationalists for too long" (188). True, the threat of de-skilling was very real. But to date, Truscot pointed out, "society has never demanded that the curriculum should be narrow" (287), which in effect left the university to determine exactly how the special honours subject was to be studied. This meant that it was still possible to define specialization in the broadest possible way, and in the process actually to *enhance* disciplinary status. Now it would be cynical to dismiss such distinctions as mere semantic quibbles or sophistries, designed to protect a certain cultural investment. Truscot, in all fairness, did maintain a commitment to general public issues – one recalls Peers' own work on the Spanish civil war. (It was a commitment that was to be lost in the next generation of Hispanists, as the space allowed for even "broad" specialization was reduced and finally eliminated.) Nor was the idea that professors might become "personalities," through public lectures, simply a pipe-dream but a real possibility in an age when the intellectual, for all his seclusion, was still a public figure (see Jacoby).

University Administration

If, as has been argued, the academic apparatus reproduces the class relations characteristic of British society as a whole, it should scarcely come as a surprise to find that much the same was true of university administration, only on an even more microcosmic level. Truscot, it goes without saying, knew the workings of this administration from close hand, and provides a detailed picture of its structure and procedures. At its summit is the University Council, which includes representatives from the local community, below which is the Senate, consisting mainly of Professors, otherwise Chairpersons or Heads of Department. Beneath the Senate are the respective Faculties of Arts and Sciences, encompassing the lecturing body as a whole, followed finally by the individual Departments. Each level had its respective committees and sub-committees.

What immediately strikes one about Truscot's view of the bureaucratic process is his very restricted notion of democracy. It leads him to characterize faculty board committees, for example, as democratic, even though the influence exerted by each member was "proportionate to his or her seniority" (1951: 92). And if this is his attitude to democratic representation at the faculty level, one shudders in anticipation of what awaits us further down the academic hierarchy. Consider, for example, the "burning" (88) issue of non-professorial representation on the Senate. Truscot's immediate instincts are not to assess the arguments in favour of such representation – he simply assumes that they are invalid – but to find ways round them. One such way, which he personally recommends, is to allow an election to take place but to exclude any senior lecturer that is known to be "difficult" (88). (Again, he simply assumes that only senior, as opposed to ordinary or assistant, lecturers are involved.) Truscot does not deign to discuss the claims of those "ultra democratic," union-inspired persons who believe that the Senate should have a student representative. If necessary, they can be circumvented by appointing a small number of graduates to relevant committees, "to represent, as it were, the student standpoint in a refined and matured form" (89). For the rest, student representation conflicts with the conception of university education that he is promoting, and "need not therefore be discussed in detail" (89).

It is only when he approaches issues nearer to home, namely as concern the relationship between the Senate and the Council, that Truscot begins to have doubts about Britain's democratic spirit. "It is often said that this arrangement works quite smoothly," he remarks later, but "so does a dictatorship – on the surface" (294). This strikes a note in Truscot the like of which we have not seen before. It is the note of the rebellious and oppressed: "In the era that is just beginning, dictators are going to disappear, and so, let us hope, is the dictatorship of Big Business, however benevolent, over education" (294). Truscot was never more wrong. In point of fact, we now know, the dictatorship of Big Business was only just beginning. What is germane to the present discussion, however, is the force of his democratic sentiments when his own rights were threatened. Even a modicum of repression, among professors who, in other respects, exerted enormous administrative power, brought the injustice of the Council's rule into focus: "But one may perhaps be allowed to inquire how a lay body came to have this all but complete control over an academic society and by what right it retains it" (294).

It should come as no surprise that Truscot's promotion of equality is more apparent than real. Symptomatically, he sees salvation in the parliamentary principle, which would dictate that the university be run by the "mature" members of the academic community and those still actively working in it, and that the Council become "truly representative of the society which it governs" (295). What Truscot objected to was not the absence of democracy, broadly understood, but interference with his own autocratic freedom as head of department. Naturally, he especially objected to interference by the socialist outside world, in the form of that "ungrammatical Alderman" on the Council (314). He himself made no secret of his opposition to the "democratic process" at the departmental level: "But it is hardly too much to say that if a question *can* be decided by an individual, it *should* be" (318). In his view individual heads were naturally inclined to act with a much greater sense of responsibility than was a committee and should be given "as much freedom as possible" (320), even when it came to the appointment of staff or faculty.

The Academy and the State

When Truscot complained that student activists, in their neglect of academic studies, were not fulfilling their responsibilities to the State, which had educated them for free from childhood (1951; 222), he inadvertently alerts us to what could be viewed as the basic presupposition of his liberal philosophy of education, namely the presupposition of neutrality of the bourgeois state.[5] The particular interest of *Red Brick University* is that, despite its author's own profession of transcendent, timeless values, it captures a particular, critical juncture in the history of the modern university, as a corporate entity. Under an early competitive form of capitalism, the State had been content simply to reproduce the general conditions conducive to the production of surplus value. During this period, it contributed modestly to the expenses of the modern university, the creation and running of which owed more to the generosity of private benefactors. Truscot hastens to express his sense of gratitude to the latter, even as he criticizes their failure to become as intellectually engaged as they were financially in the daily affairs of the University. Under monopoly capitalism, the state began to intervene more directly in relations of production and, by the same token, in public education, at the primary, secondary and tertiary levels. As Truscot explains, all universities since the end of the 1914-18 war had been receiving modest amounts of money through the University Grants Committee. The reforms he

---

5.   For a good general treatment of the relations between the State and education, see Carnoy and Dale.

advocated would require state aid "to an extent hitherto undreamed of" (297). He justifies this on the grounds that state capitalism had "crippled" the university's private benefactors with Income Tax, Surtax, Excess Profits Tax, Capital Levy and Death Duties.

Without entering into ideological collusion with Truscot – his heart, as always, bleeds for the highly taxed rich – we concede that he was signalling important changes in the world economy. It was not simply financial ties that were binding the University increasingly to the State. As the State itself became a producer, it began to incorporate specialists and professionals, as its own functionaries and employees. This led to the creation of a "new petty bourgeoisie" drawn from sections of the working class. The archetypal instance of this upward mobility is the scholarship boy himself, further confirmation, if any is needed, that class issues are the weft and warp of the state apparatus.

Now while the trend towards increased state involvement was something of which Truscot approved, and which he set out to foster, it also constituted a threat to his cherished sense of independence. His fears were understandable. State intervention towards the end of the Second World War was already giving notice of a shift towards a greater involvement in the way the nation was educated: neutrality was simply not on the government's agenda. "The other day," Truscots reported, going to extremes to demonstrate his own impartiality, "I heard two members of the Redbrick Council declaiming against a so-called 'Socialist' newspaper editor who had said our civic universities should be controlled by the State. Redbrick, they said, must at all costs remain autonomous" (296). What such comments bring home, albeit indirectly, is the extent to which the State was a condensation of class relations, as opposed to being the instrument of a single class, and that, furthermore, in 1945 the balance of power within it was tilting in favour of the underprivileged.

Truscot's predicament can be concisely expressed: he wanted the State to hand over more money but to continue to respect what he saw as the university's autonomy when it came to spending it. In other words, he wanted to have his cake and eat it, and he knew it: "Once more, the *status quo*, even if as anomalous and illogical as many other British institutions, seems on the whole preferable to any innovation that can be envisaged at the present time" (302). Any attempt to transform universities, he believed, would have disastrous consequences. Amongst other things, teachers would become civil servants and irresistible financial pressure would be brought to bear on research. Such an argument, Truscot realized, was vulnerable to the objection that there was nothing within its logic to prevent universities using block grants however they saw fit, "regardless of any national policy." But he remained unfazed: a strong convention and tradition, and the determination to make the system work were, he insisted, sufficient to prevent abuse.

One's impression is that Truscot was perfectly sincere in all of this. But he clearly did not expect others to agree and urged fellow academics to brace themselves against a demand for control which, if it came from the tax-paying community, could not be entirely disregarded (299). Indeed, there was already evidence of a growing feeling that the life and work of the university should be more closely connected with that of the nation (299-300). The business community, it was painfully obvious, was again asserting its muscle, not, it is true, through individual benefactors, otherwise the owners of family firms, but through the representatives of "Big Business," that is, large firms run by boards of directors, whose operations were both national and international.

Truscot, it is true, did his best to look on the bright side. He suggested, for example, that lecturers might benefit from outside inspection and being criticized "to their faces" for the first time in their lives; that inspections would have a salutary effect on the students, "who would think, as boys and girls at school always think, that it was they, not their teachers, who are being inspected" (301); and that inspections would, in any case, given the specialist nature of university work, prove impractical. Quietly, he took satisfaction from the university's capacity to limit the influence of private benefactors in the past, and had every confidence that government interference could be similarly restricted in the future.

Needless to say, Truscot himself would have viewed recent market-driven initiatives with horror and incomprehension, along with their associated demands for "accountability." In his own day, he feared that the situation would be arrived at in Britain in which, as in the United States and on the Continent, the government would dictate research projects and university life would be tied to the vicissitudes of political parties (298). But he feared even more the deleterious impact of a predatory capitalism, operating through market forces. Quite simply, commercial interests were incompatible with a principle that was, for him, sacrosanct, namely the disinterested pursuit of Truth.

This liberal defense of the autonomy of the university was then, and remains now, a compelling one. But is it valid? Clearly, it is undeniable that tertiary institutions are now required to cater for and to meet the technical needs of a more advanced capitalism. But it is doubtful whether the discussion is best framed in terms of such needs or, for that matter, of university autonomy. For if the raison d'être of educational institutions really depended upon their capacity to produce know-how, then surely they would have gone out of business long ago. Their knowledge, over the ages, has generally been "useless," to the extent of holding back the development of the forces of production. What has happened, so this alternative argument runs, is that in order to better "manage" the social relations, a technicist ideology is increasingly replacing a humanist one (see Lerena 354 ff). The interest of Truscot's work is that it shows to what extent this transition, which we are inclined to associate with the 1970s, was actually underway much earlier. On this basis, what is at issue is less the degree than the type of ideological control exerted by the State over the university. The issue of degree is largely an optical illusion that occurs when the educational system and the state are out of alignment in their relations. And like all illusions, it can be variously interpreted, as proving that the educational apparatus is never autonomous of state power or, alternatively, that the distance that separates the schools and universities from the economy is absolutely necessary, if educational institutions are to function, ideologically, as they should.

Marginalized Women, Excluded Proletarians

There exists, we indicated earlier, an intimate bond between the scholarship boy and women. Even in the home environment, they shared the same domestic space, in which he "worked" and she worked, and forever after, within the academy, they found themselves in each other's company. True, academic women were not the "same" as the girls back home, but they were driven, for all their privilege, to renegotiate their passage through university in a manner reminiscent of the scholarship boy (cf. Kelly and Nihlen). Given his interest in the latter, Truscot was bound, sooner or later, to address the role of women in the academy, a subject on which he boasts of holding "really strong views" (1951: 320).

By some measures, they were. Women lecturers, he protests, could be excused from believing that they were not really wanted in the academy. Of course, there were limits, and pretty severe ones, to such enlightenment: Truscot saw no role for women in business management and, more importantly, never felt compelled to address the obvious absence of the "scholarship *girl*." Indeed, he seems confused in certain respects about the kind of women that emanate from Drabtown. They appear, on the whole, to be a "better type" than the men, having been educated (the argument runs) at good schools and provided with facilities at home for undisturbed study (33). One can only assume that Truscot had girls of another class in mind, who shared nothing with the scholarship boy beyond a tendency towards industriousness and "swotting" (46). For all the evidence suggests that parents are less likely to invest in a girl's education than in her brother's (see Kelly and Nihlen 173, 175). Anecdotal impressions confirm that she was unlikely to be favored as regards accommodation. In the crowded conditions of the working-class family, there was no "room of one's own" to be had by anybody, girls included.

Be that as it may, women had not yet entered the university profession in sufficient numbers to affect its status adversely (as they were subsequently to do) or to offer any kind of threat to patriarchs such as Truscot. Indeed, the latter even expressed disappointment over the failure of women within the academy to press their claims (327). The implication is that, at a professional level, there could be no conceivable objection to being joined by what were essentially like-minded individuals.

The working class's role in education, it goes without saying, was an entirely different matter. True, certain obligations needed to be met, relating to "man's" universal need of education. But it is clear that, as far as the working class was concerned, this need extended simply to the kind of vocational training that had little to do with university education, as Truscot envisaged it. The exception proves the rule: entry into the academy is possible for the scholarship boy but on condition that he de-class himself. For the rest, Truscot was principally concerned to "discipline," and thereby neutralize, the subversive energy he was only too willing to encourage in women of his own class: "What university teachers can do for working people above anything else is to initiate them into the habits of disciplined thought which they themselves have formed and which govern all their activities" (368). Liberal discipline involved the ability to "to think clearly, examine thoroughly, to judge dispassionately, to pronounce impartially, to stand for what is good, to show contempt for what is bad, to keep an open mind about what is uncertain – above all to develop, feed, and sustain a passion for knowledge and to remember that, however much one may learn, it is of small volume beside all of which one is ignorant" (369). Its ideological virtue, from Truscot's standpoint, is its capacity to re-contain passion at the same time as it unleashes it, to neutralize it even as it stimulates it, thereby ensuring that change occurs without any threat to prevailing social structures. In this way, ruling-class hegemony can be passed off as the common good: "The great achievement of the union between scholars and workers has been the following and nurturing of this ideal, and each party has benefited from the union" (369).

This pure distillation of bourgeois ideology was never more needed than at the close of the Second World War, with the Labor movement flexing its muscles and threatening to place the need for a genuinely inclusive culture on the national agenda. Evening classes and adult education began to expand under the auspices of WEA, and briefly the possibility of a permanent education, extending over an individual's whole life-span, became feasible. But when the suggestion was made that this work should be linked with the universities, Truscot made clear his opposition (370). One suspects that although he admired the "earnestness" and "industry" that adult proletarians shared with the scholarship boy, they proved, in their maturity, rather less manageable and were best kept at a safe distance (cf. 1945: 39-40). And all in the interests of that objectivity and impartiality which has always been the hallmark of the petty bourgeoisie: "So much has been said of education for the working class that it may be feared the more leisured have been forgotten" (1951: 372). As things transpired, Truscot had little cause for concern.

Conclusion

Writing in the wake of a whole series of White Papers and Reports on education, notably those by Fleming, Norwood and McNair, Truscot fully realized that the Britain of his day was, educationally as in other respects, poised at a cross-road. His own intervention in national policy-making, in the form of several major works, a number of radio broadcasts, and his own service on different committees and advisory bodies, was both calculated and timely. It contributed to, and was affected by, the general climate of excitement and optimism regarding a future that was – on this everyone could agree – in the making. Yet, in any final assessment of the direction that this intervention took, the accent must fall on the fundamentally conservative function that it performed. In anticipation of a "Battle of the Bulge," following demobilization, Truscot set out to strengthen class defenses, in order to keep out the hoards of less privileged students threatening to flood the university. The principal dikes were the numerous types of alternative tertiary institutions at which, as Truscot explains, these students could be better and "*more appropriately*" educated (1945: 39). Demands that the university should address "problems of citizenship," as these relate to an enlarged, more socially diverse student body, constitute a "dangerous doctrine," not because these things should not be done, but because the whole idea of a university that such demands presuppose is "out of focus" (108). The phrasing, as always in Truscot, is exquisitely oblique, and had to be, if it was to make palatable the class prejudices and injustices that lay, and continue to lie, at the heart of the British educational system.

3
The Making of a Hispanist

"a self-taught man, and we all know how distressing they are, how egotistical, insistent, raw, striking and ultimately nauseating" (Virginia Woolf)

I was born in Derby, for most of its history a small market town situated at the point where the River Derwent breaks from the foot of the Pennine Range and cuts southwards across the North Midlands plain to join the Trent. The latter, more stately, describes an arc across this same plain, dividing traditionally the North from the South of England, before flowing into the Humber Estuary. Up these rivers the Norsemen traveled in days gone by, to oust the resident Saxons, who themselves had taken the place of the Roman legions. Chester Green, within the present-day city limits, is the site of an old Roman fortification, and the road along which for several years I traveled daily on my bicycle, from Friargate up the long incline to Rowditch, followed the old Roman road, straight as an arrow and merciless into a head wind.

It is an old land, steeped in history. Through the forests that lay to the east in the direction of Nottingham and north to Lincoln, Robin Hood had led his band of merry men. It was in Derby market place that Bonnie Prince Charlie rested his troops and sharpened his swords before proceeding southwards to the Trent at Swarkeston Bridge, where suddenly he stopped and began to retrace his steps, for reasons that – so our history teacher informed us – should be obvious to anyone who looks southwards from the Bridge and imagines that he has just walked all the way from Scotland. They were certainly obvious enough to me when, one hot afternoon, the path I was following while fishing that stretch of the river suddenly issued onto the high ground leading up to the Bridge, and I found myself gazing across the same endless expanse that would have greeted Bonnie Prince Charlie and his men centuries earlier. The afternoon breeze was cool on my brow, but the shimmering horizon seemed to recede and fade away imperceptibly. It was, to be sure, not a sight for sore legs.

But if this was the land of Roman, Viking, Saxon and Norman, it is to modern historians, more familiarly, the setting of the early industrial revolution, testimony to which is the site of Derby's silk mill and Arkright's mill that still sits astride the Derwent at Cromford. Even more familiarly to lovers of English literature, it is the setting for parts of Jane

Austen's *Pride and Prejudice* and Charlotte Brontë's *Jane Eyre*. On a clear day, from the front windows of our north-facing house, I could look towards Wirksworth, the location of *Adam Bede*, where the sandstone gives way to the limestone. In the gray days of winter, this horizon seemed to close in and leave visible only the more adjacent factory chimneys that dotted the urban landscape like isolated hairs on a charred scalp. But in fair weather and in foul, this was and remains for me, as for D. H. Lawrence, the most famous, if one of the more irascible, of its sons, "the country of my heart."

Strange as it may seem, I know rather less about my immediate than my distant forebears. My knowledge of the Read side of the family is particularly scanty. The only recollection I have of my great grandmother dates from the 1950s, at which point she was already well into her nineties. She was living at the time in the vicinity of Stockbrook Street, in a house that she had rented for the past sixty years. It was a very rough working-class district, even in my own day, consisting of a labyrinth of terraced housing, "entries" and back allies. Violence was endemic, particularly between the inhabitants and the police. My grandmother recalled finding a policeman's torn-off number on the ground outside the house one Sunday morning. The houses had earth closets or toilets, which were emptied by "night-soil" men once a week, when all windows had to be closed. On more than one occasion, drunken husbands would have money slip from their pockets, while they were crapping, and the whole family would be called out to empty the containers on the ground, in order to retrieve the precious coins.

The one comment of Gran Read that I recall from that last meeting, as she peered down at me, was that I would be "short and stubby, like 'is mother." In this, she proved to be correct. Doubtless, she had seen it all happen before, as any person would who vividly recalled the day when news arrived of General Custer's defeat on the banks of the Little Bighorn, and whose surviving relatives, in her girlhood days, included soldiers who had fought at Waterloo. According to my father, she also claimed to remember the barred windows of the bedroom of her eldest uncle, a Peeler in the 1830s, which served, when necessary, as a holding cell for his prisoners.

The old lady originally came from Bicester, in Oxfordshire, and kept the speech mannerisms and accent of that area till her dying day. "Don't go to bed when you're badly (ill). Folks doi (die) in bed." And with five children of her own to feed, she was nothing if not a survivor: "Get that eaten. If you don't eat, you won't shit. If you don't shit, you'll soon doi." She was full of earthy sayings of this kind. Another favorite of hers was:

"What's in the bone will come out in the flesh." Her family itself was very poor, and often had to lie low, collectively, when the rentman called. Any child that dared raise its head would be dealt with quickly: (Thump) "Duck, you bugger, duck." People in the district regularly had recourse to Gran in the laying out of corpses, which were only buried on Sundays. She attended systematically to the body's seven orifices, as she once explained to my morbidly fascinated father. "Seven?" "Don't forget that thing you pee through, lad." Of Gran's husband, my great-grandfather, I know virtually nothing, except that he died ringing the bells of St Luke's Church in Parliament Street in Derby and was remembered for his gentle refinement: "Nell, there's no need to swear at the children."

I know little about the Hayes, my grandmother's side of the family, except that they were Irish, noticeably intelligent by all accounts, but given to fighting and drinking. My grandma told how her mother died in childbirth, after being chased by her husband and jumping out of a lower-story window. However, Great Gran Read denied this to my father: "The story I heard was that she was drunk and fell." One of grandma's brothers, Jack, fought on the Western front, and used to infuriate his sister by enclosing an enormous body louse in the pages of each of his letters.

Of my grandma herself, I preserve two photographs. One is a studio portrait of an attractive, dark-eyed young woman, posing alongside her young husband or husband-to-be. Another, from her second son's wedding, shows the face of an embittered, sour, middle-aged woman, almost lost in the crowd. Seemingly, they are not of the same person. Since her death, in the 1960s, much abuse has been poured on her. Uncle Ted, when I asked him about her, recalled simply that "she was a terror." My father, more forthcoming, insists, and insisted to a hospital psychologist, that her treatment of her youngest son, Hayden, was such as to have mentally traumatized him. For example, in addition to periodic duckings, she would allegedly scream into his ear for him to stop crying, as he lay in his cot. I was appalled the first time I heard this. But having since this time raised three children of my own, I am inclined to be rather less judgmental. I am really in no position to say, but I find it tempting to weave a somewhat different narrative from the one which prevails in family circles, concerning an intelligent woman who, for reasons of class and gender, found herself caught in a web of frustration and hopelessness, lumbered at a late stage in her life by one more unwanted child. Whatever the truth may be, her side of the story died with her.

Of my grandfather, I know very little, which in itself is probably significant. He was, according to my father, a man of notable wit but very gentle – and afraid of his wife. "Ted," his mother called to him on one occasion when his wife was half-drowning her youngest son, "Go and stop her. She'll kill that little boy." "She'll kill me if I try and stop her," came the reply. At which point Gran fled the scene of horror. My grandfather held a skilled job in Royce's and managed to provide quite well for his family, even during the 1930s. But he died at a relatively early age, from causes that have never been clearly established. A rumor concerning syphilis has never been substantiated. According to my Uncle Ted, my grandfather simply shook hands with his children one day from his hospital bed, wished them all the best, rolled over and died, early the following morning, to the utter amazement and puzzlement of the specialists.

My knowledge of the Wests, that is, of my mother's side of the family, is far more detailed and direct. My grandfather, who was not brought up by his own parents, was of London stock and, correspondingly, took a life-long interest in the fortunes of Fulham Football Club. He enlisted for the First World War while still under age, serving as a machine-gunner in Flanders. When on his first leave, in the Second World War, my father happened to mention proudly that in a training session his team had assembled an old Lewis machine gun in fifty-six seconds, my grandfather complimented him, but added that, under fire, he and his comrades performed the task in twenty seconds. For the most part, however, my grandfather was always reluctant to reminisce about the War, in which respect, in my experience, he contrasted with veterans of the Second World War.

On returning from the war, my grandfather began working on British Railways, where he remained all his working life. He was a militant socialist, who still smarted from the fact that, in the 1930s, cod had been dumped into the North Sea while people starved. He ruled his wife, four daughters and one son in the patriarchal fashion typical of his generation. His slippers and supper were always punctually ready for his arrival from work, and I recall, as a small child, having hurriedly to vacate his chair by the fire. At the same time, he was a self-educated man of the old-school, who prided himself on being scrupulously fair and honest. In his spare time he was a passionate gardener and fisherman, and as a young man had also been a more than useful soccer-player. The soccer skills which I was later to exhibit, he proudly pointed out to his friends, were attributable to the West stock, and in no way connected with Tommy Powell, the famous Derby forward, who married into the family. Soccer, as it turned out, was partly his undoing, since an old, untreated knee injury eventually became arthritic. The condition was aggravated by having to work all weathers on the roofs of British Railways —retaliation by the management for his union activity. By the age of retirement, he was virtually immobilized. I could always pick him out in the distance by his stiff-legged gait, as I waited for him at the corner of the road sometimes, of an evening. He was, of course, a drinking man, but not excessively so. Befuddled and happy on Friday evenings, after a visit to the "Grandstand," he was accustomed to hand out generous sums from his wage packet to his family members, only to retrieve them, in a more sober frame of mind, the following morning.

All his daughters inherited my grandfather's intelligence, and were to become the backbone of socially ascendant families in the 1950s and 60s. Ray, his only son, was somewhat less endowed, possibly as a consequence of which he remained content with his lot and devoid of all social pretension. You had to take him as you found him, and one invariably found him busily dismantling his motor-bike on the kitchen table. He was happily married to Nellie, a simple working-class girl, and reared a close, devoted family. Like his father, he worked for British Railways, where, amongst other things, he was charged with removing the asbestos lining from carriages. As a consequence of this latter activity – except of course in the eyes of the management – he contracted a lingering cancer of the spine which, by the end, had reduced him to a fetal ball weighing only sixty pounds, into which was distilled a pain of unendurable proportions. Nellie tenaciously supported him in his request to die at home, and struggled to preserve his dwindling dignity.

In most respects, Ray took after his mother, my grandmother, who was distinguished by a profound suspicion of all things "foreign." Even when I visited her as an old lady, she refrained from addressing my New Zealand wife directly, asking me whether "she" would like more tea or another piece of cake. Her suspicions took a more insidious turn when they centered on the "blacks," in evidence, from the 1950s onwards, in Derby's East End. Her whole world did not extend far beyond her semi-detached council house with its bog in the backyard. She constantly warned us children against the dangers of meddling in religion and politics. I remember her chiefly for the importance she attached to a lilac tree, which bloomed intermittently in the back garden and gave forth a delicious perfume on summer evenings. I have the impression, rightly or wrongly, that she was given to stirring up trouble between her daughters.

I was born in the City Hospital just as the Second World War was drawing to a close. The war itself had left Derby relatively unscathed in terms of actual material damage, although German planes, on the return leg from Manchester and Liverpool to the Continent, were in the habit of off-loading their remaining cargo en passant. Moreover, as the war progressed, Royce's itelf became the object of direct attention, a fact of some consequence for my father's immediate family, which subsequently had taken up residence in the network of workers' houses in the factory vicinity. Casualties were recorded among their neighbors. Nor were the Wests unaffected. In my earliest years, adults still recalled cold nights spent in the air-raid shelter at the top of my grandparents' garden, and the sound of the air-raid siren, then used as a fire-alarm, had everyone glancing instinctively and uneasily up at the sky.

My parents were but seventeen or eighteen when they married. It took my elder brother, in his early teens, a series of delicate computations, after furtively consulting relevant family documents, to discover that, as he explained secretly and triumphantly to me, he was "within three months of being born a bastard." I say "triumphantly" because at the time my father, concerned about my brother's growing interest in girls, had taken to lecturing him in high moral tones on its possible consequences, career-wise. Years later, my father recalled the righteous indignation, even vindictiveness, with which grandma West had reacted to his and my mother's "mistake," and expressed his own quiet satisfaction on discovering subsequently that the old lady herself had been "in the family way" when she was married. We all have our little secrets.

After the war ended, and my father returned from active service in the air force in Burma, the family moved onto a new estate of "prefabs" in Littleover, on the outskirts of town. There had been considerable opposition to their construction in what was basically a middle-class neighbourhood. Indeed, I once heard them referred to by one enraged local inhabitant as "those rabbit hutches." Although allegedly built to last a mere ten years, they are still used today, as old people's residences. They were somewhat flimsy – my brother and I used to stand on the back of our bed and lift up the interior ceiling – and had a damp problem, but they were blessed with an open fire that heated up the water, and a refrigerator, in those days a luxury even in middle-class dwellings.

I naturally remember very little about those early years. A few faded family photos show me waist-high in the deep snows of 1947. A feeling still lingers of intense conviviality within a large close-knit working-class family. At Christmas-time we would all gather at my grandparents'. There was endless card-playing, smoking, drinking, jovial conversation, and good food. I was patted and fondled by my aunts and held high up in the air by Uncle Ray till I screamed to be put down. In those early years, we still sometimes took annual holidays together, usually on the Yorkshire or Lancashire coasts. Family photos show a large gathering on the beach, the men with trouser legs rolled up to the knee and newspapers or handkerchiefs, knotted at the corners, perched on their balding heads, and the women struggling to keep their skirt hems pulled down over their knees.

But not all was joy and conviviality in those cold, bleak years of continued rationing after the war. To begin with, there was the ever-present problem of poverty. My father, who, on leaving school, had worked as a bricklayer and butcher's assistant, had returned from the war to a job in the Co-op. My mother, of course, stayed at home to look after my brother and myself. At the time my parents were solid Labour supporters, and indeed my father was something of a socialist. I was indebted to him for a rough "labor" history of the industrial revolution, with its horrendous tales of social deprivation and work-related accidents and mutilations. Some of the few books we had around the house were political pamphlets by George Bernard Shaw and H.G. Wells. My father used to tell us that a time would come when the idea of one man employing another would be judged as objectionable as the burning of the Christians by the Romans.

Part of this socialist tradition was the importance attributed to self-education, which showed itself in my father in a number of ways. For example, he introduced my brother and myself very early on to the wonders of astronomy: we spent many a clear winter evening gazing starward in search of the Square of Pegasus, the Belt of Orion, Castor and Pollux and the Plow, and I still recall my early frustration and confusion at not being able to see the figures of bulls and swordsmen etched on the firmament. Similarly, on our bike rides through the countryside, my father revealed his remarkably detailed knowledge of native birds and trees. We were particularly urged to listen to the call of the yellow hammer, with its "little-bit-of-bread-and-no-cheese." The subsequent transition from this more popular learning to a pretentious high culture, as part of our social ascent, was gradual but very real.

Our formal education began at the age of five. The school we attended was in one of the roughest parts of the town, described above in connection with my great grandmother. All the kids wore boots, heavily studded or "segged" on the soles. It was a concrete jungle in which you had to fight to survive. And how I fought! Nothing held back my punches except, according to family legend, the snotty nose of one particular boy who bullied me mercilessly. There existed a vigorous street lore of rhyming songs, games, and stories. One game, I recall with vivid affection, was called "football lurky." Like all other games, it began with "dipping," to establish who was "on." Then a ball was kicked up the street, to be retrieved by the person "on." Once the latter had returned the ball to its original position, he proceeded to search for the other kids, who, naturally, had used the intervening period to go and hide. If one of them was discovered, the person "on" ran back to the ball and hoofed it up the street and his place was taken by the kid he had discovered. But if he wandered too far from the ball, anyone in hiding was permitted to scurry forth and do the hoofing, in which case the whole procedure was repeated.

As children we lived an intensely communal life on a "tip" adjacent to our prefab estate. This consisted of an old block of allotments that had been abandoned and become overgrown. Here we played Germans-against-English until late in summer evenings, and in the winter, cooked stolen potatoes over open fires inside our dens. In those days, one frequently came across such wild oases, within an otherwise largely urban setting, that often boasted a pond and associated wild life. Most of them have since been claimed by developers. Since we were on the edge of town, we also ranged deep into the adjacent countryside on our bicycles, down still relatively car-free country lanes, through Findern, Willington, and even as far as Repton. As children we watched the huge power station, which now dwarfs this landscape, gradually take shape.

A spirit of neighborliness reigned on the prefab estate, most of whose dwellings contained young families of the same age. When next-door acquired a new radiogram, we were invited to go and listen to their records. It was there that I first heard Al Jolson, Bing Crosby, and singers and musicians of the fifties, like Ruby Murray, Max Bygraves, and Eddie Calvert. One highlight of the year was Guy Fawks Night, enjoyed alike by young and old. The late 1940s and 1950s was also the heyday of the cinema, which we attended at least once a week, not counting the Saturday morning matinee. "Have you seen every film that was ever made?" my children still ask in amazement, as we sit watching TV screenings of old movies. "Every single one," I reply, only half in jest.

While life gradually improved, in material terms, it was still far from being easy. On one occasion, hurrying to arrive at his evening class on time, my father omitted to lock his bicycle, and when he returned later it had been stolen. This was a terrible blow from which it took the family some time to recover financially. Socially aspirant adults were invariably exhausted and over-worked, and barely a week-end seemed to go by without some family row. But we never ceased to pull together, particularly during the three years when my father was away at college in Sheffield, living off a small state grant. During this time, my mother worked endlessly to keep us afloat. An old lady once stopped me at the bottom of the street to observe: "You're very lucky to have a mother like that. She's always running, from the bus, to the bus."

One feature of my father's generation of socialists was the considerable degree of equality that prevailed between the sexes. Thus, once my mother returned to work, as an usherette in the Cosmo cinema, household chores were evenly divided, including the cleaning, cooking, and washing of clothes and dishes. Of course, the family system continued to be patriarchal, but in a very real sense the women functioned as the fulcrum of the family unit, orchestrating the activities of the men from, as it were, behind the scenes. I have no doubt, for example, that in reality my mother was the moving force behind our own family's social ambitions. I say this despite the fact that it fell to my father to spearhead our ascent into the petty bourgeoisie by working his way through night-school and teacher-training college.

Working-class women managed to combine extreme social timidity with considerable aggression and tenacity when cornered or when they felt their family was being threatened or not getting a fair deal. My mother was the epitome of this ambivalence. Once, she accompanied me all the way across town to Reginald Street Swimming Baths to ensure that I was given an opportunity for a time trial for a free season ticket. After ascertaining what the procedure would be, she withdrew to wait for me outside. I emerged, an hour or so later, to find her sheltering from the wind and rain in a shop doorway some way up the street. When she died tragically in her early forties in a traffic accident, it was this silhouetted image of her which, for some reason, came back to haunt me.

I consider myself to have enjoyed, on the whole, a happy, if by no means, care-free childhood. The food was poor and in short supply – few members of the family ever managed to top five feet five – and relationships were sometimes stormy, but there was also much support, love and warmth. I remember particularly the long winter evenings when, at the end of a hard day's work, my mother would sit down and read to us. I later discovered that she did not read with ease, but we never noticed as kids. Our favorite was *Wind in the Willows*, and even now any page of that work is resonant for me of those dim and distant days. Of course, I realize that our literary appreciation was, as my university colleagues would say, problematic, perhaps overdetermined. If we warmed to the idle (Edwardian) life of Mole, Rat and Badger, with their comfortable parlors, wainscot, and endless supply of beer, cold meats and pickle, our immediate middle-class neighbors would have seen more obvious parallels between ourselves and the weasels and ferrets of the Wild Wood. Toad's splendid mansion had an obvious objective correlate for us in "Sky Line," a luxury residence not far away, through whose doors and windows we – parents and children – used to peer enviously on our Sunday walks.

But it would be wrong to imply that books were readily available around our house. They were not. My favorite reading matter, in very early years, was an encyclopedia, lent to us by our next-door neighbors. It consisted of two thick volumes, and was full of the most wonderful pictures. Naturally, I was particularly impressed by those of prehistoric animals and the early cave men. This section also contained a poem that I especially loved and used to recite aloud. It began: "Tubal Cain was a man of might / In the days when the Earth was young." The flow of books increased as my father proceeded through college. I spent hours poring over an anthology of poems, one of his "set texts," of which my favorites were "Horatio on the Bridge" and "The Pied Piper of Hamelin."

The reasons for the family's social mobility are complex and difficult to determine. My father told how an older person at the Co-op took him on one side and sowed in him the seeds of his social aspirations. Doubtless the account is somewhat over-simplified. To begin with, it fails to take into account the important role of my mother, upon which I have already insisted. Apart from supporting my father in his career, she herself was not lacking in ambition in her own right, which can be traced back to her own family history and circumstances. Indeed, she became manager of a confectionery stall in the market and, ably assisted in turn by my father, eventually came to have her own stall. Indications are that from very early on both my parents had a plan to change their station in life. The decision to transfer my brother and myself from our inner-city school, I now realize, was a calculated move on their part to help "better themselves" and their children.

The slow ascent out of the working class gathered momentum from the middle 1950s when my father returned from college and began teaching across the other side of town. We acquired a car and made a strategic shift from the *Daily Mirror* and *Sunday Express* to the *Manchester Guardian* and *Observer*. Significantly, these changes coincided with the onset of squabbles with relatives. The causes were varied – the failure on the part of children, for example, to write "thank you" notes for birthday and Christmas presents – but all of them were symptomatic of something more profound. While the sisters increasingly competed, through their husbands and their boys (and by biological chance all the cousins were boys), not all nuclear families progressed at the same rate. In the rush to "get on," those who made it first were ostracized for their pretensions, doubtless both real and imagined. This ostracism was used in turn by the more successful to justify breaking away. I recall being puzzled to hear my father protest that one should be able to choose whom to associate with, be it friends or relatives. Quite suddenly, both my parents were attending elocution classes and much more attention was devoted to clothing and table manners. We continued to live in the prefab, but relationships with our neighbors also deteriorated, as a result of which we became progressively more distanced from them. Again, it bore all the signs of being a tactical withdrawal. Visitors to the house became less frequent, and were not encouraged. And, of course, the day arrived when we made the inevitable move to a detached house.

By the early sixties, both my parents' careers were flourishing. My father had quickly made up for the delayed start to his teaching career through a series of promotions. He became a headmaster at about the same time as my mother set up her own business. Naturally, life became easier, in material terms, and with this improvement the tenor of family life began to change more noticeably. To take but one example, whereas restaurants had at one time been avoided, eating out now became a Saturday night routine. But more striking were the negative consequences. The battles that had erupted earlier between the sisters and brother were reproduced within the nuclear family. Rows, as I have indicated early, were nothing new, but there was a qualitative shift in their nature. The late 1950s and early 1960s witnessed the explosion of youth culture. Jazz, blues, skiffle and rock-and-roll soon became the stuff of every-day life, along with Teddy-boys and drain-pipe trousers. My brother bought a plectrum guitar and took music lessons at Wishers Music Co. in town, and began to ape his heroes on Top of the Pops. Our new-found material prosperity enabled him to freely purchase gramophone records. Increasingly, the model grammar school boy became a headache to my parents, whose social aspirations were threatened by his weird hair styles and iridescent, lime-green socks. So much had been invested in him, so much expected of him. He was to have the university career that my father had never had. And of course the more my parents did to impose their own agenda on him, the more Mike resisted. In the end, he seemed possessed by a veritable will to self-destruct, as the only way of thwarting the wishes of parents and teachers who knew only too well "what was good for him."

Part of the problem was that, in spite of their airs and graces, both my parents preserved essentially working-class tastes and habits. Inevitably, they found themselves encouraging their children to imbibe a culture and learning that they could only "exhibit." As teenagers, my brother and I were quick to pick up on this phoniness. We were especially sensitive to the compromising of principles in an effort to "get on." For example, prior to his interview for the headship of one village school, my father, who was fiercely anti-religious, attended a service in the local church, in anticipation that it might stand him in good stead at his interview. When my brother and I joshed him about it, he turned upon us fiercely, in what was obviously a show of guilty conscience. He was quick to point out that we children did not spurn the material benefits that accrued from his little acts of betrayal. Collusion with the enemy, I was to discover during my career in higher education, is the staple diet of the social climber.

As the second born, the pressures upon me were fewer than upon my brother. Of course, my parents were bitterly disappointed when I failed to pass the 11-plus, but it was hoped that I would eventually make good. Although always in the "A" stream at primary school, I flunked regularly at math. The "A" stream itself was literally divided into two halves, the dunces and the elect, and much of my energy was spent on cheating at mental arithmetic to get on the side of the elect. Certainly, I was good at some things, such as art and sport, and on one occasion, when a teacher trainee asked us to write a story, produced a piece of imaginative prose which astounded everybody. But since I was alienated by the endless grind of intelligence tests, which were the only thing that seemed to matter, I had few opportunities to shine. So it came as no surprise when, on one occasion, I overheard the headmaster explaining to my father that "we just have to accept that, unlike Michael, Malcolm hasn't got what it takes." Well, I'd punched many a kid on his nose for saying a lot less than that about me, but I resolved to bide my time. Daily life in the concrete jungle of the inner city had taught me never to enter a fight that you didn't have a pretty good chance of winning.

Anyway, life at the secondary school to which I moved was not without its advantages. I dominated all the team and individual sports, representing the school and county at soccer and carrying off the school and Trent Valley free-style championship at swimming. Moreover, some of the teachers continued to encourage me academically. One occasion stands out particularly in my mind in this respect. One Friday afternoon, after the final bell had sounded, it happened that I was the last pupil to gather together my things and set off home. Mr Palin, the form master, I couldn't help but notice, was looking tired and drawn, after a hard week's work, and I supposed that he was anxious to see the back of me. But as I was walking out, he stopped me and, making what was obviously a conscious effort, engaged me in a discussion of the latest story of H. G. Wells I had read. I was deeply touched and never forgot his kindness. It is strange how such seemingly insignificant gestures can count for more with a pupil than hours of formal tuition.

So it was that, although I followed closely behind Mike, I avoided his destructive confrontations with Authority. When I started to learn the guitar, it was the classical guitar. And my parents were more than willing to take me occasionally to concerts by the Derby Light Orchestra. Here, drivenness found a respectable outlet, to the extent that by the age of fifteen I had mastered a small repertoire of pieces by Villa-Lobos, Albéniz, Tárrega, Granados and others. I gave my first recital for Derby Music Club in the Art Gallery, looked down upon by the pictures of Joseph Wright of Derby, with their captivating interplay of light and dark. Shortly afterwards, I played in a concert at Spondon Park Grammar School. This was a particular triumph, as can well be imagined, for a secondary modern-school boy. I eventually began giving guitar classes at Wishers, on Tuesday and Wednesday evenings and Saturday mornings, which brought in some useful cash. As a result of such activities, I emerged far less scarred from adolescence than Mike, who by his early twenties was in effect a broken personality, and in later years, became isolated socially by the very mechanisms that allowed others to ascend. He eventually sank into a lonely, eccentric, poverty-stricken life of unemployment in Manchester, where, with little to sustain him, materially and emotionally, he died in early middle age.

Nevertheless, it is important to understand that, for many years, I myself appeared destined to collapse back into the working class from which my parents had struggled to drag themselves. Indeed, for a while it seemed that professional soccer was my only chance of escape, after Nottingham Forest and Derby County fought to sign me up as an apprentice. However, I had already seen enough of this profession to know that it was a dirty game, both on an off the field, and only one step up from factory employment. The latter acquired fresh meaning for me as we school leavers began to make visits to Qualcast, British Celanese and other major industrial complexes. The glowing maws of the blast furnaces, fed by bare-torsoed, sweat-glistening figures, filled me with a kind of cosmic dread. Fortunately, I finally made good academically at the age of fifteen, when I won a place on a full-time "O" level course at the Derby College of Technology. Only some five or six of the class from secondary modern school went with me. Of the rest, some had had their fill of boring old school and were eager to start earning some money, whereas others were given no option by their parents. Needless to say, the "B" and "C" streams were simply fodder for manual labor.

It was at the Tech that I started to learn Spanish. The other subjects I took were Maths, Geography, Economic History and English. The lecturers at the Tech were, on the whole, more interesting than those I was to encounter at University. I can offer no reason for this, other than to suggest that, before tertiary education opened up in the 1950s and 60s, many gifted teachers, particularly on the left, perforce took up appointments in more marginal institutions. Mr Darbyshire, our English teacher, clearly fell into just such a category. He was the author of a series of text books on English grammar and of several useful introductions to linguistics and stylistics.

One particular incident concerning him stands out in my memory. My father, who, as it happened, had also been taught by Mr Darbyshire a decade or so earlier at night school, told me that if Darbyshire were ever to ask what was the "meaning of meaning," I was to reply "a response to stimulus." He gave me this advice on the basis of an extended discussion they had once had in one of their classes, with reference to Ogden and Richards' famous book on semantics. Sure enough, one day Darbyshire entered the lecture theatre, stared at us fixedly, and, after a decidedly pregnant pause, posed the fateful question. Obviously and not unreasonably, he expected nobody to reply, and was visibly surprised when my hand slowly went up at the back of the room. But not as taken aback as he was when I solemnly declaimed my answer. It is the memory of that occasion which has led me to be circumspect in my own teaching when it comes to rhetorical questions. Of course, further interrogation by Darbyshire revealed that I hadn't myself read a word of Ogden and Richards. But to his credit he did see the joke.

Another one of my favorite lecturers was Mr Trippett, the Spanish teacher. More than once he informed the class that the red tie he habitually wore had no political significance, which always amused me since, with his austere mien and three-piece suit, there could be no doubt as to his political allegiance. While I was always grateful for his support and interest, he sometimes annoyed me with what I took to be excessive timidity and conservatism. On one occasion, I took him to task for meekly accepting the condemnation, in a national report by the GCE examiners, of the widespread use of "without doubt." I realized that Trippett's motives were for the best, and in essence pragmatic, but they were not *simply* pragmatic, and that was what irked me. Ideological issues apart, our exchange brought to the surface a conflict between the scholarship-winning, circus-horse mentality, practiced unthinkingly by Trippett during his many years as a grammar-school teacher, and the raw energy and intransigence of someone who, while wounded by academic "failure," had not been tamed by the system.

I called to see Mr Trippett just before I "went up" to University. He lived in a quiet, secluded house just off the Uttoxeter Road. His wife answered the door and, fussing round me pleasantly, ushered me into the front room, where her husband sat at a magnificent-looking piano, playing a piece by Liszt. It was always necessary in performing on any instrument to *relax*, or so at least he informed me as we sat down for coffee. We talked of the future, and briefly of the work of A. A. Parker, to which he had introduced me. When I was leaving later, he shook me by the hand. "How old are you, young man?" (He was always so very formal and correct!) I replied that I was eighteen. "Marvelous age, marvelous age!" he commented, dreamily. I hadn't a clue what he meant at the time, but I understand him well enough now. Some years later I was saddened to hear of his death, but touched to be told by his son of his enduring pride in my achievement and the interest with which he had followed my career. He would not, I fear, have approved of some of the turns that the latter was due to take.

During my years at the Tech I became a voracious reader, working my way through the classic authors such Conrad, James, Lawrence, most of American Literature – I particularly enjoyed Steinbeck – and the Russians, not to mention the currently popular "angry young men," such as Sillitoe, Amis and Wain. I also read widely in philosophy, notably the works of Bertrand Russell (to whose work my father had introduced me). Indeed, I had what could only be described as an obsessive desire to master the totality of knowledge, not in the liberal sense of a "general culture," but in a Marxian sense of non-alienated knowledge. The latter included not only what I was able to derive of benefit from formal education but also from my socialist heritage, with its tradition of self-education. Of course, I would have found it impossible at the time to theorize what I was about, but I did discover early on that unusual connections paid off. For example, our lecturer in Economic History rewarded the use I made of George Orwell's *On the Road to Wigan Pier*. I was able in this way to turn my general reading to good account. This habit stayed with me at university. Other students, who had come through more orthodox channels, were amused by my tendency to attend all kinds of lectures.

My colleagues at the Tech were a mixed lot, in terms of ability, but alike in their determination to defy a system that had in effect written them off. Stovsky, for example, who was of Russian immigrant stock, was weak at language but brilliant at math, a combination which had obviously confused the local Educational Authorities. Being uncertain what to do, they had decided that, all in all, he was to be categorized as a no-hoper. Mike Dommett, who had come with me from the secondary modern school, was also a close friend, with whom I fished every river, canal and lake in the area. I was always envious of the ease he showed at math and sciences, which promised a smoother, because more culturally unencumbered, access to university. There was also poor old Scott, who struggled at most things. On one occasion, when stuck over a Spanish word, Mr Bayliss, our teacher at that time, tried to help him with information regarding the corresponding roots and etyma in Hebrew,

Greek and Latin, to the secret, intense amusement of the rest of us. Ever afterwards, whenever Scotty was again put on the spot, we would whisper totally spurious etymologies to him, from the most exotic languages imaginable.

Another close friend was Travis Walker, who, like Scott, was one of the students who traveled down from north Derbyshire. He had a strong regional accent, the most notable feature of which was that all definite articles were glottalized. Like me, he was more interested in the arts, but suffered from what I can only describe, in rather hackneyed terms, as rural simplicity. In contrast, we urban kids were, as the saying went, as cunning as shit-house rats. It was not that Travis was any less intelligent, but just that he faced added cultural barriers to those which were common to us all. Having negotiated so many hurdles on the way to university, he fell at the last one, the Latin requirement for entry. Travis' father, who I met in later years, was a miner and a deeply committed Stalinist, whose political convictions had been confirmed by a trip to Russia. Like many of his kind, he saw nothing problematic in the proletariat's demand for a "good education," the general acquisition of which, he believed, could only further its class interests. Qualifications, or what he called "them bits of paper," were what you needed. He swore, in a manner whose violence somewhat took me aback, that he would "chop off" his son's legs rather than see him go "down t'pit."

Of the girls, I was most friendly with Christine Tucker, who used to arrive every day on an old black bicycle, with her long scarf flapping behind her in the wind. Although a pleasant girl, she always struck me as being a swot and a goody-goody, and far more pliant and cringing in the face of authority than us boys. Significantly, she was an ardent Christian, and we used to have endless, rather silly arguments about the existence of God. Her ambition, more humble than the boys', was to go to Training College to become a school teacher. I now realize that to the burden of class was added, in Chris's case, that of gender. Separately, they could be borne. But not in combination.

Possibly my best friend at the Tech was Stan Guy. Like myself, Stan was a lad of solid working-class stock, who lived in perilous proximity to the inner-city suburbs. Indeed, he had attended a secondary school far rougher than mine. At the time I got to know him, Stan used to share a cold front room with his aged grandfather, for whose benefit he used to recite whole chunks of Shakespeare while the rest of the family watched the telly in the kitchen. His specialty was King Lear raving on the heath. During one of these performances which I myself witnessed, his grandfather lent across, tapped me on the knee and whispered with a chuckle: "'e's a card, aint 'e?"

When *Waiting for Godot* was performed at the Derby Playhouse, Stan auditioned for and won the role of the Boy.

Both Stan and I did better than we had dared hope at "O" level, even in math, at which we were both weak. I do believe that the only algebraic problem I ever got to work out was in that exam, which was indeed most fortunate for me. Naturally, we sailed through Spanish and English. That same summer, partly to celebrate, Stan and I spent a month traveling down the Mediterranean coast from Barcelona to Valencia and then on to Madrid. Stan wanted to continue south to Cadiz, but I had a girl I wanted to get back to in England.

However, Stan didn't last long at "A" level, not through lack of ability but, I suspect, because of a need to break out of the closed atmosphere of what was, in contrast to mine, a non-mobile working-class family. He was soon packing his bags to take up a position in the Foreign Office in London. I called to see him once at his London digs – I was on my way back from Spain at the time – and he took me to work to introduce me to his colleagues. It was a hell of a business getting into the building for security reasons, which, I sensed, Stan hoped would impress me. But I wasn't impressed by his colleagues – two superior types, recently graduated from Oxford, who treated Stan as the office boy he was. I knew Stan wouldn't put up with that kind of treatment, and was not surprised when a few months later he appeared in Derby to inform his friends and slightly alarmed family that he was going to go and live in Spain. True to his word, he set off for Madrid a few weeks later, knowing nobody and with scarcely a penny to his name. I could not decide at the time whether it was the bravest or most foolhardy thing I had ever seen.

Predictably, he found it hard-going for a while, but by the time I saw him again in Madrid the following summer, he had established some connections and was well set up. I was impressed by Stan's Spanish, but not by his expat friends, who seemed on the whole to be a morally degenerate version of his colleagues in London. It was in Madrid that Stan eventually got to know a sweet Japanese girl. Re-appearing in Derby the following year, he informed me of his resolve to follow her to Japan and marry her. By this point, his family had given up any thought of standing in his way. I recall during his final days in England we went for a day's hike up Monsal Dale and over the Derbyshire moors. We talked the whole day through, Stan about his future in Japan, me about mine within the academy. We both sensed, I think, that we were coming to a parting of our ways. And so, by a strange quirk of our personal destinies, at the precise moment when Stan was setting off to make his way by rail across the steppes of Siberia, I was preparing to make my way through tertiary education, one of the most deadly mine-fields within the British class system. It was a toss up which, if either, of us was going to make it, but for neither could there be any turning back.

4
Writing in the Institution: Malcolm K. Read and Paul Julian Smith

Introduction

The intellectual trajectories of Malcolm Read and Paul Julian Smith will be approached for the insight that they afford into two contrasting situational logics, viewed against the backdrop of modern British Hispanism. Very broadly, Read can be shown to operate in terms of what Margaret Archer has called the principle of *competitive contradiction*, whereas Smith, by way of contrast, conforms much more closely to the alternative principle of *contingent complementarity*.[6] What this means, on the surface, is that Read welcomes confrontational situations, in which the dynamics of class conflict can be enacted, in some kind of agon. Not surprisingly, he has made no secret of his own proletarian origins or of his passage through a "secondary modern" school. His combativeness is that of the marginalized intellectual, engaged in a desperate rearguard defense of a working-class culture that has been radically transformed in the post-war period. Yet his career path is not without its complications and contradictions. While clearly a product of the revolutionary 1960s, academically Read began his career firmly wedged within the positivism typical of his discipline, whence he progressed, ideologically, through a number of medial positions. He finally "broke" with the latter to identify with Marxism, at a time when many Leftist members of his generation were travelling in the reverse direction. The paradoxes do not cease here: a scholar who has consistently attacked the postmodern turn within his discipline has become, through his own ambulant life-style – he has taught in various national academies – a "floating intellectual" of an eminently global kind.

Smith's career, by way of contrast, exhibits all the signs of what used to be called the "grammar-school boy," whose passage through to Cambridge was always reasonably assured and predictable. The beginning of his career

---

6.   For a full discussion of competitive contradiction and contingent complementarity, see essay 6.

in Hispanism coincided with the deepening crisis of capitalism, whose repercussions upon the academy induced many senior Hispanists, struck dumb by the ideological assault upon them by Thatcherism, to take early retirement. Those that remained saw in Smith a means of arriving at some ideological compromise with the forces of neo-liberalism. Like Read, Smith needed to work his way out of the conservative forms of liberalism that dominated his discipline, but not through class conflict – Smith will increasing distance himself from Marxism to the point of assuming anti-Marxist positions. Smith's equivalent "break" will take the form of "coming out" as a gay Hispanist. The moment was opportune: the new social movements, notably feminism and queer studies, were peaking in popularity. Confrontation in these circumstances could only have been as counterproductive as it was unnecessary. It sufficed for Smith to go with the flow, which would bear him, by a happy coincidence, in the direction he wanted to go, which was away from traditional Hispanism, towards post-structuralism and postmodernism. Significantly, and in accordance with the logic of complementarity, he has refused to respond to Read's direct provocations.

In the Prison-House of Empiricism

In a recent work, *Transitional Discourses*, Read reminds us that he began his career, in the late 1960s, in theoretical linguistics. This was the period of impassioned debate between a burgeoning group of Transformational Grammarians, led by Noam Chomsky, and the dominant Bloomfieldians. The two sides were divided at the philosophical level, between the mentalism of Chomsky and the behaviorism of Bloomfield. As Chomsky himself illustrated at the time, in his books *Cartesian Linguistics* and *Language and Mind*, his "thick" subject was in point of fact the culmination of a much longer tradition, rooted ultimately in medieval thought and passing, allegedly, through Cartesian thought, the Neo-Platonic tradition, Kantianism and, ultimately, certain philosophical and cultural strains of Romanticism. The Bloomfieldian tradition was similarly rooted in pre-20th century thought, notably the British empiricist tradition, stemming from Locke and passing through Hume, which equated the mind with a *tabula rasa*. This stimulus-response model was taken to extremes in the early 20th century by Skinner. The attraction of this debate for the Hispanist was the importance that Chomsky attached to two 16th-century Spanish writers, Juan Huarte de San Juan and Francisco Sánchez de las Brozas. Huarte was to be the subject of Read's first book.

Huarte was the author of only one work, *Examen de ingenios para las ciencias* (1575), which was largely known among Hispanists as a possible source for Cervantes on the subject of madness. (Several of Cervantes' characters, it will be recalled, not least of all Don Quixote himself, are afflicted by mental instability of some kind.) In contrast, Chomsky was fascinated by the importance that Huarte attributed to human creativity, which chimed perfectly with his own insistence that human language could not be reduced to the kind of stimulus-response model favored by the behaviorists. Undoubtedly, this was a very partial reading of a very complex and contradictory work, which, the references to creativity notwithstanding, was driven by a compulsion to reduce faculty psychology to bodily functions, understood in Galenic, humoreal terms. Indeed, as a careful reading of the text reveals, creativity itself is ultimately seen by Huarte as rooted in bodily functions, leading thereby to charges of materialism by the Inquisition, which lost no time in placing the *Examen* on the Index. Huarte's son subsequently produced a revised edition, in response to the requirements of the censors, but at considerable cost to the work's integrity.

Read seemed uncertain of which direction to take, in his *Juan Huarte de San Juan*, with respect to the position mapped out by Chomsky. Indications are that he found the linguist's emphasis upon creativity not only ideologically congenial to his own literary sensibility but also historically justifiable, in the case of Huarte, insofar as consonant with the general Renaissance preoccupation with the "dignity of man." Having said which, the very detailed exposé, in chapter 5, of the relevant sections of the *Examen* demonstrates fairly conclusively that Huarte not so much *explains* creativity, in the manner suggested by Chomsky, as explains it *away*, in terms of "temperamental imbalance." Confirmation is found in contemporary theological views on "fallen man," which are shown, on the basis of textual evidence, to have impacted considerably upon Huarte. The two contrasting approaches to the *Examen*, that of Chomsky and the reductivist alternative argued by Read, are never directly juxtaposed. Instead, the Hispanist struggles to strike a balance between what he takes to be conflicting allegiancies and contradictions internal to Huarte's text, in terms that are redolent of modern ideological oppositions:

> Huarte's exaltation of the dignity of man, particularly with respect to his ability to control his own destiny, suggests a personal commitment to a philosophy of liberalism. The extent of his commitment, however, is deceptive, for the author of the *Examen* gradually emerges as a scholar who, in an attempt to extend the realms of science, undercut many key terms in the vocabulary of liberalism. Indeed, his ultimate goal seems to have been nothing less than the exorcism of the "ghost in the machine," and, in order to achieve this, he believed that it was

necessary for the scientist to carry investigation into a realm beyond freedom and dignity. (Read 1981: 71)

Now this is all very confusing. What, precisely, do "liberalism," a 19th-century political ideology, and classical mechanicism ("ghosts in the machine"), not to mention the reference in chapter 8 to "Brave New Worlds," have to do with 16th-century Spanish culture?! Read's principal difficulty, we suggest, is that while he was able, from a positivist perspective, to *describe* fairly accurately what the *Examen* actually says, his theory-laden terms start to unpick themselves once any attempt is made to *explain* the contradictions in the text, at which point the underlying idealism of Read's conceptual categories makes its presence felt. An additional complicating factor is that Read's text is no less contradictory than Huarte's, at the ideological level, although for very different reasons. For whereas the *Examen de ingenios* is arguably over-determined by substantialism, the dominant ideology of feudalism, and by animism, the emergent ideology of mercantilist capitalism, Read's dominant empiricism – the ideology of the classic bourgeoisie – was radically compromised by a residual animism, functioning, in modernity, as the specialized ideology of the petty bourgeoisie. Animism was the very tradition that, coincidentally, Chomsky himself was trying to resuscitate through, amongst other things, his partial misrecognition of Huarte, and that would furnish the conceptual means through which Read would subsequently "break" with positivist and empiricist ideology.

Hegel without Hegel

In his next work, *The Birth and Death of Language*, Read included articles that had first appeared in the 1970s, but which, with the help of newer material, were now woven into a broad narrative that swept from the feudal epic to the Baroque. A story unfolds of birth in medieval literature, maturity in the Renaissance, and of death or, to be more precise, a "sense of ending" in the Baroque. In the medieval epic, it was argued, all meaning is exteriorized in visible signs, particularly in the body. The interior remains inaccessible except insofar as it is expressed externally.

> ... language looks essentially towards the outside, to the concrete world of action, rather than inwards towards the world of the spirit. The repercussions of such a tendency are considerable. Principally, the medieval commitment to the visual dimension tends to impede, if not preclude, the exploration of inner experience not amenable to representation at this level. (Read 1983: 16)

Thus, for example, the bard is precluded from exploring that supremely lyrical moment at which the Cid confronts the small girl, who bears the message that the whole of Burgos has barred its doors against him. "The cross-examination teeters on the edge of a psychological abyss," Read writes, "and then retreats into a more manageable discussion of external, tangible embodiments of honor, namely, beards" (18). During the Renaissance, man's inner world is opened up and explored, notably by Erasmians and mystics, with their emphasis upon inner prayer and spirituality, in opposition to an increasingly secular society, culminating in Don Quixote's descent into the cave of Montesinos and Gracián's endless conceptual play, the latter in an attempt to bridge the gap that had opened up between language and the world, and between the internal and external.

Nicholas Round, in a review of *The Birth and Death of Language* in the *Bulletin of Hispanic Studies*, recognized that it is an unusual work to come out of British Hispanism and even went so far as to lay his finger on one of its most symptomatic features, namely the blurred distinction between paraphrase or summary and critical commentary (Round 1986: 150, 151). The difficulty lay, to elaborate, in the manner in which what was obviously a resumé of an author's ideas flowed seamlessly into outrageous reconfigurations of the same, using concepts drawn, for example, from psychoanalysis. But beyond this, Round was unable to proceed, predictably so in that he himself was hamstrung by the very ideology with which Read was trying to break. From our standpoint, the causal mechanisms involved appear complex, contradictory and over-determined. At one level, that of the ideological unconscious, Read's "fascination with the object" was giving way to an attempt to theorize the diachronic transformations of a manifestly Hegelian Moving Spirit, which was seen as unfolding through a process of increasing interiorization. More consciously, Read was also anticipating complaints from empirically-minded critics to the effect that, through his free-wheeling theoretical speculation, he was "getting away from the text" or, alternatively, "imposing his own ideas on the text." Viewed thus, the close weave between commentary and summary was something of a defensive device, with which to disarm his ideological opponents. The same protective function could be attributed to the array of positivists sources displayed in the footnotes (which manifestly served to legitimate the hermeneutic, psychoanalytic and even Marxian texts that jostled alongside them). Anyway, whatever the causes, the outcome was the same: Read clung to the rock-face of the text, with the tenacity of any positivist critic, even as he struggled to pull clear of it.

Such tactics, is has to be said, were largely successful, and taken together with the sheer sweep of Read's narrative, made it uncommonly difficult for positivist scholars to mount a critique of his work. And yet

Read's theoretical basis was, in fact, incredibly vulnerable to charges of anachronism, not at the localized level, although even here issues of relevance remained to be seriously debated, but in the last place either empiricist or idealist critics were likely to look, namely the "subject" itself. For if Read had partially broken with empiricism, it was only to assume another variation within the bourgeois ideological canon. What all these variations have in common is the importance they attach to the category of the subject, which is treated as a universal, transhistorical category. Needless to say, the animist "beautiful soul" is not to be confused with Cartesian Reason, nor this Reason with the Kantian Transcendental Subject or its Hegelian counterpart, and these, in turn, differ significantly from the empty subject of Humean empiricism. But what is never brought into question is the centrality of the subject itself. For which reason it never occurs to Read that, objectively speaking, there was no "subject" under feudalism, only "lords" and "serfs." And that since there was no "subject," there could be no split subject, which is why duplicity must be exteriorized or rather "substantialized," in conversations, between *two* Jews and *two* Infantes. And if the same bard proceeds sometimes in the totally aperspectival manner that Read describes, it is because his text precedes the birth of a literalism that will lead authors to remorselessly view the world from the standpoint of a "free," internalized subject. Ideologically, we are saying, *there is no inner world for the author of the* Cid *to explore.*

Postmodern Beginnings

Like Read (although at a later date), Smith began his career firmly lodged within the bounds of British empiricism, but unlike Read he will never "break" with the dominant ideology, which explains why he will negotiate the relevant transitions far more smoothly. Traditional scholars would have been more than satisfied with the positions assumed in *Quevedo on Parnassus* (1987), a work distinguished by its opposition to "modern prejudices" (Smith 1987: 194), references (in the highest tradition of liberalism) to "the general truth of the human predicament" (174), the relegation of "extra-poetic" considerations, not to mention its rejection of the "psychological theories" used by modern critics (170-71). These are not simply tactical devices to distract attention from the post-structuralist allusions to "epistemic anxiety" and the "dissolution of the self" (23, 139), but evidence of principled positions. What Smith deems objectionable about modern psychological theories is that a Golden Age poet could not possibly have had access to them. The argument, from our perspective, has significant implications: Smith, like all empiricist critics, draws no distinction between the critical concepts or tools of his own theoretical apparatus and the object of analysis; the subject, through the gaze, identifies itself with the object.

Once again, then, the familiar positivistic "fascination with the object," but re-affirmed and indeed strengthened, in Smith's case, through an insistence that the love lyric be read strictly "in its own terms." This kind of technicism proved incompatible with the "unconscious" preoccupation with literary "sensibility," based on an "expressive" view of language, that was the hall-mark of prevailing neo-Kantian literary practice, and Smith proceeded to castigate the latter in the severest terms. But if he had arrived at the edge of the dominant ideology, Smith wasn't quite certain of what he was seeing. The emphasis on "authenticity," he realized, was ideological through and through, but he sought to neutralize it by giving one more twist to the empiricist spiral, in other words, by submissively collapsing criticism further into its object, defined in terms of the critical reception and consumption of Quevedo's text by his contemporaries. It never occurred to him that the "existential" imperatives that some readers saw "in" Quevedo's text were perfectly compatible with his own technical imperatives, given a sufficiently *stratified* view of the universe (and of texts within it). Such an approach would have required a philosophical critique of empiricism, including the unthinking identification of thought about an object with the actual object, and Smith, by virtue of his ideological location, was not up to this task.

The kind of break with traditional critical practice that an Althusserian critic, such as, say, Juan Carlos Rodríguez, was forced to engineer, in the context of Fascist Spain, was simply inconceivable in Britain, where the reformist practices of the Labour Party broadly marked the limits of the Left. But the price that empiricism would exact was always going to be enormous, particularly when it came to history. And significantly, history was the one thing that would *never* figure on *Smith's* agenda, as he himself was intelligent enough to realize: "I may ... be criticized for a lack of concern for history, in the traditional sense of the word," he conceded in his next work, *Writing in the Margin* (1988 [ii]: 8). What this meant, practically speaking, was that Smith was always able to work within the bounds of a contingent complementarity. Breaks, staged in competitive terms, were undesirable and, moreover, unnecessary, for the simple reason that neo-Kantian criticism of the traditional kind was as anxious as Smith to avoid any contaminating truck with material, historical considerations: "Yet it is clear that historical incident or epiphenomenon does not determine a literary text in any direct way" (8). Or in any indirect way, insofar as Smith was well on the way to severing what residual ties the empiricist critic recognized as existing between the text and its (background) context. In other words, the anti-Marxist bias that had characterized traditional British Hispanism could be carried to new heights of idealism, as discursive formations slipped their material moorings in reality, and became free-floating.

Its commitment to ontological realism notwithstanding, Althusserianism was the site at which this slippage occurred more generally, within Western "theoretical" practice. The new "true socialism" that was emerging in the 1980s was characterized above all by the autonomization of ideology and politics, signaled by the drift towards the establishment of language or "discourse" as the dominant principle of social life. Lurking behind this drift was the dissolution of social reality into discourse; the replacement of the working class by a "discursively constructed" plural subject; and the subordination of socialist struggle to a plurality of "democratic" struggles in which "democracy" is indeterminate and abstract. As Meiksins Wood has perceptively noticed (Wood 76 ff), one general principle underlies these themes: the randomization of history and politics, whereby, once the grand Marxist narratives are displaced, history emerges as *pure contingency*. Rather, there is no history, no determinate historical *conditions, relations, processes*. Althusserianism, from the standpoint of its critics, thus constructed a bridge which many, led by Barry Hindess and Paul Hirst, crossed into the various post-Marxisms, where they were once again able to rejoin social democracy and even to indulge in various forms of neo-liberal rhetoric, notably its anti-Marxism.

This was the context in which postmodernism began to be cultivated in British Hispanism. Particularly revealing in this respect is Smith's deployment of Althusserianism in a "political" reading of the *Buscón*. The relevant pages deserve a closer reading than we have the space to permit ourselves here, not for their content – Smith's application of the Althusserian notions of the ISA and RSA is confused and perfunctory – but for the evidence of the guilt and bad faith that haunts a generation of scholars that have surrendered to reformism: "Social circumstances do not 'produce' writing in any direct sense. The very variety and proliferation of picaresque texts [...] is proof enough of this perhaps unpalatable fact" (Smith 1988 [ii], 119). What a more detailed analysis would need to tease out is the subtle shift involved in the transition from the traditional emphasis on Culture, as standing above material reality, to a linguistic turn that would in effect sever all ties with that "reality": "writing is manifestly multiple, not coterminous with, but relatively autonomous from, the social practices within which it finds its meanings" (120). Sophisticated Althusserians would wish to argue that all this has little to do with the real complexities of Althusserianism.[7] But the fact remains that their seeming inability to resolve the tensions between their epistemological conventionalism and ontological realism was conducive to Smith's brand of idealism: "... there is no theoretical or empirical link between the supposedly discrete areas of art and life" (167). Such statements confirm the suspicion that "mediation," "ideology" and "relative autonomy," in the wrong hands, simply eased the transition from New Criticism to postmodern deconstruction and into an ontological skepticism according to which "any access to a 'real' beyond [literature] is problematic indeed" (8).

A Star is Born

From the beginning, Smith's work was influential and generally well received. Some critics, it is true, were driven into competitive postures, notably those who, like Gareth Walters, picked up on the conservative dimension of Smith's quest for a more "authentic" reading of Quevedo: "one is reminded of the unremitting drone of period instruments" (Walters 1990: 189). At the same time, Walters is hamstrung by the same ideological dynamic. Knowledge consists of the gaze of a "free" subject directed towards an object: "[I]t cannot be seriously claimed that *quevedistas* lose sight of the text" (189). What Walters cannot "see" is that the challenge to critical orthodoxy, and the reasons for its success, had less to do with the past – Smith's promotion of baroque readership was, to this extent, deceptive – but with the present or, to be more exact, with the future, where postmodernism was discovering a subjectivity every bit as fragile and fragmented as its pre-modern counterpart. The leap from one to the other was performed in a moment, at least by a critic as unencumbered by material baggage as Smith.

The grumblings of some older Hispanists nothwithstanding, others more correctly intuited the "lie of the land" and the need to seek some accommodation with the new world order. Moreover, they were perceptive enough to realize that Smith, if properly supervised, offered a means of converting their cultural capital. Thus, for Peter Dunn: "Readers accustomed to more traditional modes of criticism – formalist, moral positivist, contextual, etc. – may yet find some reassurance in a certain pragmatism as different aspects or levels of a text are brought into focus and set besides the schemas of, for example, carnival (Edmond Cros) or social surveillance (Foucault). Not being an absolute purist myself, I am prepared to judge by results, and I expect that other readers will do the same" (Dunn 165). In other words, Smith could be read as an updated

---

7.   See Resch, chap. 5 for a definition of "fiction" as ideology to the second power.

version of liberal pluralism or eclecticism, which was the perfect accompaniment to the rainbow politics of the new professional classes. The problem was, as Dunn himself pointed out, that the theoretical schemes on offer were so radically diverse as to raise issues of incommensurability and consequently of *real* effectivity: "The absence of dogmatic attachment to one totalizing system may leave doubts concerning the relative power of the several paradigms that are set up" (165-6).

If pluralism of the traditionally liberal kind had been less haunted by the specter of relativism, it was because its various positions were undergirded by the all-encompassing concept of "Man." But it was precisely this concept that Smith's work set out to critique, along with its thinly disguised analogue, the unity of the text. Somewhat disturbingly, Smith had the backing of a global capitalism every bit as anxious to deconstruct the myth of subjective unity – how otherwise was it going to recycle individuals through a variety of jobs in the course of a single lifetime? Intimidated by this combined show of strength, Dunn willingly confessed the sins of the traditionalist, and conceded the existence hitherto of "unexamined ontological or aesthetic assumptions" and "hidden ideological agendas." However, liberalism was not without a comeback. Evidence suggested that post-structuralists themselves operated in practice with an unspecified sense of basic identity, which, among other things, enabled them to attach their names to their books, in a fairly unproblematic manner. And certainly, outside the academy, ordinary people could not endorse the reduction of being to language, nor could they continue to function, on a day-to-day basis, without a continuous sense of the self. In the context of such practicalities, Dunn spotted that individual identity needed affirming and reinforcing as a necessary precondition of activity (including active resistance): "But unity as such is difficult to dismiss, since it is one of the terms for order, and in all our activities (not only as artists, critics, historians, theoreticians, etc.) we strive to make structures that will have a place and a continuity and will, at some level of perception, have a relevance to one another. Indeed, we cannot *not* do so" (173).

Of course, the terms of Dunn's debate must remain those of liberalism – his veiled references to Marxism ("as we used to say ...") is sheer leftist posturing. But it is significant that, even judged by their own conservative standards, liberals were not slow to spot a rightward bias beneath the celebration of postmodernity. It was a direction diametrically opposed to that of Read, who was, however, running into problems of his own.

The Matter of Freud

Visions in Exile, continuing Read's early project, simply pressed Ernest Becker's and Norman Brown's social psychology to its materialist conclusion. Its Freud is not the Freud of desire, of erotic *jouissance*, linguistic displacement and the phallus, but of "wishes," violent anality, and the penis. The whole of Spanish culture, from the Golden Age through the Enlightenment, was pressed through a model whereby Read tracked down the glories of "civilization" and "culture" to their inglorious source. The anality – the "filth" and "dirt" – that Read discerned undoubtedly served the purposes of competitive contradiction, vis-à-vis a class-ridden idealist culture, whose works of art students were taught to revere and respect. In this sense *Visions in Exile* was clearly designed to provoke and scandalize. Indeed, psychoanalysis stood in lieu of a Marxist discourse that, unaccountably, Read only engaged obliquely at this stage.

The *Bulletin of Hispanic Studies*, the lynch pin of British Hispanism, deployed several strategies of reception when faced with a problematic text of this kind, which fell on the wrong side of the ideological divide marking the limits of empiricism. The first consisted of foregrounding stylistic mistakes, minor inaccuracies, spelling errors, etc., in an attempt to delegitimate the work's content. The second, to which recourse was had when the first proved insufficient, was to enlist the services of a foreign, usually North American, critic. This particular tactic allowed British Hispanists to acknowledge a work's existence (as every good liberal should) without having to problematize their own ideological parameters. (Only in the last instance will liberalism totally ignore a text, an extreme measure that smacks of repression and overt censorship and so infringes the norms of the liberal community.) The second strategy was deployed in the case of *Visions in Exile*, which the *Bulletin* placed in the hands of Paul Ilie, an American scholar specializing in the 18th century.

The co-option of a North American scholar, for review purposes, must itself be adequately framed and explained, in ideological terms. The claim is not that North American Hispanists, en masse, had been able to break with empiricist ideology: indeed, operating as they did within a more developed form of bourgeois society, unencumbered by the relics of feudalism, these Hispanists were even more firmly embedded within liberalism than their British counterparts. But to the extent that this empiricism was itself undergoing significant changes, North American scholars were equipped to problematize basic empiricist tenets and to raise theoretical issues in a way that was inconceivable in Britain. For example, and with respect to Read's text, Paul Ilie correctly indicated that at some point criticism must address the status of its concepts, together with the truth value of its interpretations (Ilie 282). As he implied, this was not as easy as traditional Hispanists seemed to believe, insofar as empiricism, applied to the human sciences, produced parodies of those sciences. A theory is not to be confused with empirical data; rather it possesses a transitive dimension that makes it self-contained and, to some degree, self-justifying as a research program: "But since all premises are subject to counter-premises, the test is how well the argumentation follows from them and sustains itself" (283). At this level, Ilie found *Vision in Exile* convincing and difficult to refute, except at one point; for while Read had expended considerable intellectual effort in bracing the psychoanalytic argumentation of his work, the same could not be said of its sociological counterpart, that appeared to have been loosely attached to the central framework of the text. As Ilie perceptively observes: "... debatable allusions to an incipient bourgeoisie in Góngora's time, or to Luzán's role as a spokesman for the middle class, demand justifications that exceed the intended scope of Read's discussion" (284). Justifications were to come with Read's following works.

Inscriptions of Desire

Smith's next book, *The Body Hispanic* (1989), appeared more or less at the same time as Read's *Visions in Exile*, and the two works were often linked together, to the extent that they were frequently reviewed conjointly. Strange to relate, therefore, that no critic seems to have perceived the obvious, namely that whereas Read was travelling towards historical materialism and a science of literary criticism, Smith was tending towards a post-structuralism that pressed the notion of the infinite openness of meaning and of the indefinite multiplicity of the text to the point at which the "orthodox claim to scientific objectivity" was deemed to be "no longer tenable" (Smith 1989:139). The exact nature of Smith's Nietzschean irrationalism, it has to be said, is partly obscured, and for several reasons. Firstly, Smith will never enter into the kind of debate necessary to support such claims intellectually, which would have meant engaging, in genuinely philosophical terms, a whole series of issues relating to epistemology, ontology, and the nature of language. Instead, we will be offered a range of postmodern propositions that, in the words of Christopher Norris, "merit nothing more than a footnote in some future anatomy of the nonsense of the times" (Norris 17).

Secondly, and more importantly in the present context, Smith will execute a diversionary tactic through which the charge of idealism is displaced onto Marx. It is hard to believe it, I know, but it is true. "Defined by Marx himself as invisible, empty, ahistorical and irrational, Latin

America exemplifies the point at which Marxism is no longer Marxist, but idealist" (1989: 142). I do not propose to enter into the details of this claim. Suffice it to say that a proper evaluation of the role of revolutionary Marxism in Latin America, in all its diversity, would need to engage a vast array of texts – a detailed consideration of Mariátegui, for example, would seem indispensable --, not to mention the record of achievement of Trotskyism as well as Stalinism (see Callinicos 1995: 189-90). Always travelling lightly and taking every possible shortcut, Smith rests content with Sheldon B. Liss's *Marxist Thought in Latin America* and José Aricó's *Marx y America Latina*. The first is a sketchy, elementary text by a self-confessed non-Marxist, but the second deserves more careful consideration, as does the use to which Smith puts it.

Smith produces a very extensive summary of Aricó's argument (1989: 141-42), the nub of which is that, whereas Marx and Engels produced subtle analyses of Ireland, Poland, Spain, Russia, Turkey and other colonized or economically backward nations, they continued to view Latin America as a land without history. Consequently, Latin America did not figure in the inversion of the relations of dependency between the capitalist center and the colonial margins that, according to Marx, made the emancipation of the European proletariat conditional upon that of the colonies. This omission, Aricó argues, had less to do with Eurocentrism than a Hegelian residue in Marx's thought. However, this is only a partial perspective on Aricó's work and, in that it pretends to be a summation of its whole argument, amounts to a something of a distortion. A fuller picture is required if we are to adequately frame the question of Marx's alleged idealism.

Aricó's central thesis is that Marx underplays the importance of politics, at a national level, in determining the fate of nations. According to this argument, it is not simply that Marx, in his concern with the dynamics of capitalist economics, left his project incomplete at the end of his life, but that he was resistant to recognizing in the State a capacity to produce civil society. Part of his reaction to Hegel, in order to safeguard determination by the economic, was to reduce politics to the level of the arbitrary. Now this is, in my view, a very shaky basis on which to erect any claim concerning Marx's alleged idealism. The boot, it seems to me, is on the other foot. The point at issue is not Marx's idealism but Aricó's and, by a process of extrapolation, Smith's. For what Aricó is doing here is inverting classical Marxism, so as to privilege superstructural, political and ideological interests, at the expense of the economic base. True, Aricó is still a Marxist, attempting to refine Marxist concepts, but it is but a short step from his position to those of post-Marxism. It comes as no surprise when, in the epilogue to the second edition of Aricó's book, we find ourselves suddenly entangled in a world "concebido como lenguaje" (Arico 204 note 1), and well on the way towards the dissolution of economics and politics into power: "El dominio capitalista, en adelante, deberá refundarse en una posicionalidad de poder colocada *fuera* de la relación 'económica' que representaba el capital" (219). By the same token, the opposition between capital and labor has been replaced by "la realidad de lo otro, de lo diverso" (221).

It is not the place here to enter into a detailed consideration of Aricó's ideas. Clearly, it is part of a broadly-based shift from Marxism into post-Marxism that has been fully covered elsewhere (see Meiksins Wood). The overall effect is to produce parodied forms of Marxism as an economism, which can then be played off against issues of subjectivity and consciousness. By severing the ties with the economy, we are left with a world reduced to discursivity, a discursivity that, through a further process of inversion, is able to masquerade as a species of materialism. It is from this position that Smith is able to critique Marx for his idealism and by implication promote himself as something of a materialist.[8]

The Ideological Unconscious

The contradictions, even incoherence, of Read's earlier works, structured as these were across ideological breaks internal to bourgeois ideology, are carried to extremes in his next work, *Language, Text, Subject,* and for one very important reason: the latter is located at the break between bourgeois and Marxist theory. Significant in this respect is the author's own reference to a degree of "disjunction," separating both the preface and epilogue from the main body of the text (Read 1992: xiii). One's impression is that the former, apparently composed at a later date, are more consistently materialist in their outlook than the latter. At the same time, one is also struck by the tensions throughout the separate components of the work. Thus, in the preface, while Read is critical of his

---

8.   Likewise, we do not have the space to enter into the broader issue of the role of politics and the State vis-à-vis the economy. Suffice it to note the following. Firstly, capitalist relations, it is true, are routinely reproduced without the use of violence or the threat of its use. This accounts, in part, for the sense that the capitalist State functions as a power *apart from* the economy. Secondly, and by the same token, the State has a vested interest in creaming off, through taxation at the secondary level, the largest possible portion of the total social surplus. Consequently, it will sometimes find itself in conflict with "its" bourgeoisie and in support of the proletariat. Having said which, it is also true that there are definite limits to State autonomy. After all, its own revenues depend upon the success of capital accumulation, with respect to which there exist a number of mechanisms, notably capital flight, that enable the bourgeoisie to discipline "its" government. Finally, and with particular reference to Marx, we would emphasize the need to rise from the abstract discussion of capital, in Volume One of *Capital,* to that of the competition between capitals, on the concrete level of the world economy, contained in Volume Three. Once this is done, the connection between global politics and the struggle between rival systems of property relations become clear. For further details, see Creaven 254-70.

own earlier psychoanalytic work, which allegedly "flowed outside of history" (ix), and of Paul Julian Smith, for reducing the world to language, he yet concedes that this same world is accessible "only through text" (x), a somewhat debatable claim by strictly Marxist standards, to say the least.

Such theoretical discontinuties extend into the main body of the text, which exhibits internal inconsistencies of its own. The theoretical parameters of an early chapter on Garcilaso are dictated by Read's indebtedness to the work of the Spanish Marxist, Juan Carlos Rodríguez, whose work had crucially historicized the category of the subject. Gone, under Rodríguez's influence, is the empiricist, technicist notion of science, which rests upon the subject/object relation. Gone also are the petty-bourgeois notions of literary "taste" and aesthetic "sensibility". In their place is a Structural Marxist concept of literature as an ideological practice grounded in the production and reception of literary texts in their determinate historical contexts. Thus conceived, science is not the duplication of its object but rather its theoretical re-elaboration, in an attempt to know the object as it cannot know itself. At the same time, Read is critical of the absence in Rodríguez of a theory of subjectivity, in which respect he refuses to relinquish his psychoanalytic theorizing. The latter is complicated by the addition of a Lacanian component to the "anal" reading of Freud, which Read still refuses to relinquish. Lacanianism, by the Hispanist's own estimation, constitutes an idealistic turn within the field of psychoanalytic studies.

One senses here the influence of personal factors, of the kind that Read himself does not hesitate to bring into play in his preface. Provisionally, one would hazard a guess that the socially mobile working-class boy found particularly congenial the significance that Althusserians attached to structures which totally transcended the level of individual consciousness. By the same token, the importance that Read personally attached to his own sense of working-class identity explains his attachment to psychoanalysis, in the face of Rodríguez's rejection of "psychology." What he does not seem to have realized is that the shift from the "anal" to the fragmented subject of post-structuralism, of the kind promoted by Julia Kristeva, was hardly more suited to grounding his sense of identity that was the total evacuation of subjectivity by Rodríguez. It is certainly not clear, for example, how Read manages to square his own autobiographical essentialism with the critique, in the second chapter of *Language, Text, Subject*, of the kind of "consistent subject" (55) deployed by British *calderonistas*.

The following chapters, on the Enlightenment, do much to compound and little to dispel the overall impression of theoretical confusion.

Although one is struck by the similarities between Foucault's notion of the "death of the subject" and the absence of the subject from feudal substantialism, upon which Rodríguez insists, Read misses the opportunity to compare and contrast the two theoreticians directly. But whereas theoretical pluralism may have been compatible with post-structuralism, its effect upon Read's Marxism was nothing less than catastrophic. One is reminded of an over-ambitious juggler attempting to keep too many balls in play at the same time. Perforce, Read eventually spills them in all directions, at the moment when he begins to put to Foucault questions that he might well have put to Rodríguez, namely how do "strategies without projects" relate to conscious decisions?

The final epilogue confirms our suspicions concerning Read's inability to reconcile the importance he attaches to individual agency with the Althusserian models that he otherwise finds so attractive. "The present work", he explains "presupposes the possibility of a subject that is imprisoned and *knows itself to be imprisoned*. The task that awaits us is the specification of the social and historical conditions necessary for the dialectical construction of this subject" (75). As things stood, he manifestly lacked the theoretical resources to initiate this project. Caught between a Marxist theoreticism that conflates downwards, so as to reduce individuals to the status of "mere supports," and a post-structuralist version of psychoanalysis that conflates upwards, from individual to social psychology, Read was straddled across an abyss. The result, in his own words, was "a Marxist analysis that teeters on the brink of solipsistic individualism" (xii).

Bodies, Bodies and More Bodies

It is not our aim, within the context of the present study, to unpack the contents of the series of works by Smith that have appeared over the last decade, nor, conversely, to rest content with the kind of critique, commonly heard, which dismisses Smith's work as impossibly glib and superficial. It is true that the works in question are most easily defined in terms of their changing *objects*, defined, moreover, as *Spanish* objects, subject to the privileged scrutiny of a Hispanist who is equipped with most sophisticated theoretical resources, the latter being of eminently *French* extraction. But while these are doubtless important issues, requiring theoretical scrutiny, they do not, in my view, get to the crux of the problem, with respect to Smith's work. My aim is rather to explore the latter's productive logic, by way of exposing the ideological unconscious whose effects and influence are unhesitatingly registered at the textual level. Let us begin, therefore, with some specific passages from one of the books in question, which, interestingly, converge on the specific issue of ideological "hiddenness." I have in mind *García Lorca/Almodóvar: Gender, Nationality, and the Limits of the Visible*, delivered as an inaugural lecture at the University of Cambridge in 1993:

> The hidden history of Camus's *Bernarda Alba* is that of a Socialist government which sponsored a cinema intended to mirror its own consensus politics, a cinema specialising in adaptations of literary classics with unimpeachable anti-authoritarian credentials. However, as John Hopewell notes of another of Camus's adaptations, unless culture is extended to include "the ugly and the awkward" the films produced will continue to be visually pleasing whatever the cost to the original material. The glossy production values of Camus's *Bernarda Alba* are thus not merely the result of an individual director's artistic temperament; they also betray the ideological commitment of the Spanish government to the celebration of a certain cultural heritage. (Smith 1993: 12)

What Smith is here arguing is that in order to explain the visual impact of Camus' film, we have to attend closely not simply to the actual individuals involved in its production, notably Camus himself, in his privileged capacity as director, but to the invisible forces that underlie it and that relate to government policy. By implication, the "hidden" element is actually the key to understanding the overall production process. Smith has particularly in mind, in the present instance, the operation of an ideological mechanism whereby the more *imaginative* elements of Lorca's work are, allegedly, *repressed*. The contrast with Almodóvar's treatment of similar themes is quite striking, or so at least we are led to believe:

> I mentioned earlier that Mario Camus systematically cuts those excessive or superfluous details of García Lorca's text which make *Bernarda Alba* a melodrama, those moments which frustrate the naturalist ambition of reproducing the real. We have seen that Almodóvar also exploits a performative surplus, an appeal to the expressive potential of language and cinema which transcends what is strictly necessary for narrative purposes: stylised camerawork, dramatic lighting, lushly sensual text and music. (22-23)

What is significant about Smith's work, to reiterate, is not so much its formulaic design as the Kantian ideology in which it is rooted. This ideology, as can be seen from the above, privileges the subject, individually (Camus) or collectively (the Spanish Government), to which social structures can be *reduced*. The result is an example of what Margaret Archer has referred to as *upward conflation*, through which social structures are reduced to the individuals who compose them or, more specifically, to their minds. For underlying this kind of conflation, we would argue, not least of all when it is practiced by Smith and the French theoreticians to whom he constantly defers, is a form of philosophical idealism, which rests upon the assumption that the ultimate determinants of existence are individuals with *thoughts* and *ideas*, otherwise consciousness, that are subsequently translated into action. The subjectivity in question, it should be added, is always *split* between conflictual faculties, otherwise a rational component, in the form of Camus' "timid naturalism," and an imaginative excess, to which Almodóvar freely gives release. And needless to say, standing as he does in the long tradition of romantic rebellion (music, Schopenhauer, etc.), Smith will support the latter.

The Kantian category of the subject, we are arguing, constitutes the ideological matrix from which Smith's work is generated. To have broken with it would have required a monumental effort, particularly in the case of a writer such as Lorca, whose presense so overwhelms his work. In such circumstances the biographical invocation of the *person* of the writer imposes itself as a critical obligation: "I have described that first meeting with Federico García Lorca before. It sounds, now, too romantic to be true; but it was true in 1919 ..." (quoted p. 1). One understand the convenience of the quotation (from J. B. Trend) for Smith's purposes, but the fact remains that it provides a particularly vivid example of a remarkable ideological phenomenon, accurately described by one critic in the following terms: "... el lorquismo está anegado en Lorca y Lorca demasiado construido por el 'experiencialismo lorquista': yo tuve los manuscritos, yo conocí a la familia [....] Casi como una herida que no cicatriza nunca" (Rodríguez 1994: 11). Paradoxically, as the same critic proceeds to illustrate, it was never more urgent to break with the subject, not least of all in its split, Kantian form, than in this particular instance. For while the repressive hypothesis – music, sexuality, etc. – exerted an undoubted fascination for Lorca, as illustrated by *Bernarda Alba*, his more mature work, notably *La comedia sin título*, arguably makes better sense if it is seen as exploring not repression but the (false but real) *production* of the subject (see Rodríguez 1993: 92-100).

Smith's response, I think, would be that his work is far from being reductively individualistic, in the way that has been imputed, and that while certainly his works are structured upon individual writers and artists, they are properly attentive to the relevant historical and social contexts. Further to which he would argue that his stated aim is to bridge the individual and social, otherwise "to reconcile the abstract and the empirical in a logic of practice which permits the cultural commentator a certain distance from his or her object" (Smith 2000: 187); that his methodological approach is properly slanted towards the *materiality* of existence, in order to expose and to historicize those elements often held to be transparent, innocent or invisible (32); and that, in sum, his work is a model of non-reducibility, to the extent that it "attempts to acknowledge virtuosity and psychic vitality" (32).

Aside from the fact that we have again regressed to the Kantian subject, split between a spiritual "sensibility" and a properly empirical attention to "technique," Smith's putative defense would seem to make sense. Let us therefore rectify the charge to one of central as opposed to upward conflation. The nuance, I believe, is important, and explains, among other things, the attraction exerted upon Smith by Bourdieu, a notable example of a central conflationist. As Archer herself writes with respect to the French sociologist: "... we are confronted with amalgams of 'practices' which oscillate wildly between voluntarism and determinism, without our being able to specify the conditions under which agents have greater freedoms or, conversely, work under a considerable stringency of constraints" (Archer 2000: 151).

The tactic, to elaborate, is to withhold autonomy from both the level of social structures and of individual interaction, on the grounds that they are mutually constitutive and therefore cannot be untied. Mutually constitutive, but with one proviso: social structures are deemed to have only a virtual reality until instantiated by individual subjects. This explains why Smith recognizes broadly defined, transhistorical processes, such as Spain's residual attachment to structuralism, only to shy away from them (Smith 2000: 31); and why he makes little headway as regards explaining the humanistic antipathy in Spain to feminism and queer studies (135). Such acts of evasion are symptomatic of a number of serious inadequacies in Bourdieu's and hence Smith's sociological analysis. Briefly, there is no discussion of the source of power relations and, even more seriously, their analyses have no dynamic, no capacity to explain how the system changes. What Martin Carnoy writes of Bourdieu's pedagogical theory can be extended to his sociological project in general: "Reform occurs, but the operation of the school system is fundamentally the same. Why did the reform occur in the first place? Why the necessity to mystify the real power relations in society and the function of the schools?" (Carnoy 105).

There is one final complication to central conflation of the post-structuralist variety. The individual that teases social mechanisms out of their ethereal status into reality is herself almost, but not quite, as insubstantial as these mechanisms, as the result of a displacement that renders her condition "fragmented", even cadaverous (the death of the author, etc.). This is the source of the anti-individualism that distinguishes the various post-structuralisms and postmodernisms from their classically liberal counterparts.

Finally, then, Smith promotes materialism of a singularly idealistic kind, in which the social, political and literary spheres remain suspended and alone, in some ontological limbo, attached to one another by gossamer threats or "fragile homologies" (Smith 2000: 76), until they are "grounded" by individuals who are barely any more material than they. It is a strange universe, and one wonders how anyone could possibly believe in it. Could the reason possibly lie in the cosmic support that it lends to Smith's particular brand of social reformism? For one thing is sure, nothing less than cosmic support is needed if the Hispanist is to achieve his social goal, which is quite simply that of "attacking injustice" from the summit of one of the very bastions of social injustice, namely the University of Cambridge.

Transitional Discourses

Read's last two works, *Borges and his Predecessors* and *Transitional Discourses* show him to be struggling with a very different problem from Smith. Whereas the latter is a central conflationist, who ultimately reduces social structures to a virtual status, Read inherited from Rodríguez a downward conflation that reduces individuals to epiphenomenal forms. But let us consider a little more carefully the specificities involved.

Althusser himself was the first to protest that he never sought to deny the existence of human beings and that he was simply attempting to grasp those broader social mechanisms whose operation transcends the level of individuals. The logic of such a position is plain enough: it makes no sense to try and grasp the law, say, of the declining rate of profit in terms of the conscious decisions taken by individuals. Yet, as Margaret Archer insists, the agency that has been repressed perforce returns through the analytic process: "... for who now does the 'grasping'? It looks as though real human beings have been readmitted (in concrete reality though not in functional theoretical abstractions), in which case why are they not deemed the real history-makers?" (Archer 2000: 29). Something like this seems to have preoccupied Read at the start of *Borges and his Predecessors*, where he argues that the structuralist notion of being entrapped by a dominant ideology "poses serious problems for those of us who, independently of any bourgeois notion of individual freedom, cherish that extraordinary emphasis on human creativity and self-creation which characterizes Marxism in its classic forms. How do we know that we do not know? What is involved in the struggle for human objectivity?" (Read 1993: 11).

However, having once raised the problem, Read turns away from it to focus on those broad processes of social transformation that had been involved in the transition from slave to feudal and to capitalist modes of production. Why?

Theoretically, there were certainly important reasons to stress the existential status of the social mechanisms involved in the kinds of transitional social formations with which Read was concerned. It is worth recalling at this point the extent to which upward conflationists of the post-modernist, post-structuralist kind were plagued by the singular ethereality of their displaced, fragmented subjectivity. For conversely, while by definition they privilege the central role of social structures, downward conflationists registered the impact of an epistemological relativism that ran the risk of reducing these same structures to idealist constructs. Indeed, the impossibility of reconciling this kind of relativism with the claims of realism, an indispensable ingredient of any Marxism, was largely responsible for the much proclaimed "fall" of Althusserianism in the late 1970s. With the benefit of hindsight, therefore, Read had every reason to stress ontology as opposed to the epistemological scepticism that, as *Borges and his Predecessors* demonstrated only too clearly, led inexorably into an all-encompassing solipsism.

But the need to avoid certain conventionalist dead-ends was not the only or even the most important consideration weighing upon Read in his new work. Indications are, from the prefatory material, that he was anxious not to fall back into the quagmire of a "postmodern Marxism", and that, to judge by his aggressively competitive attitudes, he was intent on laying his Marxist credentials on the table. Seeming to forget his own excursions into French thought in his recently published *Language, Text, Subject*, the new convert to Althusserian Marxism can now be found condemning liberal scholars for flirting with a "rampantly idealist" Foucault (28). How do we account for this left, materialist turn? The immediate stimulus, to judge by Read's own comments, appears to have been his radicalizing experience of a Third-World academy, in Jamaica, overdetermined by the effects of working-class culture. The latter, as we suggested above, could not but promote in the socially mobile individual a "lived" and lively sense of his material emplacement. After all, it is one thing for professionals from bourgeois backgrounds to celebrate their personal "freedoms," which they experienced on a daily basis; it is quite another for academics of proletarian origins, who have instilled in them, according to Read, a profound awareness of their own powerlessness in the face of barriers, real and metaphorical, that block their access to university campuses.

What, then, is to be deduced from the logic of Read's own development? Perversely, that the reality of working-class experience is the site at which structural determinism begins to unpick itself, unless, that is, it is properly mediated through other concepts that respect and, more importantly, theorize the initiative of socially mobile individuals. Doubtless, such considerations were not a thousand miles away from Read's own mind when, in the opening pages of *Borges and his Predecessors*, he raised the issue of individual agency. For the sheer fact of his having arrived where he had – Read was, after all, the privileged holder of a personal university Chair – hardly squares with the power that Althusser attributes to the dominant ideology. By the time of Read's next work, then, agency was, not surprisingly, back on the agenda.

In the opening pages of *Transitional Discourses*, Read talks of a "crisis in my thinking" as a result of the contradictory tendencies relating to the categories of theory and experience. At a time when the notion of the subject, partly under the stimulus of Althusserianism, had been stripped of all sense of individuality, he writes, "I found myself increasingly attracted to a testimonial style of discourse that foregrounded the issue of personal identity" (Read 1998: 11). It was to be a conflictual opposition that Read refused to resolve by reducing either side of the structure/individual equation to epiphenomenal status. And so, as his commitment to structural Marxism deepens, so also does the importance that he attaches to issues of agency. In this way, autobiographical elements within the preface of *Transitional Discourses* flow over into the Introduction, only to be resumed with a vengeance in "Some Postmodern Encounters," which concludes the work. Such was the frame that Read placed around his attempts, in the main body of the text, to theorize the question of structural causality, as mediated through the psychology of the individual.

In a series of chapters, Read sweeps from the Baroque, through the Enlightenment, to Romanticism, focusing on the way upon such canonic writers as Tirso de Molina, Gracián, and Larra, the non-canonic Pedro de Montengón, and upon contemporary cultural and linguistic theorists. In the opening chapters, which deal with the Baroque, Read is able to demonstrate, with some success, how the relevant texts are over-determined by substantialism and animism, allegedly the dominant ideologies of feudalism and mercantile capitalism respectively. Moreover, the notion of the ideological unconscious is complicated by that of the libidinal unconscious, taken over from Read's earlier psychoanalytic explorations but deepened through his subsequent encounter with the psychoanalytic Marxism of Eugine Wolfenstein. In these chapters, the ideological implications of the psychoanalytic schemata press less urgently for consideration, for the simple reason that Read abides by his earlier injunction not to treat pre-modern individuals as "case studies." Thus, "it would be premature to present [Don Juan] as an interesting 'case study.' At this stage, the unconscious best lends itself to analysis as it is projected onto culture at large" (89). Gracián is treated in the same way, in that his "persona" is theorized as a compromise version of the subject, between a substantialism that makes no use of the subject, as an ideological category, and animism, which articulates subjectivity in its proto-subject form, otherwise the *alma bella.*

All these theoretical moves are, in themselves reasonable enough, but their broader implications deserve to be pondered further. For example, do they not run the risk of reproducing the liberal notion of subjectivity, a subjectivity that is gradually hollowed out and enriched, and, it goes without saying, becomes "freerer"? One's suspicions are aroused when Read moves on to the 18th century, and directly introduces the notion of individual psychology, with respect to Cadalso and Montengón. Indeed, it is at this point that he activates the Hegelian notions of the Unhappy Consciousness and Stoicism/Skepticism, which he has taken from Wolfenstein. What exactly is being claimed here? That in the pre-modern period, individual psychology did not exist? Or that is was so radically incommensurate with its modern counterpart as to fall outside the latter's conceptual parameters? One accepts Read's suspicions, inherited from Rodríguez, regarding the "subject" as an ideological category, but what is to be gained by substituting it with "individuality," if we have no psychological theory of that individuality?

The problem comes to a head in the chapter that deals with the suicidal Larra, whose richly individualized subjectivity clamors for theoretical recognition. Departing from his Althusserian basis, Read concedes that psychoanalytic knowledge is not directly or immediately political knowledge (235). This is tantamount to insisting on the need for a stratified view of individualities, which would allow for the level of individual psychology and for the social structuring of the self. In spite of which, Read cannot prevent his narrative from degenerating into incoherence when, in "Some Postmodern Encounters" he suddenly protests the absurdity of any attempt to combine Marxism and structuralism, in the sense that a structure of thought, imposed on all members of a class or society, is incompatible with the spontaneous creativity of real men and women (239). Fine! But how exactly does one reconcile such proclamations with the profoundly Althusserian legacy of Read's own work, as mediated through Rodríguez?!

At the root of Read's problem, we suggest, is his indebtedness to a form of Marxism that had itself been profoundly influenced by the (post-)structuralist dispersal of "human nature," in other words, of a "species being." Of course, one sympathizes with the Marxist's anxieties. The bourgeoisie has always been willing to use the notion of human nature, which it fills out shamelessly with its own ideology. But there is a severe price to be paid for surrendering the concept to the enemy, and indications are that Read was finally unwilling to pay it, for the simple reason that it flew in the face of his own sense of individual identity, rooted as this was in the lived experience of his passage through the academy.

Freedom to be Exploited

While Smith sometimes engaged in the kind of exchanges characteristic of competitive contradiction, he has preferred relatively easy targets, such as James Parr, a marooned traditionalist who "shows no sign of having read the theorists he dismisses so blithely" (Smith 1991: 331). As he moved on from Golden Age studies to the cinema and gay studies, and thence, more recently, to architecture and journalism, Smith was able to avoid such potentially bruising encounters. From the beginning, he exhibited a willingness to make the most of newly discovered contingent complementarities. Precisely what attracts him about the new areas being opened up is the absence of entrenched élites and established expertise. The innovative thrust of the migrant meets no resistance, as it surges forward over the terra incognita. It is a no-(wo)man's land, in which one can travel all day without seeing another living soul. Significantly, it corresponds with the global impulse of a capitalism intent on colonizing those domains that still remain outside its reach. It also chimes perfectly with the new world of consumerism, in which theories could be picked up and dropped, like yesterday's clothes. All that matters is to shorten the turn-over time of capital.

Within the global scenario, a work such as *Laws of Desire*, which appeared in the Oxford Hispanic series, is marketed in the most radicalizing terms, beginning with Smith's general introduction – composed in his capacity as general editor – in which he speaks of a recent "revolution" in the humanities, together with the "upsurge of exciting new work" (Smith 1992: vii). Likewise, in the introduction to his own volume, he takes credit for introducing a "new and challenging subject area into Hispanic studies" (9). It is doubtful whether either of these claims can be sustained, at least when compared, say, with the kind of innovatory work that was conducted in the 1960s. The challenge to established curricula, integral to the original liberatory thrust of Cultural Studies, has been dissipated in the preoccupation with "required courses." The need for respectability and recognition is likewise very much to the fore in *Entiendes? Queer Readings, Hispanic Writings*, which contains articles that are "scrupulously attentive and respectful" to the letter of the classics, and show an "irreproachable respect for scholarly proprieties" (Bergmann and Smith 1995: 3).

Smith's pretensions to respectability are very much class-based in that, ideologically, his imagined readership consists of middle-class feminists and queer theorists, whose concerns extend to "personal politics," "careerism," "women against violence" and the textualities of desire, but not to daycare, domestic help, health care, police harassment, job losses, wage and benefit cuts, homelessness, provision for the elderly, and other issues that are painfully relevant to lives of working class women and gays. To this extent one is sympathetic with the impatience expressed by Nicola Field, in her *Over the Rainbow: Money, Class and Homophobia*, towards a postmodernism that "is the embodiment of abstruseness because it has 'given up on' the real world and offers to hopeless cynics an avenue of debate which does not require much reference to the workings of the material world" (Field 127). On Field's reckoning, we are dealing with the radical shortcomings of a gay movement that, since its revolutionary beginnings in the 1970s, has come to operate within the structure of capitalism, on the basis of a reformist program: "Its rhetoric claims to be revolutionary. But tragically, whilst often powerful and poignant, cultural activist art displays an idealism which counters its own revolutionary aspirations" (121).

The same class bias emerges in Smith's celebration of the "eclipse of Marxism as a political and theoretical force" in *Vision Machines* (Smith 1996: 60), a work which reads Spanish and Cuban cinema through the lens of Foucault and Deleuze and provides a timely reminder that, despite their commitment to a number of progressive causes, these Parisian masters ultimately "espouse an egoistic individualism that degenerates all too easily from postmodern dissidence to neo-liberal conformity" (Resch 253). It is a sorry sight but adds one more fittingly shoddy chapter to the history of British Hispanism. Support for the Castro Revolution must necessarily be conditional upon the rejection of a ruling monolithic party and bureaucracy that at no point has made any move, beyond the charade of "direct democracy," to build institutions of accountability and power rooted in the mass of the people. At the same time, the defense of socialism also requires the recognition of Cuba's achievements in health care and education and warns against the dangers to these gains embodied in the present concessions to the market by the Cuban regime. No socialist can fail to object to Smith's concern for democratic rights, together with his "vision of a newly democratized civil society" (Smith 1996: 97), in the absence of any reference to economic equality, or to the Cuban Miami millionaires and gangsters waiting to re-assume their former control of Cuba.

To conclude, there is no reason to accept the progressive teleology that Smith wishes to impose upon the theoretical confrontations between Marxism and postmodern critical social theory, but every reason to suggest that Smith's downgrading of class in favor of gender is symptomatic of his own emancipation from the material realities of class subordination. The same freedom from class restraints, we would argue, also explains the prominence he accords to the relatively marginal, although very real, disadvantages of being gay. Undoubtedly, there is a degree of self-deception involved, but one wonders to what extent Smith's celebration of a manifestly *middle-class* gay community, and his dismissal of working-class militancy, also betrays a degree of class opportunism. The promotion of the body, as a site of sexual freedom, also needs to be approached with due caution, and for the same reasons. The element of self-deception is again obvious enough: what Smith fails to see is that transgression and liberation are the traps that capitalism laid for the unwary, that the only freedom that is at stake is the freedom to be exploited. But the opportunistic element is again in evidence. For Smith is part of an influential fraction of younger academics who no longer perceive their goal as fighting against exploitation, in the name of socialism, but simply of seeking the best (professional) strategies through which to minimize their own discomfort.

5

Who walked a Crooked Mile

There was a crooked man, who walked a crooked mile
(English Nursery Rhyme)

Finally, the long-awaited day had arrived on which I was to "go up" to Bristol University, arguably Britain's most elite university after Oxford and Cambridge. As the train trundled around Derby, before heading southwards, I could not help but reflect on the advice given by my primary school headmaster to the effect that I was not "suitable material" for an academic career, and that the most that could be hoped for was that I might become a tradesman "of some kind." Needless to say, it was advice repeated much nearer home, more sensitively but no less pragmatically, by friends and relatives. Their motives, to be sure, were in part for the best: they were genuinely concerned about the consequences (and likelihood) of my failure. But there were also elements of suspicion towards somebody clearly in the process of abandoning their community. And finally, of course, my behavior doubtless posed for these same people problems of which, till then, they had been blissfully unaware and which related to their own (in every sense) unrealized possibilities. What, after all, if I were to succeed?! Repressed fear, anxiety, annoyance, envy – a whole gamut of emotions – lurked behind their dire warnings about the dangers of "getting above oneself."

I was certainly under no illusion about these dangers, or of my chances of survival. Clearly, if nothing else, my unorthodox and uneven academic preparation prior to university was going to lead to some problems. And sure enough, these quickly began to unfold, with their only too painful logic. Less expected were the advantages with which I was favored from the outset and which, in the end, would make all the difference between "success" and "failure." They included, to begin with, an incredible capacity for sustained and disciplined hard work, which was qualitatively distinct from that possessed, as a general rule, by middle-class students. It was, I guess, the intellectual equivalent of that labor power of which working-class men boasted: I well recall being invited to prod their firm, bulging biceps ("Get a gleg o'that, lad"). More was at stake than simple exhibitionism: all that such individuals had to sell was their physical strength and endurance. My natural instinct, on finding myself at last in the academy, was to reapply this capacity mentally, and I did so, to telling effect.

However, it would not only be unflattering but wrong to give the impression that I was all brawn and no brain. For in fact I brought with me into the academy very specific qualities of an intellectual kind, qualities all the more valuable for being again unusual and rare among my fellow-students. The latter moved through the world "as if they owned it," which to all intents and purposes some of them, or at least their fathers, did. One unforeseen and unfortunate side-effect of their proprietorial "ease" was a fundamentally unquestioning attitude towards the world. The university was an extension of their social round, with all the privileges that this entailed, and which they had every reason to accept as it was. True, many of these students were also women, who tended to congregate in the Humanities, and who were disadvantaged to the extent that they had to negotiate a patriarchal system. But they "naturally" disposed of the class ethos necessary to extract concessions, and proceeded to do so, increasingly, throughout the 1970s and 80s. In contrast, I found the academy to be a totally alien environment, and was compelled by sheer force of circumstance, including the constant possibility of betrayal by my instincts, to operate both *in* and *upon* the world. It was this compulsion to make sense of the world that, I think, has annoyed postmodernists in recent years, who have complained about my vulgar insistence upon "getting things straight." The implication is that I lack their mature insight into the complexity of things, which, together with their ironizing appreciation of the fluidity of boundaries, protects them from such unseemly behavior.

What was perhaps my key advantage over fellow students, however, related to the choice of Spanish as my honors subject. Spanish was at the time the poor (wo)man's option, taken by those students who specialized in English, French and German but found the competition in those subjects too stiff, as a result of which, as sociologists euphemistically put it, the student body was "under-selected." Admittedly, some students, such as the offspring of diplomats, were only seeking to make the most of their linguistic skills, typically acquired through exposure to Spanish at home or abroad. But these were largely of a technical kind, eked out by social or "cultural" graces, and as a general rule were in no way an indication of exceptional ability or even average intelligence. The tactical considerations that dictated the options of "late developers" were of a rather different kind. It was reasonably felt by our advisors at the Technical College that we could not be expected to compete in French and German with grammar-school pupils, who had the advantage of years of preparation. In contrast, Spanish, towards which pupils at grammar school were channelled at a relatively late stage, constituted something in the way of a level playing field. More importantly, and in this consisted our basic differentia, Tech students were the product of "over-selection," massively so in the case of anyone who survived to reach university. In this respect, I was, to put it arrogantly, literally one in thousands. Of course, it could be argued that "failure" at the age of eleven was in itself sufficient proof of my mediocrity. But the fact remains that for my peers, at university, Spanish had invariably been a soft option: for me, it has been the only option I ever had.

What was true of students majoring in Spanish was also true of their lecturers or professors. British Hispanism was, and still is, a discipline in which faculty members were, on the whole, intellectually inferior to those in, say, English or Philosophy. While I was not particularly alert to this at the time – after all, a plodding empiricism was fairly widespread in the British academy – I began to suspect very early on that something was amiss. Take, for instance, the course on Spanish philology. A supplementary reading list included Bloomfield's famous book on language, a text that I worked through carefully and systematically. The chapters on the phoneme, morpheme and semantics impressed me immensely, and seemed light-years ahead of what was routinely presented to us under the guise of "Spanish philology." Stimulated by my earlier encounter with theoretical linguistics, I began to read more widely – R. A. Hall Jr's *Linguistics and Your Language* proved especially stimulating. My interests were not simply theoretical: sociolinguistics dealt crucially with "accent" and "correctness," in short, with issues of class which were vigorously repressed from literary studies and to which I could relate personally.

So marginal did Bloomfield appear to other students, who were trained to focus on passing exams, that they simply ignored him. They thereby saved themselves certain puzzles. To begin with, Bloomfield's impersonal behaviorism was impossible to square with the neo-idealistic emphasis upon individual creativity, characteristic of our Hispanic texts, not to mention the contradiction between the linguist's anti-prescriptive bias and the value judgments on language rampant in our literary studies. But even stranger was the general contrast between the effervescence of theoretical linguistics – the Chomskyian revolution was by this time firmly underway – and the fact-grubbing myopia of Spanish philology. It did not escape my attention that the latter proved attractive to students and lecturers of a certain "hard-headed" type, or that these same people were drawn to medieval literary studies for the same reasons. What they sought was a way out of lit. crit., with its threatening onus upon "imagination." What they feared, in the last instance, was "emotion." My own attraction to linguistic theory, I would now suggest, was ultimately rooted in the same fear, the fear of being "found out" or "shown up," culturally speaking. In lit. crit., sensibility was something you had to be "born with," a peculiar feminine attribute which, frankly, "you either had or you didn't." Theory, in contrast, while "higher" and more demanding than philology, was still something one could "master" and "work at" in a very concrete way. Here, crash courses were more feasible and, consequently, class-barriers less insurmountable.

Such issues were not confined to the heady realm of abstraction. On the contrary, they sometimes irrupted with a vengeance into everyday academic life. I recall one such occasion very well. I was attending a philology class in which an elderly Spanish lady began to puff up with pride when the lecturer indicated that Castilian was the "most innovative" dialect of the Peninsula. Far from questioning her subjective bias, the lecturer appeared to collude with it. When eventually I could contain myself no longer, and questioned whether this kind of evaluation was appropriate, I was brutally silenced and told to "go and do a course on aesthetics, young man." Such encounters were invariably resolved in this way, and left me quietly simmering with rage. I was particularly vulnerable to the one cultural card that philologists were able, and did not hesitate, to play, namely a "scholarly" knowledge of the classical languages. Lacking a grammar-school education, I had studied Latin only to an elementary level at evening class. To "put down" such an individual, particularly when they were "difficult," was easy, and doubtless tempting. What made matters worse was that, deep down, I knew that these were not rational debates, that what they were about was not what they were about.

The study of literature posed comparable problems. An earlier generation of scholars, the aging disciples of Allison Peers, was in the process of being displaced by a younger generation, the epigones of Alexander Parker. As students, we were dimly aware of the conflict between the faculty, although as always happens, disagreements were personalized and reduced to the level of corridor gossip. Or more exactly, they failed to rise above this level. As with linguistics, my private reading took me beyond the boundaries of Hispanism – I recall reading Auerbach and Ernst Fischer – but not in any systematic way. There was certainly no space within Hispanism in which to develop or "work through" any unorthodox approaches to literature. Of course, liberalism encouraged us students to "say what we thought," to "express our own opinions," but it was a foolish person who took it at its word. I was such a person. For example, after having read a searing attack upon academic criticism by D. H. Lawrence, I dared to refer to it in one of my essays. Severely reprimanded and threatened darkly with expulsion, I withdrew into silence, nursing my wounds.

Such moments of potential violence were relatively rare. As a general rule, lecturers exercised control over students not directly, upon what was said, but indirectly, via the conceptual tools with which they equipped us and which we were taught to apply to literary texts. Needless to say, I am not referring here to the conscious attitude of individual lecturers. Most of them were thoughtful, kind and helpful. Moreover, they thought of themselves as being open-minded, and were, within limits. It was just that these limits corresponded largely with a trenchantly conservative ideology, of the kind expounded by the likes of Parker. It seems hard to believe, in retrospect, the awe in which such people were held, a warning no doubt to younger Hispanists who now enthuse so readily about advances made by the "New Hispanisms." I realized, intuitively and half-consciously, that we were being sold an ideological package, but simply lacked the resources to critique it, intellectually. One came to operate almost bilingually, holding apart in a state of permanent tension not only received and private knowledges but also emotion and intellect. It was possibly this experience which was to make it very hard for me to assume in future years that oppressed people are simply the dupes of a dominant ideology.

We spent the first two of our three undergraduate years on Golden Age Literature. Only in our final year did we study "modern" literature, which, for reasons that were never specified, was understood to have come to an end in 1936. I have no recollection of studying literature of the Romantic period, except for Larra, which is a fair indication of the influence of Parkerian criticism. Despite its limitations, in terms of those liberal constraints to which I referred above, I enjoyed the tutorial system whereby we were given the opportunity, in small groups, to argue over our "set texts" and discuss our literary essays. Latin-American literature was also taught, but in a far less rigorous manner. We went to the Department of History for lectures on Latin-American history, which struck me as qualitatively superior to the banal "culture and civilization" fodder that we were fed locally. Our language teaching consisted of conversation classes, given by Spanish tutors, and translation classes. At one of the latter I was ridiculed for wanting to translate "amigo" as "mate," at which point I ceased to attend. I was already convinced that such classes had little to do with learning Spanish. To improve my own linguistic skills, I made extensive trips to Spain every summer, traveling from town to town, with a rucksack on my back. My own vision of Spain was largely indebted to the work of Gerald Brenan, whose Bloomsbury version of Spanish culture was infinitely more palatable than that filtered through Parkerian scholarship. Predictably, *The Literature of the Spanish People* became the bugbear of British academic Hispanists.

Even so, the past refused to let me go and would constantly return to disturb the present. I have in mind those moments when, quite suddenly and unexpectedly, there came upon me the sense of being lost. I recall one such occasion very vividly during my undergraduate career, while reading Gerald Brenan's *The Face of Spain*. I was particularly charmed by the work's concluding section, with its evocative juxtaposition of Spanish and English societies, in all their intimacies. Such a powerful antidote to the sterility of much academic work! It was impossible not to succumb absolutely to Brenan's distillation of an essential, timeless Englishness, symbolized by the country lane, in the "slow English twilight," with the rooks in the elms, and the notes of the blackbirds, sweet and prolonged, sinking gradually into the "thick silence."

"There is then the class aspect." The lurch in the narrative was unexpected and, I confess, completely caught me off guard. In the blink of an eye the idyll faded, leaving me confronted by a mass of urban inhabitants, "rootless, amorphous, and disease-ridden." Despite the veil of prejudice and distortion, I recognized immediately the community in which I had spent my childhood: "they bring with them nothing but a few moral notions founded on the ethics of the football field and the boxing ring"(Brenan 267). The insidious mastery of Brenan's style betrayed me back to the dense network of terraced housing, in the vicinity of Derby County's ground, to the milling crowds, the thrill of expectancy just before kick-off, the sense of camaraderie, the endless flow of badinage and witticism. But part of it too was the excitement of the actual game, the individual ball control, the quick perception of geometric patterns, the even quicker ability to act upon them, in all of which I saw the vivid gestures of a theatrical agon.

Necessarily, the discrepancy between Brenan's attitude to the working class and my own began to pose certain problems. For example, why was Brenan so eager to denigrate proletarian culture? And why was I so eager to embrace the culture of a man who simply parodied mine? Suddenly, my academic surroundings took on a strange, even alien, appearance. Like anyone who is lost, my instincts were automatically to retrace my steps. But only to just round the last bend. And so, over the years, similar scenes would be re-enacted with an uncanny sense of *déjà vu*.

At Bristol I lived a socially very isolated life. I was pathologically shy, felt awkward in any social situation, and made friends with difficulty. At week-ends I went to concerts, particularly when a classical guitarist was performing. During my undergraduate career I saw Segovia, Bream, Williams and, an experience that still lives with me, the guitar duo Presti-Lagoya. (Tragically, it was to be one of Ida Presti's last concerts – she died shortly afterwards.) Sometimes I would go to the cinema. I recall seeing *Life at the Top*, John Braine's sequel to *Room at the Top*, one of those angry-young-man novels that I had read some years earlier. Lawrence Harvey's portrayal of a successful but jaundiced working-class boy resonated with my own situation. Often, however, I treated myself to a good novel and spent an evening in front of my small gas fire in my digs in Cotham Vale. I shared the kitchen facilities with a Polish refugee, who I called Joseph, after Joseph Conrad, one of my favourite writers. "What are you studying at the university?", he would ask. "Spanish." "Ah, the great Miguel de Cervantes. [Pregnant pause]. Do you know he never finished *Don Quixote?*" This puzzling exchange seemed to take place every time our paths crossed in the kitchen.

Once or twice a term I returned home. My parents had by now moved to a detached house in a more secluded middle-class area of Littleover. Ties with the larger family, on both sides, had been largely severed, although tentative relations had recently been re-established with my grandparents on my mother's side. Within our nuclear family, my brother remained a constant source of friction. He had left school and taken up a position as a clerk in the County Offices at Matlock, much to the displeasure of my parents. The family atmosphere was tense and unpleasant. When at home, I steeped myself in my academic work, and went for long walks. One of my favorites was down a footpath between the Manor and Burton Roads, which afforded a panoramic view of the city. Immediately below was Ricknald Rec and the rough working-class districts around Stockbrook Street, where so much of my early life had unfolded. Significantly, it was a world that I now looked down on, literally and figuratively, from a distance. At the same time, I was not at ease in the middle-class world in which I now moved. It came as something of a shock later to discover, on reading Hoggart's *The Uses of Literacy*, that this crisis of identity was not as exquisitely unique as I imagined it to be, but integral to a trajectory only too familiar to sociologists.

Whenever I was back in Derby, I would always find time to call to see the Figuerolas. The Figuerolas were an exiled Catalan family, who had come to live in England after the Civil War. Señor Figuerola was a manual worker at Royce's, Señora Figuerola a cleaner. They had a son called

Floreal, who was originally one of my guitar pupils at Wishers Music Co., where I taught part-time. Floreal's lessons proved to be something of an ordeal, since he refused to practice, a fact that did not escape his father. The latter would sit at the far end of the room and fix his eyes on his trembling son. At each fluffed chord he would strike his forehead with the palm of his hand – a curious gesture – and unleash a stream of abuse, in Catalan of course. Floreal, wandering extraterritorially between English, Catalan and Castilian, used to protest his innocence. In order to derive some personal benefit from this unhappy situation, I agreed to give Floreal lessons for nothing, provided that Señor Figuerola gave me conversation practice in Castilian. Thus I became a regular visitor to their home. On these occasions, Señor Figuerola talked freely about his life and his experiences as a soldier during the Civil War, with one eye trained on the television, which was always blaring away and to which Floreal remained glued. He had been an anarchist, and, to judge by what he told me, had seen plenty of action. Once he produced an old broken knife, his only memento from the war, which he gave me to look at. I observed perfunctorily that it must have been very difficult to impale a man with that. "Not at all," he replied, more interested in the television, "it was very easy." I gave it back to him very quickly.

Unhappily, during my second year at university, Señor Figuerola suffered a stroke. During my first visit to see him, after he had been hospitalized, I innocently drew his attention to the label "Catholic" above his bed, placed there by the nurses, presumably for purposes of pastoral care. Señor Figuerola seemed not to have been aware of its existence until this moment. His eyes visibly widened and in a matter of seconds he was transformed from a prostrate, corpse-like figure into a wildly gesticulating anarchist, rearing up out of the bed. The hullabaloo soon brought the matron running. She informed us that it would be "irregular" not to indicate any religious affiliation. But there was no stopping Señor Figuerola, who was raving on about being shot at by Catholic priests, and from church towers no less! Just when he was on the point of throwing another apoplexy, the matron suddenly gave way. On the way out later, I came across her complaining to one of the other nurses that she had felt "personally insulted."

Another incident concerned the activities of Señora Figuerola. During my second visit to the hospital, the same matron took me on one side and informed me, in a loud whisper, that the "Spanish woman" could not visit her husband whenever she liked and for as long as she liked. There *were* visiting hours! Poor Señora Figuerola! After twenty years her English was limited almost literally to "yes, m'luv," "no, m'luv." I did my best to convey to her the extent of the "irregularity" she was committing, but to no avail. When entry was barred to her, she would lurk around the hospital, laden with baskets of *tortilla* and *salchichón*, peering through windows and doors, waving to and smiling at her beloved Ramón. Within a few weeks – it was the middle of January and the snow was deep on the ground – the hospital was forced to relent, and Señora Figuerola was given permission to come and go as she pleased. The po-faced matron always avoided my eyes whenever by chance we met. Clearly, she was not a woman who was used to being crossed and two defeats in a matter of weeks were more than her psyche could stand.

I not only survived my undergraduate career, but did so with flying colors. Through a massive, personally crippling over-investment in academic work, I gained a First Class Hons. degree in Spanish, one of only two in Britain that year, I seem to recall from the listings ("Brains of Britain") in the *Times*. Of course, my parents and old teachers were overjoyed and I was made much of in both the local and national press. But while my own satisfaction was real enough, I refused to be paraded as a model of "achievement." Indeed, I trembled to think that others might be encouraged to follow in my footsteps. One of the failings of my parents' generation was to turn their children into their own personal projects. Of course, it is reasonable to take pride in the successes of our children. To watch their development and share in their sense of fulfillment is one of the greater joys of life. But it becomes, however unwittingly, an exercise in sadism to pit young people against a class structure which, even in the climate of relative economic prosperity that prevailed in the 1950s and 60s, disposes of hidden mechanisms designed specifically to frustrate their efforts. And it is ultimately immaterial whether parental motives are selfless or selfish, well-meaning or self-centered, or, as is more likely, mixed. It may be objected that young people can always refuse to assume such burdens, and do in fact find ways of resisting authoritarian impositions. But experience suggests that their resistance can assume forms tragically even more damaging and self-destructive than acts of accommodation. People's energies are better employed collectively, in my view, through political action aimed at dismantling a hierarchical system based on such insane competitiveness.

At all events, the celebrations were cut short that summer by a traffic accident in Spain, in which my mother was killed. The effect of this accident was to shatter the precarious unity of the larger family unit – rows immediately blew up over the funeral arrangements or lack of them – and, eventually, of our nuclear family itself, of which my mother had been the lynch-pin. In the confusion, I let slip invitations to do graduate research in America and at Oxford. At this time I also received an invitation to apply to the Foreign Office, doubtless on the assumption that any student with a First Class degree would exhibit the appropriate pedigree. I was tempted to present myself for an interview, just to see the look of horror on their faces. In September (1967) I drifted back to Bristol, but so belatedly that I had to accept some inconceivably grotty digs down Hotwells. I used to work late at the university or sit reading and drinking scrumpy cider in a local pub, in order to avoid having to contemplate the water that oozed through the wall of my bedsitter during a cold Autumn. These were miserable days. After Christmas I fled to Madrid, where I spent the whole winter working in the Biblioteca Nacional. I returned to England in the late Spring, to continue my research in the British Museum. During this period, I applied for a position in the University College of Wales, Aberystwyth, and was duly appointed.

My career as a graduate student was, let us say, different. Conditioned by their grammar-school environment, most of my colleagues dutifully "chose" the most mind-numbing topics, whose only recommendation was that a successful candidature, if you stayed the course, was virtually guaranteed. In practice, needless to say, the drop-out and non-completion rates were amazingly high, since many students basically died of boredom. Boredom was the one thing that never afflicted me. I have spoken already of my need to "live" academic work, in the sense that this work served to guide me, practically, through the unfamiliar world in which I found myself. I don't mean practical in the vocational sense – given my background and career trajectory, vocational work stood for manual work, and I viewed it with profound suspicion – but in the sense of a self-directed "general education." I wanted to know everything, I needed to know everything. Somehow, everything related to everything else, and finding out how was the only way of making sense of my situation. It was a way of thinking about the world that would eventually blend into a Marxist synoptic vision.

Yes, it is hard to know which was more astounding, my naïveté or my arrogance. Yet there was method to my madness. While, as I have explained, arguing from a position of personal commitment sometimes provoked difficult encounters, this commitment also served to energize my work in a way that, to their credit, my lecturers at undergraduate level had been prepared to recognize. The sterile, unimaginative grammar-school or scholarship student was left floundering in my wake. Understandably, I adopted the same proven tactics when it came to research. Soon I was deep into Renaissance linguistics, then Western linguistics and, ultimately, philosophy. What I was feeling my way towards was the study of epistemic regularities across literature, history and linguistics. Highly sophisticated work of this kind was being conducted in France at the time, but that might well have been on the moon, as far as British Hispanism was concerned. The reality of my circumstances can be succinctly stated: I was mired in a non-theoretical culture, was beginning virtually from scratch within my discipline, and had no experience in advanced research of a large-scale kind. Moreover, I received little or no supervision and, it has to be said, did not actively seek it, since in my experience it always amounted to nervous efforts to re-contain my intellectual energy. What made matters worse was that, since my work was vaguely "linguistic," I found myself having to submit it for evaluation to philologists and medievalists who were deeply hostile to any "metaphysics."

In this way, I replayed the brushes with authority that had occurred during my undergraduate career, but now the stakes were higher. I was more stubborn and my liberal opponents, feeling more threatened, were more vengeful and unforgiving. Although I was coming up with interesting results, supervisors and examiners homed in on the undeniably crude residues in my work, the broad sweep of which meant that I sometimes had to cut corners. And of course methodologically I was always feeling my way. However, the problem never lay so much with my ideas, any doubts concerning whose potential would eventually be dispelled through my articles and books. The scholars with whom I was dealing were petty-bourgeois intellectuals, obsessed by niceties of technique, "presentation," "bibliographical reference," editorial styles, etc. In this respect, the verdict was unanimous: I was sloppy, careless, slap-dash over details, unable to spell, even unable to "write." But if they stood at one extreme, I stood at the other. Mine was a typically proletarian truculence, based on a refusal of any form of "propriety": proper dress, proper speech, proper manners, etc.

One of the British Marxist historians, Christopher Hill I think, or it may have been Hobsbawn, once observed that a Leftist's scholarship has to be impeccable because "they" are watching for the slightest slip. I was being watched alright, and knew it. But there was just one little problem: I was no Western Marxist of impeccably bourgeois extraction, ready to scramble for cover if capitalism went onto the offensive and to distance himself from the proletariat, but a working-class academic, in the sense that, however declassed and seduced by my bourgeois environment, I remained by habitus and instinct working-class through and through. I could no more change my work habits than I could my North-Midlands accent or my table manners.

Once I had finally finished my Ph.D., I went on a year's exchange to New Zealand, which I enjoyed immensely. Being outside Britain meant having a space in which I could think. It was at this time that I became familiar with the work of Ernest Becker and Norman Brown, aspects of which I incorporated into my history of ideas, so as to lend it an existential dimension. And, of course, following upon my reading of Becker and Brown came my first direct encounter with Freud. I began to feel excited that my work could be developed in different ways, and on a grand scale. While colleagues who had taken short-cuts with their Ph.D.s were running aground, and looking to move into administration, my research program began to pick up momentum. By this time, I had refined my dialectical technique of moving freely between individual experience and abstract general concepts. All the risks I had taken started to pay off.

But in other respects, not all was well in my life. While, intellectually, the clash between proletarian and bourgeois culture had been profoundly energizing and enabling, it had always proved stressful and difficult to negotiate, at a more personal level. And things were not getting any easier. By the late 1970s, I had been socially adrift for almost a decade, a free-floating intellectual, cut off almost literally at his roots, and the effects were beginning to show. Despite my productivity – at this time I was publishing two or three articles a year in leading journals – I had the impression that my work was becoming ideologically one-dimensional. I looked to psychoanalysis to provide an element of scandal, but the converse of my discovery of Freud, it has to be said, was a creeping bourgeois solipsism and individualism. Unhappy with the direction in which I was tending, I turned increasingly to Marxism, at first filtered through the humanism of Eric Fromm but subsequently in its classically economistic forms. I am at a loss to explain fully the reasons for what finally amounted to a radical *prise de conscience*. Certainly, the sense of having been co-opted never left me. Nor did the feeling of not being "at home" in the academy. Doubtless it was a feeling over-determined by other factors, both personal and political. To begin with, I was less vulnerable, professionally speaking, and able to afford, literally and otherwise, the luxury of facing certain unpleasant truths, including the class betrayals and compromises that had underwritten my early career. Curiously, I saw these betrayals magnified a thousand-fold in the world of national politics, where a rightward-swinging Labour Government was busy undermining working-class institutions. Reformism in all its forms, it seemed, was running aground.

I was in a bleak frame of mind when in 1980, I drove from Wales to Nottingham to attend the National Conference of British Hispanists, at which I was to give a paper. Since my route took me through Derby, my reflexive mood deepened. I drove through the city, transformed, or should I say ravaged, by urban projects of the 1970s. Almost without realizing it, I found myself picking up the old Nottingham Road, now almost a residential street, shadowed by the new motorway that ran alongside it. Within a few minutes, I was winding my way through the backstreets of Chaddesden. They now seemed strangely shrunken, as places do when we visit them as adults, after having known them as children. Now other children played in them, outrageously oblivious to the ghosts that haunted them. Eventually I arrived at Radnor Street, where the Wests had formerly lived.

There was nobody at home, but I could tell immediately that my grandparents no longer lived there. The garden was overrun and the paintwork on the house peeling. I called round next door. "The old man died a year or so ago," the neighbor informed me, "They moved Mrs West to the old people's bungalows, on the new estate." From the directions she gave me, I soon found the house. My grandmother opened the door, clearly nervous to have a stranger calling. I introduced myself. "Well I'll be ...," her mouth literally dropped open. "I was only sayin' to our Gladys the other week ... Well I'll be ..." I explained that I'd called round at Radnor Street first. "Oh, it's gone to the dogs down there. Blacks and Pakis. You don't feel safe in your own 'ome any more." Anyway, she ushered me inside and made a cup of tea. Soon the events of the last decade were unfolding, in a rambling kind of way, as my grandma leapt from past to present, and then, bewilderingly, back into the past again. "'E could 'ardly walk at the end, with 'is knee. After 'e'd 'ad the stroke, 'e just lay there. I told our Babs, I'm not goin' in there ... I'm not well mesen these days. Me rheumatism's killin' me. All down me back, 'ere ... What's Mike doin'? Still in Manchester? 'E was never the same after ya mother was killed ... Did ya not get married?..." etc. etc. I stayed for an hour or so, then left, promising to keep in touch. She came out and stood in the road, while I turned the car around. "It's goin' to rain, mark me words," she called, "I can always feel it in me bones. It'll be rainin' stair rods before the afternoon's out." I waved. She turned and hurried inside. In a matter of seconds, I knew, she'd don her coat and be on the way to the phone box at the corner, to call one or probably all of my aunts.

I gave my paper in Nottingham later the same day, on money and alienation in Juan Ruiz's *Libro de buen amor*. It would eventually become a chapter of *The Birth and Death of Language*. They had a problem about finding someone willing to introduce me, I could tell. I went slowly and confidently, but it wasn't the usual medieval stuff they were used to, and I could sense their hackles rising. My mind wandered for a while towards the end. I was imagining the conversation between my grandma and Auntie Val. "You'll never guess who turned up today. Marj's boy. The younger one, Malcolm." "Go on with you!" "Says 'e's thinkin' of movin' to Australia, no, 'old your sweat, New Zealand. That's it." "What's 'e goin' there for? I thought 'e 'ad a good job?" "It'll be 'is father in 'im. Mad as March 'ares, the Reads, the whole lot of 'em. That's what I always thought, any road." There were questions. Somebody pointed out that the comparison between words and coins, which I'd taken to be symptomatic of a market mentality, had already been made by the Greeks, which rather disproved my point. It certainly had nothing to do with Marx or Freud. One or two people laughed quietly. They despised me, I realized, but they no longer had the capacity to intimidate me, as they once had. I could now see them for what they were: a fraction of the petite bourgeoisie which had managed to carve out a comfortable class position for itself, and whose members were convinced that, whatever its other defects, capitalism certainly rewarded those with talent and initiative, such as themselves. But in the early 1980s, the vision of capitalism with a human face was fading fast, leaving this same fraction fiercely defending its meager (intellectual) assets against "devaluation." Inexplicably, the days of prosperity had ended, and a populist right-wing government was attacking the academy.

Funny how one had always thought of it all as a ladder, when in reality it was more like a merry-go round. I could see a younger generation of graduate students, mostly feminists and postmodernists, patiently queuing up. The music would stop shortly, a few places would be relinquished, and several newcomers would eagerly clamber aboard. Unburdened by outmoded ideological baggage, notably economic determination and class struggle, the postmodernists looked particularly sharp and professional, and were obviously set on giving it a whirl. They would be welcomed by some of their senior colleagues, increasingly traumatized by government policies, who saw in the younger generation a means of revitalizing the discipline. Perhaps such optimism was justified: at the very least, these younger Hispanists looked like people who, unlike their befuddled elders, were consumer-wise. But already indications were that collective resistance was not on the postmodern agenda: power was everywhere, and could only be resisted individually. If, that is, you thought it was worth trying to resist, which it wasn't. For my own part, I also wondered, briefly, whether I might have something in common with these younger Hispanists, if only a sense of marginalization. But as I looked at them, pushing and jostling each other in the queue, any thought of collaboration quickly dissipated. Literature was the *love* of their lives; and their conference papers, one after another, bore witness to a curious erotics of literature. What drove me forwards was not love but hatred.

Somebody else was asking a question, well not really a question, just raving on about my reference to the late medieval "crisis." People were always talking about crises. The term, he protested, was over-used. But to be perfectly honest I wasn't listening any more. Through the window I could see that the weather had closed in and the stair rods were bouncing off the roof tops.

6

In the Meantime: British Hispanism and the Rise of Cultural Studies

In the winter, in the summer,
Don't we have fun?
Times are bum and getting bummer
Still we have fun.
There's nothing surer:
The rich get rich and the poor get poorer
In the meantime,
In between time,
Ain't we got fun?
(Popular Song)

Indications are that British Hispanism is currently undergoing a shift of far-reaching, paradigmatic proportions, through which the discipline is being restructured under the guise of postmodern "cultural studies." The extent and pace of change is dictated by local considerations and varies from university to university, and from department to department, but its effects are easily discernible, at a daily level: a curriculum that previously engaged Literature, within a framework of universally recognized canonic norms and clearly defined periods (medieval, Golden Age, etc.) or epochal styles (Renaissance, Baroque, etc.) is being turned on its head. Departments that, at one time, privileged the pre-modern, and for which "modern literature" largely excluded anything post-1930, are now focusing primarily on the cinema and other non-literary cultural forms in the post-Civil War and, indeed, in the post-Franco period, in an ongoing process of reconfiguration that has culminated in the emergence of Hispanic Cultural Studies. Attitudes to these changes have varied: while die-hard conservatives predict and bemoan the "death of literature," others are attempting to bridge the old and the new, to the mutual benefit of both, whereas younger scholars celebrate what they perceive to be a market-driven displacement of older departmental structures.

Broadly considered, Cultural Studies is the product of non-elite, extra-mural higher education in Britain, formally institutionalized at the Centre for Contemporary Studies at the University of Birmingham in 1966, where it has been subject to periodic review and redefinition (see Turner, Brantlinger, Diworkin). Its extension to North America and accompanying metamorphoses have been monitored and commented upon (see, for example, Ohmann). The turn to mass culture within Hispanism is largely the localized expression of a "boom" or "explosion" that the discipline is currently experiencing throughout the Anglo-Saxon academy and indeed at the global level. The call for a "moment of clarification" – Stuart Hall's phrase (Hall 199) – has met with some response, notably from Michael Sprinker and, within the realm of Hispanic or more strictly Latin-American Studies, from John Beverley. Grossberg, Nelson and Treichler speculate, with reason, that "the *future* of cultural studies will include re-readings of its past" (Grossberg, Nelson and Treichler 10). However, it is fair to say that necessary stock-taking has yet to be undertaken by many of its practitioners (see Grossberg et al 3), a fact that Fredric Jameson attributes to the "anxieties and dreariness" that would inevitably result (Jameson 41). Peninsular studies, while participating enthusiastically in the curricular reforms, has progressed little beyond the pre-theoretical level of reflex response, with only the promise to make good the omission of any discussion of the history and development of the discipline (see, for example, Coffey 265).

The limitations observable in the States are compounded in Britain, where, with the exception of a flurry of activity in the early 1990s, Hispanism has remained, as throughout its history, notably and stubbornly unreflective about the conditions of its own existence. We will be arguing below that they are the result of structural incapacities that operate at the ideological level.[9] To this end, we will be concerned to construct, on the basis of a relatively limited amount of data, a theoretical apparatus that will facilitate an explanatory purchase on the disciplinary changes adumbrated above. Our key concepts are derived predominantly from the tradition of Critical Realism associated with the name of Roy Bhaskar,

9.   Doubtless, they will also be found to transcend the level of disciplinary boundaries. One wonders, for example, whether Hispanism's deficiencies are connected, in some underground and suitably mediated form, with the singularly uncritical approach to the British State that Colin Leys discerns in so many academic treatments of British politics. Who exactly are the people who man the State (including the University) apparatus? From where are they drawn, socially speaking? Evidence, as Leys confesses, is fragmentary – "and it is interesting to speculate why no comprehensive study based on direct observation has appeared" (Leys 291) – but indications are that they are drawn from the same homogeneous, extremely narrow social stratum, and that the higher up the bureaucratic ladder one progresses, whether in the private or public sector, the narrower it becomes. Hence, presumably, the "anxieties" and "fear" that, in the British case, would attend the discovery that the British State (and its universities) still continues to be run by people who, for the most part, have passed through one of its six major public schools and Oxford and Cambridge.

eked out by others drawn directly from the Althusserian tradition of Structural Marxism. Tactically, our aim is to familiarize British Hispanists with a philosophical tradition committed to an ontological realism, to be off-set against the dominant Parisian relativisms that have dominated their discipline in recent years. Critical Realism is, in the genuine sense of the term, a *transdisciplinary* enterprise, which already boasts a variety of practitioners, including Margaret Archer, who has been principally responsible for articulating a critical realist paradigm within sociology.

Realist Social Theory

The crux of Archer's work is the distinction drawn between social structure and human culture. Failure to recognize their autonomy would lead to distinctive levels being "clamped" together, and so to "eliding the material and the ideational aspects of social life" (Archer 1996: xi). Similarly, it is vitally important, within the domain of culture, to distinguish the "parts" from the "people," otherwise the *Cultural System* (CS) from the *Social Cultural* (S-C) level. The former is best imagined as a library of ideas or logical-propositional components, the latter as the agents who, through their personal, interactive relations, make up the Socio-Cultural level. Their elision leads to a number of unfortunate *conflations* within modern social theory, notably *upward* conflation in which, say, society is seen as a conglomerate of individuals; a *downward* conflation, in which individuals are seen as mere bearers of social structures; and a *central* conflation, in which autonomy is withheld from both "parts" and "people."

The distinction between the CS and the S-C level is strictly one of analytic convenience: "Clearly the Cultural System and Socio-Cultural life do not exist or operate independently of one another, they overlap, intertwine and are mutually influential" (xix). Archer is emphatic that the morphogenetic perspective is not only dualistic but also sequential, dealing in endless three-part cycles: structural conditioning followed by social interaction, followed in turn by structural elaboration. Agents arrive on a scene that is pre-structured – they are shaped by the conditions in which they find themselves – but which they subsequently transform, sometimes unconsciously, by their actions. The distinction between parts and people is thus not only between two kinds of entities but between two kinds of causal powers. Having said which, only people are responsible for efficient causality, in that all structural influences are mediated through people. The reality of stratification explains the existence of "structurally emergent properties" within the CS, and of "people's emergent properties" at the S-C level.

To the extent that the CS and the S-C level are not co-existent through time, any approach that amalgamates them precludes the possibility of examining their interaction over time. The general outlines of this interaction are as follows: "Generically it is how contradictory or complementary relations between 'parts' of the Cultural System map onto orderly or conflictual relationships between 'people' at the Socio-Cultural level which determines whether the outcome is cultural stability or change. This means that we need to specify, first, which Systemic relations impinge upon agency and how they do so; and, second, which social relations affect how agents respond to and react back on the Cultural System" (xxi). On this basis, Archer will proceed to distinguish between various kinds of relations: *constraining contradiction*; *concomitant compatibility*; *competitive contradiction*; and *contingent complementarity*. Let us briefly consider the defining characteristics of each.

By *constraining contradiction*, Archer has in mind the tension within a discipline, at the level of the CS, between two irreconcilable yet mutually related elements (A and B). As Archer herself explains: "Strategically top priority goes to the concealment of the contradiction itself. Indeed such concealment is a precondition of a group 'a' defending A itself, for unless B is hidden from social view it remains a permanent source of S-C pluralism and confrontation" (190). Dominance is achieved through a series of "containing strategies," through which certain works are branded as careless or unscholarly, and therefore unworthy of extended consideration. However, there are a number of drawbacks to such authoritarian tactics, not least of which is the very dependence of A upon B. This dependence can result in a variety of outcomes: B can be corrected so that it becomes consistent with A; A and B can both be corrected so as to become mutually consistent; or A can be corrected so as to become consistent with B (158 ff).

Archer specifies the broad dynamics of *concomitant compatibility* as follows: "[I]nvoking A also ineluctably invokes B, but since the B upon which this A depends is consistent with it, then B buttresses adherence to A. Consequently A occupies a congenial environment of ideas, the exploration of which, far from being fraught with danger, yields a treasure trove of reinforcement, clarification, confirmation and vindication – because of the logical consistency of the items involved" (153). The consistency of the relative components makes exploring B deeply satisfying to the proponents of A, both ideologically and psychologically speaking. With relative ease, students reach out and colonize one more area, as part of an ongoing mopping-up operation in which the original insights of the Master are systematized and reproduced. Yet, as Archer also perceptively warns, the ensuing "cosiness is the close ally of closure," to the extent that "[o]ver time the situational logic fosters a feed-back loop which discourages alterations in the felicitous cluster of items making for concomitant consistency" (157-58). Closure, in turn, generates a reactive formation, otherwise an innovative impulse that, in conjunction with external factors, unleashes a disorderliness that heralds the onset of *competitive contradiction*.

The situational logic of competitive contradiction is very different from that of either constraining contradiction or concomitant compatibility (245 ff). Neither the correction nor incorporation of B is at issue, rather its elimination. The most obvious symptom that we are entering a period of competitive contradiction is the increasing prominence of activity at the S-C level. The dynamics are no longer those of dialogue but of what Archer refers to as "barbed interchange." The shift is from making the best to making the worst of a situation. Peacemakers are universally detested.

Contingent complementarity, like competitive contradiction, is distinguished by a certain ebullience at the S-C level. However, in contrast to competitive contradiction, its exponents exhibit dissatisfaction with, rather than antagonism towards, cultural developments in their own area. And it is this dissatisfaction that drives them off in search of "foreign" material, which they proceed to incorporate within their own discipline. As Archer observes, "[t]he payoffs at the point of break-through are often enormous and prove enormously attractive" (221). Apart from initial and occasional brushes with conservative scholars (attached to A), the heat of the battle (characteristic of competitive contradiction) is generally avoided. The emphasis is upon innovation, not upon confrontation. True, S-C élites will to try exert some degree of control, through commentary, but since the new material is not explicitly oppositional to their own activity, it is generally not perceived as a threat. Everyone is left to pursue his or her activity undisturbed, or until it is too late. The result, as Archer indicates, is a decline in consensus without any proportional increase in conflict. However, the situation is transitional: marginal groups gradually repudiate their traditional ties to convert their cultural capital, whereas traditional practitioners find their own capital increasingly devalued. At the same time, specialization affirms its hold: the situational logic remains one of opportunity and free play (258), to the extent that, within a relatively short period, disciplinary practice can be totally transformed.

One other important aspect of Critical Realism is the attention that it gives to the ontological status of social structures or laws/mechanisms. A dominant empiricism, as we will be considering below, has always insisted on the need to translate collective properties back into a series of observational statements about people. It was precisely the progressive demise of empiricism that, beginning in the 1970s and 80s, opened up a space in which the various post-structuralisms and postmodernisms flourished. This same space was also the condition of possibility for Critical Realism, which, in the face of the epistemological relativism of the Parisian schools, has reasserted the centrality of an ontological realism. The realist claim is that, while science perforce operates within an internal or transitive domain, without any immediate access to the real, its laboratory activity and indeed its progress are conditional upon the existence of *real* mechanisms. From this it follows that science cannot be restricted to the level of observable events: constant junctions are rare even in the hard sciences. What interests scientists, or so critical realists aver, are the real sources of phenomena, not the contingent combinations of disparate elements from different strata, which happen to manifest themselves at a given time.[10] More problematic is the ontological status of social laws and mechanisms within the human sciences, given the difficulty of establishing the theoretical equivalent of laboratory conditions (see Bhaskar 1989; also Archer 1995: 144 ff). Suffice it to note, in the present context, the significance that critical realists have attributed to the *effect* of mechanisms, as a way of establishing their reality.

Some Problems and Re-definitions

This, then, is the broad outline of Archer's ideas. Our goal is a practical one: to *apply* these ideas to the recent, post-war history of British Hispanism. In the process, however, we are bound to *test* them, to the point of problematizing them, theoretically. We would draw attention particularly to Archer's discussion of the way in which structure "impinges" upon agency. While emergent structures admittedly condition us "involuntaristically" and "in semi-awareness," social structures are never to be envisaged as "hydraulic pressure" operating upon the individual (see Archer 1995: 152, 195, 197, 209, and passim). The danger of reification, we concede, is certainly very real, and the importance that Archer attaches to "efficient causality" a powerful corrective against it. At the same time, we would argue, efficient causality betrays a continuing attachment to the centrality of the subject and of individual consciousness: significantly, the "people's emergent properties" theorized by Archer lack an "unconscious" level. The effect is to marginalize the role

---

10. The foundational Critical Realist text is Roy Bhaskar 1978.

of the ideological (not to say Freudian) unconscious, a concept that is essential to the analysis of social conditioning.

Archer would doubtless protest that her CS is emphatically a process without a subject, as opposed to the S-C level, which deals with causal relations between subjects, and that, moreover, she warns explicitly against the dangers of omitting any reference to the material and ideational factors that condition the activity of agents. For when all is said and done, to take her own example, victims of educational discrimination do not necessarily suffer from any lack of "discursive penetration" of the situation in which they find themselves but from the restrictions that objectively limit the range of alternative courses of action available. But to equate "parts" with "propositions" and "having reasons" or "ideas" is, in our view, equally to court discursive dangers, and invites an idealism that the "push" and "pull" of hydraulic pressure effectively circumvents.

It is worth recalling, to pursue the ramifications of this discussion, that Roy Bhaskar, in his early days, was considered to be something of a "closet Althusserian" (Resch 1992: 377 note 1). From Archer's perspective, Althusser is a classic exponent of what she refers to as "downwards conflation." Ideology, in Althusserian terms, is an *objective* form arising from the requirements of production and not the creation of a particular class or individual subject. "The drawbacks of this approach [Archer comments] are similar to those of its Parsonian counterpart; there is no explanation of what generates the appropriate ideology but rather a lapse into the teleology of correspondence – there is no account of independent human agency, for the Socio-Cultural level is eternally encased in ideology, which orchestrates it just as heavily as did the central value system" (Archer 1996: 47). Now while it is true that Althusserians were sometimes guilty of talking of individuals as *mere* supports, the whole process of "interpellation," as theorized by Althusser, was far more complex than Archer allows. Moreover, the converse of the neglect of subjectivity – if that indeed is what was involved – is a profound sense of the workings of the "ideological unconscious," which is precisely the weak point of Archer's system. To the extent that we need to take account of these workings below, with reference to British Hispanism, let us pause at this point to remind ourselves of the key features of Althusserianism.

Within the context of Althusserianism, the economic function is held to be determinate; that is, the mode of production is understood as constituting the deep structure or the *matrix* of the relevant social formations. Economic determination refers to the causal effect of the social formation, as a complex whole, on individual structures and relations. The social formation, in other words, constitutes the intransitive conditions of existence of individual structures, even as it owes its "complex unity" to the transitive influence of these same structures. Social formations are "structures of structures" integrated or articulated into a meaningful whole. Although relatively autonomous, individual structures and levels are inscribed in a hierarchy of determinations that assigns them a place and a function. Clearly, determination in the last instance was never intended as a unilateral relationship of causality. The primacy of the economy does not, in other words, explain the political and ideological instances in such a way that they can simply be read off the structure of the mode of production. "In the last instance" means that a social formation is "always already" there, in the form of a causal influence effecting all its component elements. The concept of *overdetermination* is the Althusserian's way of expressing the historical effect of the ensemble of contradictions on each individual contradiction. The strength of Structural Marxism, on this basis, "is its ability to hold these seemingly contradictory positions in productive tension: to establish firm relationships between concepts of the social whole and concepts of its component structures while maintaining throughout an awareness of the discrete levels of analysis appropriate to both" (Resch: 35-36).

What causes social relations to change? At the level of analysis of the social formation, the economic, political, and ideological instances exist as a system of interrelated, interdependent practices. Althusserians call this simultaneous unity of distinct and unequal modes of determination "structural causality," of which overdetermination is, in effect, a variation. Althusserianism departs not only from the empiricist notion of linear causality but also from the Hegelian notion of expressive causality. As practised within British Empiricism, linear (otherwise transitive) causality imagines causality as involving collisions, between irreducible but atomized elements, after the manner of billiard balls. Such a model precludes both the transformation of elements and the interplay between the complex whole and its parts. By way of contrast, expressive causality views social phenomena, from the economy to, say, lyric poetry, as the exteriorization of one internal principle that is the essence of those phenomena. Structural causality differs from its linear and expressive counterparts in that it "forces us to recognize that social structures must be conceptualized along two dimensions, one that stresses the structured whole as the reciprocal effectivity of its elements, but also a second that investigates the structure of the elements themselves with the intention of discovering their particular effectivity" (51). In the case of structural causality, we are not talking about subjects – say, the number of bourgeois citizens in a particular social formation – but about a process without a subject, that involves new political, economic and ideological structures – say, the liberal state.

In our view, which we will be substantiating with reference to British Hispanism, the Althusserian notion of structural causality, otherwise the matrix effect, affords a depth of analysis that is unavailable to Archer, for all her emphasis upon stratification.

Constraining Contradiction: the Parkerian Tradition

British Hispanism, as it developed in the 1950s and 60s, during the heyday of Alexander Parker, provides a singularly vivid instance of the phenomenon that Archer refers to as "constraining contradiction." The dynamics of the latter, we recall, is envisaged as the interaction between two irreconcilable yet mutually related elements. We will construe these elements, in the case of Parker, as correlative with (feudal) Catholicism (A) and (bourgeois) Liberalism (B), whose interaction forms the fault line across which Calderonian scholarship, of Parkerian ilk, was built. Even as Catholic conservatives such as Parker attempted to draw B back to A, so other, younger scholars slowly nudged A towards B, often under the discernible influence, at the transitive level, of North-American scholarship. The *Bulletin of Hispanic Studies* of these years furnishes numerous examples of the dynamics in question, but we will focus upon the work of Professor Gwynne Edwards, a student of Parker who, during the 1960s and 70s, undertook to "liberalize" the Parkerian paradigm.

Edwards' review of a work on Calderón by P. Halkhoree provided an occasion on which to articulate his own concerns. While believing himself to be a faithful exponent of Parkerian doctrine, Halkhoree "unconsciously" subjected *El Alcalde de Zalamea* to a secularized reading that emphasized "Man's" existential aloneness and vulnerability to an irresistible force of destiny: "... if only men observed the Law, if only they exercised their Reason responsibly, if only they acted in harmony with Nature, life on earth would be happier. Agreed; but can they?" Edwards picked up on the slight but significant departure from Parkerian orthodoxy implicit in Halkhoree's rhetorical question. It was a departure of which Edwards approved, in that it brought Calderón's work into line with liberal notions of what constitutes "true tragic drama": "What remains for this reviewer is the niggling question itself, perhaps the most valuable contribution in this lucid, well-organized and intelligently written critical guide" (Edwards 169).

When, in 1978, Edwards came forward with an elaboration of his views, in a work entitled *The Prison and the Labyrinth*, Parker responded with a review that, in accordance with the dynamics of constraining contradiction, attempted to draw B (Edwards' position) back toward A (Parker's original formulation): "The fact that Dr Edwards follows a well-trodden path would not, of course, matter, if he had brought a new and significant insight into Calderón's conception and handling of tragic themes" (Parker 1982: 340). The clear implication is that the student has nothing new to add to the insights of the Master. However, as we have suggested, Edwards had in fact pushed A significantly in the direction of B. A reading of Calderonian drama that foregrounds the "total image of [Man's] tragic helplessness" was a nuance with profound ramifications, whose originality Parker was obliged to acknowledge: "If we could discount the loose conception of dramatic symbols and misguided method of analysing them, there would be much to admire in this unexpected Calderón who emerges from Dr Edwards' collaboration with him" (343).

Let us elaborate further upon the dynamics of this interchange. Since the relation between A (Man's subservience to God) and B (the Freedom of the Individual) is a genuine logical contradiction, it is incapable of direct resolution. The corrective exercise that aims to repair the inconsistency necessarily requires a redefinition of one or both elements. The onus was upon Parker to furnish a reinterpretation of B or an explanation of how Edwards had arrived at his own (misguided) formulation. The key move, in this respect, is Parker's attribution to Edwards of a certain "looseness," which can be readily extended from the analysis of dramatic symbols to a person's moral being: "His imagination is, in fact, creating *metaphors* (imprisonment in the labyrinth of the world) which get even vaguer until they carry Dr Edwards away." Parker views this willingness to be "carried away" as symptomatic of a weakness that he is prepared to track down to its source, in the moral degradation of contemporary society: "Is it the advent of a permissive society that considers wife or husband to be *imprisoned* in their mutual fidelity?"(342).

Let us pause and consider, more in abstracto, some further aspects of Parker's reading of Edwards' reading of Calderón. The psychoanalytic implications are obvious enough, particularly given the presence, in the same edition of the *Bulletin*, of Parker's article on "Segismundo's Tower." In the shadow of the latter's darkly phallic resonances, Parker emerges as an authoritarian father-figure, out to castigate his illegitimate son for certain onanistic practices: a short, sharp rap across the knuckles, one might say. Nor, given the contemporary context of political turbulence (in the 1970s and 80s), would one hesitate to pose this challenge to patriarchal authority in broader, social terms. At this level, however, we are obliged to confront the workings of an unconscious that, correspondingly, needs to be broadly conceived, at the level of the ideological unconscious. For, on reflection, what strikes one as most intriguing about Parker's review is its commitment, at this level, to enact a struggle between the forces of Morality and Reason, on the one hand, and the wayward (Romantic) Imagination, on the other. The presence of this manifestly neo-Kantian agon confirms our suspicion that A cannot entirely relinquish B for the simple reason that it is firmly implicated in it. To unpack the social dimension of this particular agon, and thereby the operations of structural causality, we turn to what is, by implication, the basic issue being debated by Parker and Edwards, namely the eminently bourgeois relation between the "individual" and "society."

The Unconscious Empiricism of Parkerianism

I have described elsewhere how Parker found himself caught in a curious ideological bind through which he was constrained to concede that individual freedom suffers some attenuation, not merely at the level of the *individual*, in her dreams and under the influence of the passions, but on account of the *social* influence of other characters (see Read 1992: 64). His solution was to refine the notion of "poetic justice" in terms of a "diffuse responsibility." What escaped my earlier formulation was the extent to which the individual/social opposition is rooted in empiricism, at the level of the ideological unconscious. For lurking behind the obvious reluctance with which Parker postulates a "diffuse responsibility" is the assumption that social theory should confine itself to observables, otherwise, in the case of literary analysis, to the "words on the page." The notion of "diffuse responsibility," we would now suggest, functions as an example of a "compositional law," of the kind that obviates the need to appeal to any social context beyond "other people" (cf. Archer 1995: 24-25). The Parkerian, as an individualist committed to social atomism, assumes that evil, virtue, guilt, etc. can indeed be identified independently of their social context. The root conviction, unstated because "unconscious," is that any collective entity is reducible to a series of observational statements about people. The result is to raise a question mark over the ontological status of "society" and its cognates.

Individualism collapses not only "upwards" but also "downwards", so that even as its "sense-data" secure the individual as a visible *organism*, they also register the effect of non-observable attitudes, mentalities, faculties, etc. On this basis, it is not clear on what ground some traditionalists were opposed to the use of psychoanalysis, or why traditional faculty psychology or "common-sense" references to "reason" and the "imagination" were preferable, in explanatory terms, to Freudian meta-psychology.

Tentatively, we suggest that such texts as those of Parker are in fact complex, highly stratified structures, that are overdetermined by at least three distinctive ideologies. Most notably, they are characterized by an opposition between a residual Kantian-Romantic construction of the subject, which preserves many of the "thick" attributes of the neo-Platonic "beautiful soul" and Cartesian "Reason", and the empiricist, ultimately Lockean or Humean subject, that has been largely stripped of its internal features to become a *tabula rasa*. Needless to say, Parker was also deeply attached to Scholasticism, which, following the Althusserian Juan Carlos Rodríguez, we will categorize as a feudal *substantialism* or *organicism*, an ideology which does not operate through the notion of the subject. This substantialism survives into the 16th and 17th centuries in the form of a recharged, non-Aristotelian organicism, whose materialism has sometimes been confused with its empiricist counterpart (see Rodríguez 1990: 55 ff).

A more detailed study than is possible here would indicate the determination of these ideologies, in the last instance, by the economic level and how they are "secreted," to use Rodríguez's term, to grease the operations of a transitional social formation (between feudalism and capitalism). Suffice it to note that substantialism does not secrete a (free) subject: its dominant categories are those of the serf/servant and the lord/ Lord. Only bourgeois ideologies boast "free subjects" for the simple reason that only capitalism requires that the individual be "free" to sell his or her labor power. The Kantian subject will eventually become the ideology of the petty-bourgeoisie, for whom it will function as the discourse of Literature and of "sensibility," whereas the Humean subject will subsequently sustain a variety of positivist discourses and thereby serve, ideologically speaking, the more philistine, technicist fractions of the bourgeoisie.

Needless to say, these ideological currents intermingle to provide a whole range of possible positions, with differing emphases (see Rodríguez 1990: 124-30). Examples of a dominantly Humean, positivist tradition, blended with neo-Kantian elements, abound in British Hispanism, particularly in such sub-branches as medieval literature, history and philology. Consider the claim by Derek Lomax, in a 1972 review, that one of the distinctive features of British Hispanists is their predilection for detail, as evinced by their "careful analysis of small sections or aspects, which they study with few or no preconceptions." Few or no preconceptions – the pressure of a dominantly empiricist ideological unconscious could not be clearer. If the focus is upon *"facts,"* in accordance with the principle of verifiability, then objectivity and neutrality are assured. The blend between Hume and Kant surfaces in the "attempt to reconcile the historical and aesthetic approaches" (Lomax 68).

The limitations that such empiricism imposes are starkly revealed whenever the British Hispanist moves from description to explanation, as when Keith Whinnom undertook to theorize the concept of the "best seller." Immediately, insecurity threatens – "deeper waters," "some very dubious territory" – as Whinnom is forced to relinquish his hold on empirical fact. Perforce, the psychological and sociological, which, in Humean terms, are "largely unverifiable," are deemed to be "pseudo" concepts (Whinnom 1980: 189). Denied the benefit of explanatory hypotheses, Whinnom is limited to confessedly "crude" suggestions and statements. The converse of such mechanical materialism is a rampant idealism: Literature bestrides everything from "primitive myth" to "modern magazines."

At this level, that of the ideological unconscious, texts are revealing less for what they actually say than for what they assume. Literature is always "given," as an object, equal to itself, whose interior never varies because it is the "expression" of "Man," who likewise never varies but simply unfolds his inner being, gradually, from age to age. By the same token, reading is an encounter between two "free" subjects, the writer and reader. The former, the peculiarities of his/her historical medium notwithstanding, is able to speak directly to the latter, who is able to recognize her/himself in the text, for the simple reason that s/he belongs to the same basic stratum.

Empiricism and Class Conflict

While Althusserianism views society as a structured whole, about which knowledge is possible, it also emphasizes the complexity of the causal process that binds together the multiple, stratified levels of structures within structures, whose vertical and horizontal displacements, in constant, dialectical movement, cannot be simplified or reduced to a single center. From this standpoint, the "unity" of the individual texts can only be a fabrication, otherwise the fevered product of an idealist's fantasy, that is belied even by the writings of the critical ideologue himself. Hence the tension throughout between Parker's preoccupation with social morality and his otherwise pervasive individualism, a contradiction that can only finally be explained with reference to the singular nature of professional labor.

Professional labor, it is important to note, is not exchanged against capital, but directly with revenue, that is, wages and profits, which means that professionals are to some degree removed from the capitalist mode of production. We would suggest, following Larson (Larson chap. 12), that the university professions represent, in fact, an extension of exchange relations into new areas of life, as an effect of the generalized breakdown of the pre-capitalist social structure. The professional ethic derives from ideals of craftsmanship, which finds intrinsic value in the work that professionals perform. Hence the ideal of universal service and the emphasis, particularly notable in the case of Parker, upon a Morality that protects the social fabric against the subversive effects of the market. At the same time, these very professionals are also the embodiment of individualism, based on the notion of the exchange of individual services. Hence also the conviction, on the part of Parker, that moral dilemmas are a purely private affair, that admit of individual solutions. It is a moral vision bolstered, ontologically, by the flat, unchanging world of empiricism, with its discrete, depthless objects, isolated in an empty space.

Class returns, then, through what Jameson refers to as the "inconspicuous backdoor" of the floating intellectual (Jameson 39), whose contradictory class positioning in the bosom of traditional society, the hallmark of the petty bourgeoisie, has been further compounded by the rise of the "new professional class" (see Callinicos 1987). This positioning, we believe, is sufficient to contextualize the curious obsession, exhibited by Parkerians, with the figure of the "rebel soldier," who appears in Calderón's *La vida es sueño*.

Rebellion is not exactly a topic conducive to constraining contradiction, in that, as we explained above, the latter's social logic promotes not revolution but correction, through procedures designed to limit the ramifications of logical contradiction at the S-C level. In this respect British Hispanism, as it operated throughout the 1950s and 60s, possessed very refined containing strategies, that made the radical transfiguration of the *Bulletin* itself, in 1954, a singularly bloodless affair. Indeed, Harold Hall, who had previously assisted Peers in his editorship, quietly disappeared from the scene for a number of years, allegedly to "spare him any embarrassment" (Sloman 189). It was, needless to say, but one more example of a paradigmatic shift that British Hispanists executed "unconsciously." But precisely because it was never theorized, one suspects, the guilt involved was never abreacted, with the result that Hall returned to tax Parker with his treatment of the rebel solider, summarily dispatched by Segismundo to life-long incarceration in the Tower (see Read 1992: 61-62).

Doubtless it was a guilt overdetermined, on the one hand, by the ongoing preoccupation on the part of the bourgeoisie with its historical acts of betrayal, epitomized by the events of 1968, which would explain why such scholars as Daniel L. Beiple and Donald McGrady returned obsessively to the fate of the rebel soldier; and, on the other hand, by the same class's attachment to the pre-capitalist formations and to the values of the organic community. Those values had never been more under threat than they were in 1976, when D. J. Gifford and J. L. Brooks took it upon themselves to offer a history of the Association of Hispanists of Great Britain and North Ireland in which the Association was promoted as one big "happy family," besieged by a bureaucratized modernity: "[w]e live nowadays in a world where human relationships remain the most important consideration in communication, where human contact matters more than easy formulae and press release, where straight affection and interested gossip count for more than all the sheets of paper" (Gifford and Brooks 97).

But this particular happy family was not all that it was cut out to be. The quality of its conference papers, celebrated so euphorically by Gifford and Brooks, was in fact belied by a pervasive mediocrity, which could be accounted for, structurally, by the process of under-selection that channeled into Spanish pupils that had underperformed in English, French and German. Moreover, disregarding the singular absence of women, the image of the Association as a happy family could be sustained only at the price of repressing the realities of broader social relations. Both objectively and subjectively, the professions are outside and above the working class—as Larson points out, teaching, including university lecturing, was the typical aspiration of socially mobile children of industrial and clerical workers. Moreover, while the Association consisted of *free* professionals, who did not traverse class boundaries, its minimal equality was grounded on the deeply inegalitarian structure of the social formation at large. The freedom of expression, of which it boasted, co-existed internally with power structures that reproduced those prevailing more generally, throughout the social formation. Such, after all, were the very conditions of possibility of constraining contradiction.

Concomitant Compatibilities

Anthony Giddens speculates that reformism came naturally to a British working class that had, by the 20th century, lost contact with alternative modes of production. According to this argument, revolutionary expectations will flourish in pre-modern societies, which have yet to lose the sense of alternative social arrangements as desirable and achievable goals, and in which, correspondingly, the contradictions of capitalist development are most keenly felt (Gidden 1973). Whatever the reason, Britain led the way in a process of political transformation that has forced all the social-democratic parties in Western Europe to become reformist parties. It is our view that these same processes of capitalist transformation, operating through the mediation of structural causality, explain the presence within British Hispanism, throughout the 1960s and 70s and, residually, thereafter, of the disciplinary dynamic that we have characterized, following Margaret Archer, as *concomitant compatibility*.

Let us remind ourselves of the situational logic involved. Concomitant compatibility is concerned with the *protection* of consistency and with ideational *systematization*. In the words of Archer, it is conducive to "a kind of adventure playground, a congenial environment which can be explored with profit (for it reinforces the original idea) and without danger (since it presents no threat to it)" (Archer 1996: 172). Its theorists are characterized by a strong aesthetic as opposed to analytical orientation, a predilection for "artistic" hermeneutics as the method for grasping the inner sense of cultural whole. As we shall see, this same hermeneutics can be effectively deployed to grasp the unity of the literary text. The emphasis upon unity correlates with the repression of time, which in turn leads to a downgrading of cause and effect, as applied to culture, since causality necessarily operates over time. Scholars actively seek identities, not contrasts or oppositions, which are subsequently incorporated not on the basis of corrective interchange, as in the case of constraining contradictions, but through the discovery of harmonious relations.

The principle of compatibility, as it functioned within British Hispanism, was particularly apparent within the central area of the canon, namely the Golden Age, from the late 1960s. From that point on, the "ferment of criticism" – the phrase is Margaret Wilson's (Wilson 1966: 200) – characteristic of constraining contradiction gradually gave way to concomitant compatibility as rising scholars sought to apply the established categories of Parkerian criticism to yet one more play by Lope or Calderón, or to refine already existing analyses. Variations in individual works are simply incorporated into the conceptual field, so as to produce a body of criticism of almost scholastic *density*. It was an activity that bore all the marks of a "mopping-up" operation, of the kind that Thomas Kuhn was concurrently theorizing with respect to the development of the hard sciences. By the 1990s, the critical trajectory was visible in all its outlines. As Wilson observed in 1992, in a review of a work by Melveena McKendrick: "The ferment of criticism of recent decades has now had time to settle, and Dr McKendrick can for the most part leave controversy behind to give an account of Golden-Age drama which will broadly be accepted as definitive" (Wilson 1992: 194).

Closure, to reiterate, appears as the last element in a sequence and never the first: the background – "literary theory or new readings of the texts" – is not excluded on principle because it is threatening but because it is viewed as uninteresting. Within the tightly-knit community of British Calderonistas, agreement and unanimity reigns, grounded ideologically in a "sensitivity" to the text and to "what is essentially dramatic and perennially true in these enactments of human experience." But ironically the closure occurs when the satisfactions of complementarity have become increasingly difficult to defend, in the context of the revolutionary turmoil of the early 1990s: "The only emphases that link her work to modern critical fashion are those on hints of feminism in plays, and on the importance of the subtext: the need to be alert to the note of subversion in which the attentive ear will detect disharmony with the apparently satisfying outcome of action" (194). Symptomatic of the breakdown at the level of social structures was the increasing inability on the part of literary critics to maintain the equally mythical conception of the unity of the text. If Wilson's review finally converges on the issue of structural disharmony and the "vast resources of poetic drama" that are deployed to off-set it, it is because, unconsciously, more is at issue that an "aesthetic flaw." Rather the interrelationship of a play's parts is the thinly disguised analogue of social harmony, not to mention the New World Order.

The principle of concomitant compatibility was operative not simply within the British Calderonian school or, for that matter, within Golden Age studies, but extended its reach right across Hispanism. To this extent, the career of Professor Gwynne Edwards is paradigmatic. As we have seen above, his early work on Calderón threatened to become a flash point, at which constraining contradiction exploded into a form of competitive contradiction. If this never occurred, it was simply because it would have required an ideological "break" of the kind that was inconceivable within British Hispanism. True, the compositional laws required to sustain individualism had visibly begun to break down, even within the conservative confines of the British Academy, but in the last instance the force of empiricism, at the level of the ideological unconscious, blocked any radicalization. Everything, including the career structures of the scholarship boy, conspired to induce a ready acceptance of a buoyant complementarity. Thus, even when coziness became a potentially asphyxiating closure, encouraging younger scholars to begin to move into adjacent fields, it was concomitant compatibility that dictated the methodological strategies, which consisted of the simple extension of those refined in familiar territory, to the new fields. In this way, Edwards moved on to write books on Lorca and other modern dramatists, not to mention Buñuel and the modern cinema.

Of course, the potential for instability remained, even within the confines of Calderonian scholarship. In particular, the opposition between North-American pragmatic liberalism and its more conservative British counterpart was always smoldering. And so when Don Cruickshank was called upon to review a work by Edwin Honig, he was forced to confront a scholar who objected to the unconsciously neo-Kantian preoccupation with moral purpose that characterized the British school. Feeling threatened and maneuvering instinctively for position, the British Hispanist gestures towards the (allegedly) numerous technical imperfections of the work under review. It is a common enough tactic, almost obligatory in the *Bulletin* in the case of problematic works. But in the present case, it remains a mere gesture, significantly recognized by Cruickshank for what it is, namely an exclusionary device (Cruickshank 168). The reasoning behind such a conciliatory approach is obvious enough: the "universal dramatist" that Honig wishes to promote is still *compatible* with the more narrowly defined "moralist" that was promoted by Parker et al: "¿qué importa errar lo menos/ quien acertó lo demás?"

It was relatively rare for concomitant compatibility to break down within British Hispanism, where it could be secretly imposed at the S-C level. However, strategies of containment that were relatively effective against vulnerable graduate students proved less so internationally, where a causal consensus was less easily engineered. Consider, for example, Keith Whinnom's review (1975) of Stephen Gilman's *The Spain of Fernando de Rojas*. Issues of substance were never at issue, and predictably so in that both Hispanists moved within the boundaries of a common liberal ideology. Their commonality explains why Whinnom discovered in Gilman a "good deal of interesting material," and could readily agree, for example, that the Spanish Inquisition was a "pernicious institution." We are only talking of different logical emphases and the disorder that they have created at the C-S level: "Gilman is guilty of an unpardonable betrayal of the best standards of international Hispanism in the way in which he expresses his disagreement with other critics" (Whinnom 1975: 160). As was to be expected, Whinnom gravitates unthinkingly towards those tried and trusted strategies, otherwise the parading of "trivial inaccuracies" that allegedly "pop up" on every page. But, as we have observed, strategies that were effective in the control and policing of undergraduate and graduate students proved ineffective against mature scholars, with the power and resources to defend themselves.

Such incidents disturbed the placid waters of British Hispanism only exceptionally during the 1960s and 70s. But, as noted above, it became progressively harder to maintain complementary relations in the 1980s and early 90s. Exactly how hard emerges from a review by Nicholas Round of a volume published in honor of Alan Deyermond, a scholar who participated actively in both the British and North-American academies. While the British predilection for close and subtle readings of texts is here held to *complement* the more intellectually uninhibited, free-ranging approach of the North-American Hispanists, Round is mildly critical of British myopia and of its products: "Yet it is no denigration of that achievement to insist that this academic mode has limitations of its own. Its schemes of interpretation tend to be constituted beforehand as 'knowledges' – holdings, as it were, of a mental library – rather than being explored as elements in the living contexts from which our texts emerge. The thrust, then is radically against any 'making strange': in consequence, the sheer strangeness of medieval literature and its world can sometimes be lost" (Round 1992: 179). The "mental library," we suggest, is none other than the library of ideas (CS) to which Archer refers, whereas the "living context" may be legitimately construed, in the present context, as the S-C level. In the early 1990s this S-C level exploded into disorder as, briefly, comcomitant compatibility was displaced by competitive contradiction.

The Emergence of Competitive Contradiction: the Case of Psychoanalysis

When the community of British Hispanism began visibly to fragment in the 1980s and 90s, a number of younger Hispanists, seizing the moment, stepped forward to proclaim the novelty of their position as exponents of "New Hispanisms." A scenario was created in which they cast themselves as radicals and revolutionaries, heroes in the elimination of an older order. In truth, when the break came, it was but the culmination of long years of conflict at the S-C level, rendered largely invisible by a dominant complementarity. One area of particular instability was that of psychoanalysis, located largely in the North-American but sometimes in the European Academy and influencing its British counterpart through a process of seepage. Typical of the mechanics of this process is the exchange between José Aguirre and Carlos Feal that was instigated in the 1976 edition of the *Bulletin* by an article in which Aguirre, a Spanish scholar resident in Britain, took it upon himself to condemn Feal's earlier deployment of psychoanalytic concepts in his analysis of Lorca.

The crux of Aguirre's opposition rested upon what he believed to be the unsuitability of Freudian or Jungian concepts for addressing "concrete" instances of dream work in Lorca. Quite simply the instrument is not appropriate, not designed, for the delicate task that that it is called upon to perform: "La suma de las interpretaciones de distintos sueños puede conducir a establecer 'verdades generales,' o mejor 'leyes generales de tendencia,' pero resultará siempre muy peligroso aplicar las mismas, sin previa y cuidadosa descriminación, a los casos concretos e individuales" (Aguirre 129). As would so often be the case, opposition to some body of knowledge rested not on familiarity with and close attention to the relevant canonic texts, but on the contrary, on broad sweeping generalities: "Cualquier psicólogo o psiquiatra, digno de tal nombre, sabe que ..."; "quien esté ligeramente familiarizado con las obras de [...] Freud," etc. The moment of competitive contradiction arrives when the patronizing, bullying tactics aimed actually at hiding B from view are resisted by somebody of intellectual and, more importantly, institutional standing. At this point, B is turned into a source of pluralism and confrontation, as when Feal chose to avail himself of the liberal "freedom" to respond to criticism.

Needless to say, it took little effort on Feal's part to undercut Aguirre's position: manifestly, any attempt to analyze individual dreams, not least of all in psychoanalytic practice, depends upon the use of general concepts, and to claim the opposite would be, in effect, to abandon methodological thought. But in a manner of speaking, propositional differences were not the key issue: what Feal protested about was the impression that his ideas had been "mutilated" and he had been "manipulated" by Aguirre (Feal 311, 314). In other words, attention focused on the process of personal interaction, at the S-C level.

Such encounters are relatively rare, given the dominant complementarity within British Hispanism. When they do occur, they are staged simply to re-affirm a sense of cultural integration within the academic community, as an exercise in phatic communion. "We" know, "of course," that psychoanalysis is suspect, notably in its application to literary texts. When, as occasionally happens, issues of substance are engaged, they relate invariably to an issue already in evidence in Aguirre, namely the general/concrete, science/literature opposition. By way of further illustration, let us consider how Alan K. G. Paterson evaluates the Lacanian reading of Golden Age drama undertaken by H. W. Sullivan and E. Ragland-Sullivan:

> [I]f, like myself, one has reservations both about Calderón's status as tragedian (unassumed by himself) and about the critical gains from applying theories of psychoanalysis – especially a system inclusive enough to make the object of analysis a matter of relative indifference – then the efforts of both writers will have been spent in vain. The series of "therefores" that leads from the general to the specific, from Lacan to Calderón (a poet with "praeternatural access" to Lacan's

analytical insight, they tell us) and to *Las tres justicias*, creaks at the joints; at bottom, of course, any theory of catharsis and any theory of the psychic nature of tragic doom are extra-textual, postulates about a psychological transaction between a play and an audience that lies beyond proof or disproof.
(Paterson 1983: 69)

One knows, "of course," that psychoanalytic criticism is inadmissible, but more importantly one "knows" that the text is separated from its context by an ontological gulf; that science consists of "subjects" observing "objects"; and that the task of analysis is to reduce collective entities to their ultimate constituents, namely the concrete individual or the "words on the page." One also "knows" – if, that is, one is fully integrated into liberal ideology – that the individual (text), stripped of all its material (outside) encumbrances, is the very image of the universal ("Man").

In sum, psychoanalytic criticism always proved so potentially devastating for the British Hispanist insofar as it constituted a form of *modernism*. I will define modernism by its commitment to ontological realism, which involved an appeal not to simple observation – the gaze of the subject cast upon the object – but to the existence of abstract structures and forces underlying empirical reality. The modernist philosopher, artist or scientist was increasingly conscious of the formal structures, not the least significant of which was language itself, that determined his or her perception of the objective world. Abstraction, in other words, far from distancing us from knowledge, actually provided a more rigorous and fundamental access to reality. British Hispanists were right to be on the alert, for what modernism called into question, among other things, were political and social theories rooted in such pre-modern, empirical views as theirs.

Conflictual Ideologies

Nothing is more revealing of ideological allegiance, unconscious or otherwise, than a scholar's very use and understanding of the term "ideology," an issue which again finds North-American and British Hispanism significantly at odds. Let us contrast, in this respect, Walter Holzinger's "Ideology, imagery and the literalization of metaphor in *Secreto agravio, secreta venganza*" (1977) with A. F. Lambert's "*El celoso extremeño*: ideology and criticism" (1980).

Holzinger's piece confessedly derives from a close reading of the work of Althusser, which dominated debate in the 1970s. "Ideologies," he explains, "are usually not homogeneous wholes, but contain internal divisions ranging from differences of emphasis to outright contradictions responding to different social forces within a society. In addition, there is usually a considerable timelag between ideology and social reality. The latter can change quickly, ideologies, on the other hand, are usually a generational attribute, traditionally very difficult to alter once acquired, especially if the acquisition has been during childhood and by way of the family" (Holzinger 212). To be sure, this considerably dilutes Althusser's original insights – for "social forces" read "class conflict," for "social reality" read "social formation," etc. – but it was sufficient to cast Calderón in a rather different light. What emerged was not the Kantian blend between religious morality and bourgeois liberalism – the "universal terms of the drama" – that typically preoccupied British Calderonistas, but a real, historicized sense of the otherness of feudal ideology, based on the notion of the World as a Book. Holzinger was alert to the novelty of his views: "My disagreement with Professor Wilson's interpretation raises larger methodological questions [...]. I suggest [...] that a great deal more attention must be paid to placing the literary work into its ideological context" (211).

Holzinger's attempt to apply Althusserian notions to the Calderonian opus may seem relatively unimpressive and even confused, particularly when measured against the comparable but qualitatively superior project of Juan Carlos Rodríguez (1974), but the details are less important in themselves than the ideological divide that threatens to separate the North-American from the British Hispanist. For as Lambert's article illustrates only too clearly, ideology as conceived by British Hispanism was, like bad breath, something we only notice in others (Lambert 224). This common-sense meaning is only tenuously connected with that which emerges from Althusser's texts, which fell completely outside the realm of British Hispanism.

The stage was set for a number of confused and acerbic encounters, as British Hispanists were called upon to review Marxist or Marxian works of North-American critics that problematized key aspects of their own ideological unconscious. Perforce, disagreement at this level focuses on causal rather than logical relations: "For four decades of innovative and meticulous critical scholarship are not going to lie down in front of a book that in the space of a mere hundred pages tries to tackle a subject as huge as reason and the passions, dealing in any depth with only nine plays" (McKendrick 395). Melveena McKendrick is here struggling to come to terms with Hildner's *Reason and the Passions*, not because the work is devoid of useful insights, because it manifestly is not, but because of the ultimately "elusive" and "allusive" nature of its thesis. Stated briefly, this thesis was, in Hildner's own words (and quoted by McKendrick), that

Calderón's dramaturgy was part of "an ideology which attempted to re-feudalise Spain as the aristocracy felt its bases beginning to slip away" (395). Understandably, such a meta-narrative left McKendrick bemused. Her claim that it was unsupported by hard "evidence" and "historical underpinning" is very unpersuasive, given the depth of Marxist scholarship – Hill, Dobb, Thompson, Anderson, Vilar, etc. – specifically on the transition from feudalism to capitalism. Any isolation or insulation to be found is a feature not of Hildner's sociology, which on McKendrick's own reckoning is characterized by a certain iconoclastic competitiveness, but of her own commitment to a concomitant compatibility that actively ignores views discrepant with her own.

More revealing of McKendrick's difficulties is the complaint that "the author does not seem able to make up his mind what manner of dramatist Calderón is; he seems now to argue for a less dogmatic, less closed Calderón, now for a Calderón intent on indoctrination who puts his art at the service of largely secular ideology" (396). Given McKendrick's commitment, at the level of the ideological unconscious, to the myth of social (and textual) integration, the concept of ideological contradiction is totally alien to her, particularly when compounded by a relative indifference to "Calderón's [conscious] purpose." The Marxist version of contradiction, or what Althusser understood as over-determination, as applied to a particular historical conjuncture, involves a dialectical mode of thinking quite alien to the British Hispanist, for whom Calderón has to be one thing or another, but cannot be both. It is at such moments that one senses behind the façade of British Hispanism a long tradition of empiricist thought, rooted in Locke and Hume, which must be off-set against the Hegelian mode typical of continental thought. Posed in other terms, it is the opposition between linear causality, which involves direct or transitive influence, and structural causality, which allows for indirect or intransitive influence.

After the Break

When Juan Carlos Rodríguez undertook to read Spanish culture through the lens of Althusserianism and to initiate what was to be, arguably, the major theoretical achievement of modern Hispanism, he began with a "break," a break that, among other things, signaled a transition to a regime dictated by the principle of competitive contradiction: "El *alea jacta* era irreversible. Mi ruptura con todos los planteamientos anteriores también: literalmente los arrojé a la calle" (Rodríguez 1990: 27). The Althusserian moment of modernism in Spain, as embodied in the work of Rodríguez, was a true example of an overdetermined conjuncture, which threw into relief with vivid intensity the distinctive outlines of feudalism, modernism and post-modernism. The contrast with British Hispanism could not be greater, as is shown by those reviewers in the 1970s and 80s who struggled to come to terms with Marxian texts. As we have seen, concomitant compatibility was the motor that drove British Hispanism, and it was significantly with the word "conflictiva" that P. Gallagher's objections began with respect to Rodríguez-Puértolas' *De la Edad Media a la edad conflictiva*: "The title, expanding upon Américos Castro's *De la edad conflictiva* (1963), I found a trifle anomalous, not only because *conflictiva* shows value-judgement and *media* doesn't, but also because the shift from one age to the other is not in every important respect as great as the title would seem to imply" (Gallagher 373).

Such terms as "Renaissance" and "Middle Ages" were, when viewed from outside the ideological boundary of British empiricism, radically subjective terms, "que sólo tienen aplicación dentro de la lógica teórica de la ideología burguesa en general" (Rodríguez 1990: 135). Viewed from within this boundary, "conflict" was unthinkable, since what was ultimately at issue was not only the unity of historical epochs but that of the liberal subject itself: " ... para esta perspectiva ideológica (repito: hegemónica, dominante), la *literatura* resulta ser [...] ante todo un 'objeto' específicamente siempre *'igual-a-sí-mismo'* ... El 'interior,' el 'en sí' de la 'literatura' no variará nunca en tanto que la 'Literatura' es la expresión lingüística ('sensible/artística' o 'sensible/imaginativa') del 'sujeto-hombre' ..." (162). Such language, one supposes, would have been literally incomprehensible to British Hispanists, who needed to break with their empiricist ideology if they were to begin to see how pervasive were its unconscious effects. As things stood, the very brevity of the *Bulletin*'s review format was itself a containment strategy, that assured the protection of this dominant ideology by marginalizing such works as Puértolas' and silencing those of Juan Carlos Rodríguez. For the rest, such reviews as Gallagher's are of interest only as laboratories in which to observe ideology in operation.

The validity of Puértolas' critical methodology, Gallagher claims, is questionable on the grounds that it addresses the "everyday reality" of "*groups* of people": "It tends to confirm what is already well known and to be impotently hypothetical about what is in dispute" (Gallagher 374). Hypothetical because the implicit norm is a positivist one, based on "observation" and "verification," which exclude the possibility of social structures that, like magnetic fields, are visible only through their effects. After all, the argument runs, "groups of people" are ultimately reducible to "individuals," in that, "though societies 'produce' individuals, it is the individuals, not societies, that produce the works of art." Here, the undeniable fact of the mediation of social structures through individuals is used to ground an ideological individualism and to question, by implication, the ontological status of social structures. "By implication" because British Hispanists will never engage fundamental issues concerning the nature of the human sciences and the status of the social mechanisms whose existence these sciences postulate. The blockage is totally disabling when it comes to an understanding of Marxism, at least of a Structuralist ilk, which insists on viewing social mechanisms not as the conscious product of groups or collectivities but as structures secreted from prevailing social *relations*. Nor do these same Hispanists possess the necessary discursive penetration to raise to the level of conscious awareness their neo-Kantian, idealistic insistence on the "thing in itself" ("the work itself," "literature ... studied for itself"). Texts, like individual subjects, are progressively stripped of their social attributes and reduced to their "concrete" form, before being paraded, in their transcendental abstraction, as the embodiment of universal values.

These moments of incommensurability are not frequent in British Hispanism, whose commitment to compatibility largely insulated it against the outside, but they occur whenever its practitioners front up to Marxist-inspired texts from abroad. Alan Deyermond, for example, in his review of another work by Puértolas, can accept the claims regarding the structural ambiguity of the *Libro de buen amor* but inevitably balks at the attempt to link this ambiguity to "a fourteenth-century crisis of the feudal system," an attempt which cannot help but seem "arbitrary and even perfunctory" to those unthinkingly attached to the principle of linear causality (Deyermond 56). Likewise, Puértolas' overall conclusion that the ballads are a manifestation of the feudal system in decay "does not seem to follow from the evidence adduced." The hesitancy betrays the uncertainty of someone dimly aware that he is in ideologically alien territory and whose standards of comparison are those of a positivism in which one "actual" event unambiguously and visibly determines another: "This failure to demonstrate a connexion between poems and their socio-historical context is all the more striking when one recalls Entwistle's success in doing this with the Trastámaran ballads, and Angus MacKay's recent 'The ballad and the frontier'" (56).

The Moment of Competitive Contradiction

While British Hispanism had remained largely unaffected by the events of 1968, it could not help but register the deepening world economic crisis of the 1980s. Britain's national situation was determined by problems that derive, in the last instance, from its early pre-eminence in the development of industrial capitalism. As technology moved beyond the relatively primitive requirements of mining and textile production, Britain found itself increasingly outstripped by other countries, notably the USA and Germany. Two factors helped stave off disaster: the revenue that it derived from its massive overseas investments and London's role within the world financial market, and the fact that its empire guaranteed an outlet for its manufactured products. The structural weaknesses that dogged British capital throughout the 19th century accompanied Britain into the 20th century. They were masked by two World Wars, the effects of which were temporarily to stall economies competing with Britain's, such as Germany's and, subsequently, Japan's, and by a period of protectionism under state capitalism. The period after the Second World War, with which we are concerned, is therefore best understood, economically, as a temporary reprieve, before Britain was again exposed to the realities of world-wide competition. In the absence of a radical restructuring, successive Labour governments in the 1960s and 70s found it increasingly impossible to "manage" the economy. It fell to successive Tory governments under Thatcher to open up the British economy to global capital (cf. Leys, chap. 2).

Bewilderment at the collapse of capitalism with a human face was particularly acute in the universities, not least in its secluded backwaters, where British Hispanism still remained attached to the organic values of pre-capitalist societies. The leaders of the field, along with other conservative liberals, were powerless to understand, much less to resist, the curtailment of their privileges or to escape its political flow-on effect – a right-wing populism that included the universities as one of its prime targets. Stripped of their moral and intellectual authority, many took early retirement. Of those that remained, some retreated into their private research, there to bemoan the increasing dislocation and sectionalism that they observed around them and to indulge their nostalgia for a time when cultural density was high. Typically, J. Alberich found himself struggling to take on board the ideological effects of globalization, emanating from the USA: "Las páginas dedicadas al burlador barroco," he wrote of James Mandrell's *The Point of Honor,* "no las entiendo ni poco ni mucho" (Alberich 232). Likewise, "linguistic excesses" and "self-referentiality" told him nothing about Don Juan, but a good deal about North-American Hispanism ("¡Vaya por Dios!"). Their effect was to drive the traditionalist to assume positions of outright rejection. Such moments mark a key passage, from the principle of constraining contradiction – how can one correct what one cannot understand? – to that of competitive contradiction.

Other traditional scholars seized the moment of disorder and breakdown to settle former grudges that, under the regime of concomitant compatibility, had found no possible outlet. Thus, in a review of Parker's *The Mind and Art of Calderón*, Ruano de la Haza castigated the Master himself for allegedly smuggling his own preoccupations and obsessions into the mind of Calderón: "el evangelio de Calderón, según Parker, tiene a veces muy poco que ver con el Calderón que vieron los españoles del siglo XVII" (Ruano de la Haza 1991: 538). Ruano's major complaint is that Parker never sufficiently attended to the actual mechanics of staging and theatre direction. At root, his review is a replay of the old opposition between philology and literary criticism, otherwise between a version of mechanical materialism and neo-Kantian moralism. Suffice it to note, in the present context, that it was directed less at exposing logical contradictions in the CS than the realities of oppression and intimidation at the S-C level ("I am right. You are wrong"). Frustratingly, until this point, these realities had been masked by the much-vaunted but in effect very limited openness of British Hispanism, or so at least Ruano implies.

Other traditionalists realized that the occasion called for more drastic adjustments. Of these, some chose to reconvert their cultural capital by moving over into administration. For those that remained, the painful task of accommodation – alien to competitive contradiction – was the only realistic option, given the reach of the ideological transformations currently underway. Doubtless the process involved its indignities, but it was not without its rewards. Thus Alan K. G. Paterson, to take but one example, belatedly discovered aspects of the Golden Age, notably the "sinister, violent side of misogyny" and other matters relating to gender and sexuality, that Parkerianism had effectively repressed. It was even conceded, albeit grudgingly, that "a psychoanalytical method could also doubtless operate" (Paterson 1993: 111-12).

As in all things, change came easiest to the young. Sensing the intellectual bankruptcy and vulnerability of their senior colleagues, some younger Hispanists began to look elsewhere for the intellectual stimulus necessary to renovate their discipline. They accepted the abandonment of medieval literature and the need to raise their publishing rate as readily as, globally, capitalists accepted the de-industrialization of whole regions and the need to increase turn-over time and raise the rate of profit. In the creative confusion generated by competitive contradiction, ideological boundaries were breached, with the result that, for the first time, British Hispanists were able to view the dominant ideology from the outside.

Thus, for Paul Julian Smith, Godzich and Spadiccini's *Literature Among Discourses* "poses an overt challenge to the unexamined positivism and empiricism still dominant in Golden Age studies" (Smith 1988[i]: 295). It became routine for younger Hispanists to castigate traditional work for its "lack of critical self-awareness" and for being "unashamedly positivist and historicist." And not without reason, in that many of the books produced in this period by these same Hispanists – those of Jo Labanyi spring to mind – show a theoretical depth and polemical edge that would have been unimaginable only a decade earlier. Some of the *Bulletin*'s reviews were exceptional, such as Barry Jordan's brilliant critique of Goytisolo's pre-Oedipal attachment to the Pleasure Principle, an attachment that the British Hispanist correctly believed to lead into a "literary and political cul de sac" (Jordan 396).

The "flow" of articles in successive issues of the *Bulletin* in the 1980s and early 90s is itself eloquent testimony of the diversity and disparity of the intellectual positions being assumed. Thus, resident and residual Parkerians can be found alongside newly arrived specialists on modern and Latin-American literature, who show themselves to be much more responsive to matters of "theory." Film studies gradually make their mark, and are a means by which older scholars are able to reconstitute themselves in a relatively painless manner. Likewise, it no longer becomes unthinkable for British Hispanists to respond positively to psychoanalysis, Marxism and, increasingly, post-structuralism and deconstruction. It is important not to underestimate the novelty of such developments: while competitive contradiction emerges through the corrective vicissitudes associated with constraining contradiction in the 1950s and 60s, the polemical encounters of the1980s were qualitatively distinct from their antecedents. The disputes no longer concern basically like-minded, traditional liberals: younger British Hispanists engage in the conscious pursuit of new material, and are prepared to transgress national boundaries to gain access to it. The result is a gradual intensification of schismatic hostilities, which culminated in a rancorous exchange of views in the pages of the *Journal of Hispanic Research* in the early 90s (see Round 1992-93).

Contingent Complementarity

And yet and yet ... it would be easy to exaggerate the polemical effervescence of this period. Indeed, it could well be argued that, given the political and economic turmoil of these years, the surface of British Hispanism remained remarkably placid. Certainly, by the mid 1990s, the indications are that the moment of contradiction has come and gone. To a great extent, the competition had always been avoided by the simple device of a division of labor. It was almost as if there existed a tacit agreement: traditionalists were left undisturbed in those areas of the canon that had always interested them, notably the Golden Age, whilst younger Hispanists were free to colonize new lands. However, even when concerns overlapped, one is struck by the relative absence of polemic. Take, for instance, Peter Evans' review of *Hacia Calderón: Séptimo Coloquio Anglogermano*, with its breezy references to "another valuable collection of essays incorporating a wide variety of methodologies applies to the analysis of Calderón's plays" (Evans 372). True, the reviewer visibly warms to Henry Sullivan's exercise in Lacanian theory: "Anyone who is still committed to the idea of Calderón's unmitigated conservatism might like to start reading here" (373). But there were words of encouragement all around as both younger Hispanists and traditionalists showed themselves to be uncommonly prepared to restrain their own aggressive impulses. Indications are that, surreptitiously, a transition was being negotiated between liberal eclecticism and postmodern pluralism. In our terms, competitive contradiction has visibly been succeeded by contingent compatibility. How and why was this possible?

Tentatively, we suggest that an explanation is to be found in the relative weakness of modernism in both British and Hispanic cultures. Modernism, we argue, is strongest in those countries where the process of modernization was most fraught with difficulties, in other words, countries in which extensive industrialization existed alongside rural communities in which the medieval peasantry still maintained a firm grip upon the land. In this respect, Britain and Spain were notable for their relative stability, in Britain's case because the industrialization process was exceptionally prolonged and advanced, and in Spain's case because it was correspondingly belated. This meant that British Hispanism, which by its very nature, bridged both cultures, was overdetermined at the ideological level in a way that neutralized the impact of modernism, along with its major exponents, notably Freud and Marx. Now modernism, we argue, was the key ingredient of competitive contradiction: as we saw, Freud and Marx were precisely the areas of tension and potential instability within concomitant compatibility. It was they who most threatened the myth of cultural integration.

Of course, there was no way back for younger British Hispanists. The nostalgic attempt to recoup the values of the organic community was limited to traditionalists. But when younger Hispanists moved on, it was not via Marx but, on the contrary, in reaction to Marxism, via the critics of modernity, notably Nietzsche, as he was mediated through the post-structuralism of Foucault and Deleuze. In these circumstances, the shift from Gramsci and Althusser to Foucault was worked through only superficially, in terms of a rather vulgar anti-Marxism. The complex legacy of Marxism, in other words, is not taken on board so much as dismissed as a site "where ideological control is simply a function of economic power and of the relationship to the means of production" (Peris 75) – significantly at a time when the Left was suffering some terrible defeats, politically, and when the successes of '68 were not even a dim memory for a new generation.

True, Foucault's works performed a very important corrective function through their focus on what Millington called the "norms of the network of power as they might function largely unconsciously and unproblematically" (Millington 73), which meant, amongst other things, that the liberal preoccupation with textual unity had gone. But by the time Foucault was taken up by British Hispanists, he had abandoned the structuralism of *The Order of Things* for the localized operations of Power in *Discipline and Punish*. This transition masks another: from what Archer terms downwards conflation to a correspondingly vivid illustration of its upward counterpart. In the process, the notion of a structural unconscious slipped from view. Post-structuralist voluntarism met no resistance from the "New Hispanisms," which lacked the intellectual resources seriously to evaluate it and had every reason to collude with it. In their anxiety to focus on "power-structure" in terms of gender, and to avoid analysis based on class, younger academics followed Foucault in effectively emptying power of any real political content. What Millington described as a "more resisting reading" was always possible, but, once it succeeded, such a reading, like knowledge itself, allegedly ran the danger of being transformed into power. One consequence, at least within the bounds of British Hispanism, was a growing sense of pessimism and passivity. Another was that postmodern dissidence proved to be a short-cut from classical liberalism, which included Parkerian individualism, to a celebration of consumerism and middle-class life-styles.

And so, after the brief interlude of competitive contradiction, during the late 1980s and early 90s, British Hispanism had once again resumed the same orderly relations, at the S-C level, that it had exhibited in the 1960s and 70s. Indeed there were signs of a new orthodoxy at the CS level as Hispanists began to congratulate themselves that the changes necessary to up-date the discipline had in effect been made. Thus, Adam Sharman was reasonably able to claim that Barry Jordan's spirited manifesto for future change, dating from an earlier period, "is itself already historical since the challenge has, in practice and in diverse institutions, already begun" (Sharman 284). Traditionalists were not slow to pick up on the concealed conservatism and to turn it to their own advantage: post-structuralism and deconstruction had simply served to recharge lit. crit., they argued, and could now be dispensed with. Thus, Ruano de la Haza, still plying his positivist trade and bemoaning the impact of "fashionable literary theory," lauds Catherine Larson when she allegedly "abandons the borrowed theoretical crutches and walks boldly into the text," as in the good old days (Ruano de la Haza 1993: 462). The implication that "theory" was simply a superficial overlay that could be peeled back, was wrong, but for once the traditionalist claim to have "seen it all before" was not entirely without foundation, as rather more progressive scholars were prepared to concede. Among the latter, Philip Swanson pointed to the continuities in British Hispanism, in the form of "old-fashioned intentionalism and what used to be called 'common sense'," continuities that the otherwise "impressive if eclectic" range of references barely served to hide (Swanson 222).

We do not have the space to explore the development of feminism within British Hispanism. Suffice it to note that it corresponds in its broad outlines with the trajectory that we have traced above. Even as they celebrated the "birth" of the Association of Great Britain and North Ireland, D. J. Gifford and L. L. Brooks failed to notice the singular absence of women. The paternalistic, finger-wagging morality of Parkerian Hispanism, it has to be said, was scarcely conducive to the cultivation of feminine values, but then again, as the interventions of Dorothy Severin and Margaret Wilson have amply illustrated over the years, one doesn't have to be a man to be a positivist or empiricist. When women's studies appeared in British Hispanism, as they gradually did, the logic of contingent complementarity was so compelling that they assumed a very conservative guise. Competitive contradiction had its moments, notably through the work of Jo Labanyi and others, but it proved on the whole to be a relatively tame affair. Nobody stepped forward to take on the patriarchal Establishment. By the time that the *Bulletin* dedicated a special edition to the Issues of Gender and Women, in 1995, the moment had gone, and the dominant dynamics assumed a complementary form.

But if from an ideological point of view, the changes were cosmetic, their cumulative impact was considerable. History slipped from view and with it the study of pre-capitalist societies. Attention began to focus exclusively upon modernity and even postmodernity, otherwise the cultural face of a globalizing capitalism. Naturally, the moment arrived when the new configuration needed to be formalized within the academy. This was the moment of Cultural Studies.

The Advent of Cultural Studies

Cultural Studies, in its beginnings in the Birmingham group, had been a political project, and indeed a Marxist project, pursued in accordance with the principle of competitive contradiction. By the 1990s, the discipline had disconnected from these historical roots and was actively promoting itself as some kind of substitute for Marxism, in complementary terms. In the process, as Michael Sprinker has perceptively noted, it "mutated from its original condition of limited but real resistance to the relations of domination in capitalist society, into one of the instruments by which those relations are, subtly but powerfully, reproduced" (Sprinker 392). One of the advantages that British Hispanism always offers the historian of culture is that it allows her to observe cultural processes on a small scale, almost, as it were, in laboratory conditions, their configurations thrown into relief by the sheer weight of the discipline's cultural conservatism. This was never more clearly demonstrated that by the repercussions, within Hispanism, of the transformations described by Sprinker. Let us consider them in their broad outlines.

It was always to be feared that Cultural Studies would assume insufficiently political and critical forms, once incorporated into a discipline such as British Hispanism, with its long tradition of Catholic conservatism and anti-Marxism. Recent developments, notably the publication of a standard text, *Hispanic Cultural Studies: An Introduction* (Graham and Labanyi), have proved these fears to be more than justified. The effect of this volume is decisively to inflect Cultural Studies to the Right. In evidence throughout is the crudest kind of idealism, which places an autonomous human being at the center of historical explanation and conceptualizes history from the perspective of the consciousness and practice of individuals. Thus, Spain's "barbaric individualism" is deemed by Rosa Montero to be "ingrained" in the Spaniard's "mentality." She proceeds along frankly populist lines: "The day before yesterday we were poor and now we are not" (Montero [i]: 319). But, seemingly, "we are learning tolerance," and are to be encouraged by the fact that Spanish women novelists have "conquered the market as well as their creative freedom" (Montero [ii]: 384). This kind of triviality scarcely calls for comment, except to point out that, in intellectual terms, it bears no comparison with earlier forms of cultural commentary available in Spain. Whatever one may personally think of the conservative tradition embodied, for example, in Ortega y Gasset, it *was* cultural criticism, and it is *there*, as a standard for comparison.

Of course, the contributions to the Anthology are uneven in form and content, and raise interesting theoretical problems concerning their "flow." The more sophisticated contributors are certainly aware of the political dangers of the irreducibility of the particular, insisted upon by postmodernism, and of the preoccupation with plural cultures "at play." But this very unevenness symptomatizes the dominance of contingent complementarity, as a unifying principle. References to the "working class," "capital," the "exchange value of the market," etc. lend a left-sounding nuance to the volume, but have been pillaged from other sources, dominantly Marxist, and are nowhere justified in terms of explicit economic and political theory. The result, in Archer's terms, is a *central conflation*, in which, by implication, structures exist as virtual realities, that are lent ontological status only through the actions of individuals. I say "by implication," since these exponents of contingent complementarity never aspire to political and sociological theory but content themselves with curiously oblique, parenthesized gestures in that direction: "In terms of prevailing political and social attitudes (dominant ideology/culture), then, Spain is ..." (Graham and Labanyi 417). Hence the disturbingly familiar feel of the "survey mode" that dominates in *Hispanic Cultural Studies*. Cultural theory made simple, as it were.

Needless to say, the Left proper is given no space. We would need to go elsewhere for a critique of Santiago Carrillo's brand of Eurocommunism and the failings of orthodox Stalinism in Spain. The force of this critique rests not, as one contributor believes, on the claim that "Franco had foreseen and paved the way for the transition" (Borja de Riquer I Permanyer 270), but on the scandal, from the standpoint of the Left, that this transition, through the active collusion of the Communist Party, found post-Franco Spain still in the hands of those who had run sections of the state machine under Franco (see Harman 336-37). Measured against these standards, the revisionist voices that are included in the Anthology, presumably on the grounds of their Leftish credentials, appear to be conservative in the extreme. Thus, Elías Díaz: "Against this rampant and profoundly anti-social individualism, the new project of a Left alliance – in Spain as elsewhere – must be to champion an alternative positive 'freedom,' defined by policies that shift the balance of social and economic power, improving the lot of the majority" (Díaz 285). Such centrists are no longer attacking "capitalism," in the name of a global working class, now numerically more massive than at any point in its history. Socialism is as absent from Díaz's agenda as it is from those so-called socialist parties that have masterminded the acceptance of neo-liberalism in Europe. True, Díaz promotes "the enhancement of participatory, representative democracy" (290), but central to any Leftist politics worthy of the name is precisely the distinction between substantive (participatory) and formal (representative) freedoms.

In sum, one feels, along with Michael Sprinker, that Culturalists have not sufficiently pondered the theoretical consequences of their dominant emphasis on the artifacts of mass-consumption societies, an emphasis that "effectively blocks a more comprehensive, historically differentiated theorization of culture" (Sprinker 390). Given its belated entry into modernity, Spanish culture is particularly vulnerable to what Sprinker refers to as the "irreducible presentism" of Cultural Studies. As what used to be called medieval and Golden Age studies, not to mention the legacies of the 18th and even 19th centuries, are lost from view, so also is the knowledge that, in other historical periods, culture occupied a very different position in the hierarchy of social practices. Thus, when cultural theorists do deign to investigate earlier periods, they do not fail to discover what Richard Pym recently discovered in Calderón, namely literary texts with "a peculiar relevance for the modern world" (Pym 275). Unfortunately, it is a discovery made possible by superimposing the fragmented subject of post-modernity upon a resurgent feudal substantialism, penetrated by an early form of bourgeois ideology, namely animism. One important lesson that cultural studies has to learn is that, while culture is definitely a social phenomenon, "it is equally – and just as a consequence of its sociality – a historical phenomenon" (Sprinker 390).

Conclusion

The limitations under which British Hispanism has labored, to the extent of defining what can and cannot be said or thought within the discipline, are determined by a system of social relations that permeate the entire social fabric. Of course, within this system, the existence of individualities needs to be recognized, and theorized, but in ways that do not lead to their conflation, at other levels, with their status as members of collective agencies. A sufficiently stratified view of humanity must also distinguish historically and geographically located aspects of our humanity from others that fall within the domain of our "species being," and, above all, recognize the function of an ideological unconscious. For, in the last instance, the source of empiricism's hegemony lies not in the attitudes of individuals qua individuals but in the way they are socialized in their homes – where women are expected to do the lion's share of the housework – and educated at schools – where the mass of the population is prepared to work for the small minority of the population who own the productive forces. At this level, contingent complementarity, as it operates within the Academy, combines unconsciously with the political opportunism of New Labour – electoral success at any price. And for one very obvious reason: both are secreted from the same source, otherwise the dominant ideological matrix. Given the pervasive effects of this matrix, which gives capital the advantage of being taken for granted, it may seem an odd moment at which to raise the possibility of alternative social, or rather socialist, arrangements. Yet it is our belief and hope that the very process of globalization that brought about the demise of "actually existing socialism" will put democratic socialism back on the agenda, but this time at a higher socio-economic level, for the very important reason that any ideology that is compelled to speak about "democracy" and "freedom" is also compelled, by the logic of its argument, to confront their absence, at the level of existing relations of production. And when that moment occurs, British Hispanists will be forced also to confront the ways in which, heretofore, they have contributed to reproducing those relations and how, hereafter, they may assist in their overthrow.

7
Placing Changes

"Did you ever know Professor Parker?"

The question came from a small Scotsman who materialized beside me. The occasion was a social function at the home of the Vice-Chancellor of the University. I was standing alone on the terrace, sipping my rum and coke and gazing up at the huge Caribbean moon.

"I never actually met him. I saw him once at a conference, from a distance."

It was true. It must have been in the late 1960s, during a conference of Hispanists. At Exeter, I think. A senior colleague, alongside whom I was sitting, pointed to the figure of Parker in the audience, seated prominently near the front.

"He was a visiting professor at Kingston, you know. Ah, such a marvelous gentleman!"

I smiled knowingly. How ironic, I thought, that I should find myself, as it were, in Parker's shoes. What I was never to understand in Jamaica was that such ironies were lost on everyone else. For them, I was just another professor from the Motherland, whose only oddity was that he had passed through New Zealand on the way to Jamaica. Unable to see myself as others saw me – glowing pink and looking rich – the endless misrecognitions never ceased to catch me unawares.

But life in the "developing" nations has the capacity to remind people, in very material ways, of their *real* location. And so, some weeks later, I sat in the university police station, recovering from a mugging and making my statement to the sergeant on duty. He wrote slowly, as children do, with his tongue sticking out between his teeth. I sat waiting for him to finish each sentence. The cicadas were buzzing incessantly outside, the fan turned slowly on the ceiling, and the cuts on my chest were starting to smart from the sweat trickling down my neck. Suddenly, the door opened and my recent assailant was projected into the room, sprawling across the floor. The arresting officer entered after him, depositing certain belongings on the table – my money (including my identity card) and a knife. The sergeant put down his pen and smiled a cruel smile. The young man was struggling to his feet. He was rough and ragged, an obvious inhabitant of Kingston's poorest districts. His eyes flashed fear and defiance, like a cornered animal. But within a few minutes he had been stripped and stood facing the wall.

"Do you recognize him, Professor?"

Recognize him? Oh yes, oh yes! I recognized him. I recognized him only too well and in more than one way.

"... Professor?"

I nodded slowly, seeing everything as if in a dream world. The boy protested his innocence, at which point a full-blooded blow from the sergeant, across his kidneys, sent him crashing into the wall, whence he collapsed into a heap on the floor. Some minutes later, as I stumbled across the compound of the police station, towards the university, the screaming began again. At home, that evening, my thoughts turned towards my family back in New Zealand. I gradually began to gather my belongings together and prepare for my return, lacking even the will to continue until the end of the semester, and so work out my notice. It had, all told, been a massive failure.

One should never arrive at any city late at night, particularly from overseas, but central Kingston, ramshackle and run-down, appears particularly alien and impersonal at such hours. It was January 1987, and I had arrived from New Zealand, with my wife and two young children, to take up a personal Chair of Spanish, in the University of the West Indies. Our first impressions of the city were confirmed rather than dispelled by the accommodation to which we were taken – smaller than we had been promised, dirty and over-run with cockroaches and, in the toilet and bathroom, with the most alarmingly large slugs. Throughout what remained of the night, I lay awake in the darkness, listening to the chorus of barking dogs, echoing against the dome of the sky. Only as dawn came and the birds began to sing out did I finally drop off to sleep.

I have to smile now at my naïveté, when I recall those early days in Kingston. Take, for example, my visit to one of the local schools, where we were considering placing our elder son, who was approaching school age. As the headmistress was showing me round, I was overwhelmed by one single and central fact, namely the utter blackness of the mass of school children, where my son's would have been the only white face. Somehow I hadn't anticipated this situation, at least emotionally, nor the hidden prejudices to which my reaction gave expression. Would my son be able to cope? By his age, I had perforce acquired the proletarian resilience necessary to survive in comparable circumstances. But was anything to be gained by subjecting him to that kind of apprenticeship? Perhaps it might be "bad" for him. In the end, after debating the matter with my wife, a bourgeois protective instinct prevailed and my son ended up being sent to a private Montessori school, in the city, along with other expatriate and light-skinned children. Here, pupils were encouraged to explore their creativity and develop their humanity, within a cultural bubble, of the kind that only money could buy. It was the first of many such acts of compromise.

Of course, one went with the best intentions – "pommy" wingeing was particularly frowned upon in New Zealand – which explains why, in those first few days, I came to find myself in the Campus bank, queuing patiently – always so many queues! – and struggling quietly to contain my rage and frustration. Suddenly, the door burst open and in strode a white woman of overwhelming presence. Despite my only too brief familiarity with Jamaican society, I could immediately place her, socially, as one of the expat group. In the weeks that followed, I would grow accustomed, at social gatherings, to their wistful evocations of Jamaica as it once was, in the good old days. Speaking loudly, and in a BBC accent that one could have cut with a knife, the lady in question proceeded to tear a strip off all the clerks, including the manageress, whom she had summoned within a matter of seconds. Why were there no exchange rates available? It was midday, perhaps they had not realized, and the rates had been available in the newspaper for hours! It was always the same! When were they going to get their act together! etc. etc. I stood cringing, but was amazed to see everyone rushing around – I had not until this moment seen anyone rush in Jamaica – to attend to the lady's every need.

Unfortunately, or possibly fortunately, neither my wife nor myself had it within us to emulate such imperialist manners, and as a result we were constantly being taken advantage of. Take, for example, the question of domestic servants, upon the employment of whom, we were assured, the local economy depended. One elderly woman felt at liberty to steal quite brazenly from us, whereas a young girl, placed with us by a relative in the university, suddenly disappeared one day, leaving a very disconsolate note – she was apparently homesick for her village in the hills – but departing also with all our toilet paper and electric light bulbs. Well, I reflected stoically, wasn't the surplus value extracted by employers from employees always *stolen*? Hadn't generations of my forefathers equipped their homes with material stolen from British Railways? (The only item missing from one toilet well known to me was the sign prohibiting its use while the train was in a station.) But, … well, I mean to say, *toilet rolls*!

We only ran into further trouble when we decided to do away with the idea of domestic help and rent out the servant's room to the secretary of the French Department. Within two weeks, this allegedly "single woman" was accompanied by an infant daughter, and shortly afterwards had a boy friend in effect living with her. When I gave her notice, she suddenly began to insist on being called Mrs. **** instead of "Mary." I was not in England now, you know, and couldn't treat blacks like dirt, etc. upon which she gave me notice, in return, of her intention to remain. I left the matter with the university lawyers for the summer, while I was away in New Zealand, but on my return discovered that nothing had been done. I was advised, confidentially, to do what any Jamaican would have done at the beginning, namely take Mary by the scruff of the neck and throw her out, into the street, along with her child, her boyfriend and her belongings. But I solved the problem by moving out of the house myself – my family having remained in New Zealand – and leaving my unwanted tenant to her own devices. Sometime later, I learned that Mary had continued her devious practices. Amongst other things she ran up a bill on the Departmental phone, through private calls to a family member in Florida, of several thousand dollars. The university authorities were shocked to find, or so my sources informed me, that prosecution was impossible since there was no law again phone abuse. Clearly, Mary was a born lawyer.

One problem, which defied solution throughout my stay, can be stated quite succinctly: how to buy a car. A fairly simply operation no doubt, by First-World standards, but not so easy in Jamaica, at least at that time, and when you were on a Jamaican salary. Cars were not often imported, and when unexpectedly a boat-load of them arrived, they came with First-World price tags, unless they were Russian, in which case they were cheaper but notoriously unreliable. On more than one occasion, I would arrange for a friend to rush me out into the distant suburbs of Kingston where, I had heard, there was a suitably priced vehicle for sale. We would arrive, hot and bothered, only to discover that what was for sale was something that, until this point, I had only been accustomed to seeing abandoned in Maori backyards back in New Zealand.

If such practical difficulties had been the only difficulties, then the situation might have been salvageable, but they were not. There was simply no way in which intellectual work could be insulated against the ideological contradictions that surfaced on a daily basis outside the academy. Of course, impressive barriers had been raised – the campus was literally ringed by a barbed-wire fence – with the aim of allowing the work of the mind to proceed unencumbered by material exigencies. But there were many occasions when those exigencies pressed ineluctably for consideration. In this respect, one particular incident comes to mind. While on my way to the university one day, I passed a recumbent figure in the street, attended by a woman who, seemingly, like myself, just happened to be passing by. One too many! I joked. The woman shook her head. Not drunk, simply starving. Look at his glassy eyes. Well, as fate would have it, on that particular day I had scheduled a seminar on Calderonian tragedy, which I joined while still flustered by my recent encounter. Only gradually did I come to my senses, enough to realize that I was being regaled with the purest Parkerian orthodoxy, which aimed to limit tragedy to the fall of kings and queens, and to locate its source in the responsibility of the individual. But if what I had just witnessed in the street outside was not a tragedy, what exactly was it?

That evening I sat at the bar of the university club, quietly turning over Parker's ideas further. By implication, the poor were actually *sinful*, and could overcome their condition by the exercise of free will and moral fortitude. Now as an undergraduate in Britain, I had always "known" that this was wrong, that there is a class bias built into liberal notions of the "death of tragedy," but I always lacked the necessary conviction to step forward and proclaim the absence of the emperor's clothes. Anyway, in Britain, in the 1960s and 70s, "poverty" had sufficiently retreated from the public sphere to allow one to worship at the altar of Culture with an easy conscience. In Jamaica, in the 1980s, this indulgence came at a price. How could one "love" Literature when people were quietly starving to death in the streets? How could one legitimately lay claim to the social wealth necessary to foster the Humanities when it meant the denial of basic human dignity to the majority? Perhaps this had always been so, even in the First World, but in Jamaica the realities of exclusion had to be confronted routinely. Where precisely lay the difference between literary critics and those barking dogs that were let out at nightfall to patrol the perimeter fences of private property?

While this soul searching was proceeding, I struggled to keep my family financially afloat, in the life-style to which they were accustomed. Amongst other things this involved receiving the income-tax breaks to which I was entitled as a *British* subject and foreign resident – or at least so I had been assured upon my appointment – and failing which our financial situation was barely viable. When a technicality arose that threatened to disqualify me from the relevant exemptions – I had actually been recruited from *New Zealand* – I found myself hastening down to the Inland Revenue in the center of Kingston to press my claims, and while less aggressive in my approach to the appropriate officials than the ex-pat lady in the bank, I was forceful enough to get the desired results. I found myself constantly caught in this kind of situation, which involved laying claim to what was, in the context of a poor country, a large slice of the social pie. Life was indeed a struggle, but a struggle to maintain what was a manifestly bourgeois life-style. To give another example, I was constantly to be found jostling with patients in the waiting rooms of the University Medical Centre, to arrange exchange deals with newly arrived medics, all of whom came laden with pounds sterling. It did not escape my attention that the other people in attendance had basic health concerns – the incidence of sickle-cell anemia was quite striking – at the side of which my own problems, large as they sometimes seemed, paled to insignificance.

How did one live the ideological contradictions academically? Quite simply, one lived them indirectly. Let me explain with reference to the Freudian notion of "anality," which I was currently developing and which was to figure prominently in my next book, *Visions in Exile*. Doubtless a preoccupation with "filth" was ultimately rooted in my experience of working-class life, and was always intended to scandalize the bourgeois academy. A materialist reading of Freud certainly pre-dates my arrival in Jamaica, as even a perfunctory glance at *The Birth and Death of Language* will reveal. If petty-bourgeois critics were so preoccupied with the Spirit, then I would confront them with the reality of the Body, or so at least I reasoned. Having said which, there is no doubt in my own mind that an encounter with Third-World culture rekindled within me a class consciousness that had been repressed for many years. This radicalization explains the importance attached to anality in my work, at a time when literary psychoanalysis, in the First World, was undergoing a Lacanian turn, which enabled critics to talk less about the material body and more about language.

Anality, then, enabled me to thematize issues that particularly confronted someone working within a Third-World academy. But what became increasingly obvious, as I pondered social reality in Jamaica, was that my concept of anality was framed very much in ahistorical and asocial terms. Indeed, the theoretical apparatus by which it was sustained was not indebted to Marx but to the existential psychoanalytic school associated with Norman Brown and Ernest Becker. In other words, there was an inescapably idealist dimension to my materialism, which is what I mean when I say that contradictions in Jamaica were lived "indirectly". One way of resolving the aporia was through a strategy of containment that consisted of superimposing, almost literally, onto the original version of *Visions in Exile* passages that suggested links between the psychical and the social. But the result, it has to be said, was very much a patched-up job, in that, theoretically, the passages in question remained an excrescence attached to the body of the text. Clearly, a serious encounter with Marx awaited me at some point.

I derived little of lasting intellectual value from my academic contact with other scholars in Jamaica, at least within the Humanities, although my sense was that some interesting work was being done in linguistics. At ground level, individuals were the product of very different backgrounds and conditions: while some – the more privileged – had degrees from British and North-American institutions, others had been educated locally, in the Third-World academy, whereas many, perhaps most, fell astride this division, in varying degrees. In spite of which, the majority were emphatically bourgeois in their beliefs and values, subject to relatively minor adjustments by way of accommodation to Third-World conditions. Much the same applied to the students, most of whom, if they could have afforded it, would have been away at foreign universities. The impression I gained of foreign scholars at the university was likewise discouraging, namely that, generally speaking, they were there because they had been unable to gain access to tertiary institutions at home, and now found themselves stuck on the outside track of the global academy, with little hope of getting back to the center. But even here there were exceptions, notably the odd individual who had married into Jamaican society.

And so I limped back to New Zealand to join my family, and to face the prospect of possibly two years' unemployment before I could resume the academic position that I had vacated at the University of Auckland. My life continued gradually to fall apart: quite suddenly, one could count one's friends on the fingers of one hand, whilst former colleagues shrank away in embarrassment and avoided social contact. The realities of professional individualism were driven home as never before. To make matters worse, I had never actually done a teacher's training course, so there was little possibility of finding employment in schools. Naturally, I was anxious to keep my research going, both to be ready to resume lecturing and also to work through the ferment of ideas provoked by my experience in Jamaica. But as anyone knows who has been unemployed, it is not a condition that can be lived in tranquillity. Being a professional actually made matters worse in that I became the special target of sadistic officials in the Social Welfare Department. There were no depths of pettiness to which the latter would not sink. On one occasion, for example, they curtailed my unemployment benefit on discovering that I had been for an interview for a Chair in Australia, presumably on the principle that I was to be penalized both for attempting and not attempting to find gainful employment.

Fortunately, after six months I returned to the University on a part-time basis, and after a year, was back on full-time. But as so often happens in life, it was not possible to "go home again." At first, I attributed the change to the professional damage inevitably caused by my premature return from Jamaica and to my general state of mental and emotional exhaustion. But it soon became clear that key institutional changes had also taken place during my absence. Of course, the academic situation in New Zealand had always been far from ideal, even during an exchange visit that I made, in 1977-78, and again, when I returned permanently to Auckland in 1980. Most scholars were, with some notable exceptions, more conservative and benighted than their British counterparts – indeed, not a few were deeply mediocre rejects of the mother country, who had used the former colony as a means of moving from secondary to tertiary education. But the simple remoteness and smallness of New Zealand meant, in those early days, that if one possessed sufficient internal resources to offset the negative effects of isolation, there were opportunities to be exploited, in terms of the relative freedom from professional peer pressure. On my return "down under," after the Jamaica debacle, I found that these opportunities no longer existed, at least, to the same extent, as a result of which it was becoming increasingly difficult to sustain the idea of "critique": negativity was giving way to positivity, as embodied in the celebration of the market. The ensuing contradictions were lived daily, but no attempt was made to resolve them theoretically.

Still, I settled down to the task of making the most of a bad job. Gradually, I began actively to retrieve the socialist legacy that had lain relatively dormant for many years. Relatively in that I was always poised to make a left turn, even during the 1970s, during which time I was systematically exploring the liberal tradition. Indeed, just before leaving for Jamaica, I had become acquainted with the work of Juan Carlos Rodríguez, a Spanish Marxist of vaguely Althusserian extraction, and its impact had been immediate, even devastating. After having read the second section of *Teoría e historia*, I became aware that much of my own work was irreparably contaminated by idealism, and needed to be radically reconfigured if not jettisoned in its entirety. Once back in New Zealand, and with *Visions in Exile* behind me (although its publication was delayed for several years), I turned to Rodríguez's work with a vengeance.

At the time – this was the late 1980s – Marxism was entering into another of its crises, but this hardly deterred me. The older people who were abandoning it were precisely the young Leftists that I had first met on arriving at University in the 1960s. Even then, I had not trusted them, not simply because at the time I was more interested in distancing myself from the working class than affirming my connections with it, but because I could see that, in any event, such petty-bourgeois idealists would not hesitate to abandon the socialist ground once the political tide really turned. And so it transpired: effortlessly, painlessly, they would relinquish Marx to take on board Foucault and Derrida, and the other post-structuralist and postmodernist gurus. They were joined by younger academics, who had only ever known socialism in a period of defeat and political downturn.

The first task was to come up with some materialist paradigm for understanding the development of Hispanism as a discipline. In this respect, I was ideally placed: within the small New Zealand academy, it was possible to analyze, as in some geological cross section, the sedimented layers of successive ideologies, as these had built up over the years. At the bottom, geologically speaking (although on top, professionally) were senior lecturers who could still boast some connection, through their teachers, with the earliest period in British Hispanism, which had been dominated by Allison Peers. These were followed by lecturers such as myself, who, while they had absorbed something of the same tradition (in my case from John Metford at Bristol), were more the product of the school of Parker, which had largely replaced the earlier tradition. In the meantime, a younger generation of scholars had arrived who were in the process of transforming themselves into academic entrepreneurs. "Literature" was still worshipped but, particularly when it came in pre-modern forms, with a growing sense of nostalgia, as something that had to be given away, if the profession was to survive. A commitment to language teaching, to raise enrolment (at any price), and to professional translation became the order of the day, combined, by way of preserving some sense of intellectual respectability, with versions of feminism and post-structuralism. The result, all told, was a heady ideological mix in which personal animosities festered, to the detriment of any sense of community. In practice, the department at Auckland became disfunctional.

In many respects these changes paralleled broader movements at the national level, in politics and the economy. New Zealand, it will be recalled, was used as a laboratory in which to test neo-liberalism or "Rogernomics," as it was known locally, after the Labour Minister that first promoted it. A Labour minister, note! The message to be learned by the Western World was that neo-liberalism proved far more palatable for the population at large when imposed by supposedly Left-wing governments. The New Zealand experiment was notable for the seeming inability of Left-wing groups to mount any effective resistance to the neo-liberal onslaught – the unions, in particular, folded under pressure. Needless to say, it was these broader social changes, impinging upon the academy, which I had registered upon my return from Jamaica.

The parallel between the Academy and the Nation is anything but contrived on my part: on the contrary, the government of the day was "consciously" engaged in working the interconnections. I vividly recall a Modern-Language conference held at Hamilton, in the late 1980s, at which a Wellington spokesperson gave a talk outlining the semantic shift being engineered by the government, as a point of policy, from a vocabulary of "care" to one of "efficiency." I recall also the bemused silence with which he was greeted by literature "specialists," who seemed not to realize that their key ideology of "sensibility," which had formerly sustained critical practice, was under threat. Not for the first time, I was struck by the intellectual limitations of so-called "critical" intellectuals within the Humanities. As for the language specialists, within the same departments, their mind-set was means-directed: the critical assessment of ends never posed itself as an issue for debate.

Just as neo-liberal ideology displaced older notions of the welfare state, so also, at the academic level, the proponents of a new "technicist" ideology, rooted in the electronic media, quickly overran the staunch defenders of "culture." And just as the imposition of neo-liberalism corresponded with a deterioration in conditions in the work-place, so, within the academy, class sizes increased and lecturers found themselves with more "contact" hours, although never to the level that I had experienced in Jamaica. This increase was associated largely with the promotion of language teaching. Incredibly, the goal seemed to be that of providing all-round immersion for language students. Little attention was given to the problems of fostering some level of sophistication in cultural analysis through the medium of "basic" Spanish. Necessarily, Hispanism remained theoretically parasitic upon such departments as English, where the vocational bias was less marked and therefore where theoretical speculation assumed a more sophisticated form.

I adjusted my own working practices accordingly. What energy I had was poured into my research. I led a very isolated existence within the university, as I slowly turned over my thoughts and worked towards a new book. Much of my reading was done in the quiet corner of a coffee bar, away from the Department. What intellectual stimulation I required I sought and found outside the university, in left-wing, working-class gatherings, invariably with Troskyist connections. Here, however, my participation was largely passive: I sat and watched, no longer trustful of my proletarian instincts, at a time when the Yeltsin coup was being hotly debated by contending groups. Academically, the work of Rodríguez remained the fulcrum around which my ideas turned. I was determined to break with the post-structuralist pluralism that was in the process of displacing the liberal pluralism that had characterized New Criticism. Part of my frustration was the sense of not being sufficiently well prepared in basic philosophy to do the kind of work that I wanted, and the realization that, in the absence of such a preparation, I would remain an unconscious Kantian, an unconscious Hegelian, etc. "Theory" courses at this time, such as those given by the English Department, ranged far and wide, but always, seemingly, at one remove from the real primary sources.

Throughout this period, I avoided administration as far as this was possible. Given the heavy language-teaching load and the kind of research that I was doing, there was simply no choice. Heads of sections and departments were increasingly envisaged as managers, in the entrepreneurial sense, just as universities were increasingly promoted as factories, which train technicians. Deans were requesting "visibility," as opposed to intellectual leadership, along with the promotion of the university in the media and "society at large." Language departments responded by literally assuming the appearance of travel agents, notably on the occasion of "open days." In such circumstances, "cultural" courses began to function as light-weight, travellers' guides to Spain, alongside language classes that were increasingly slanted towards commercial Spanish. Corresponding adjustments were made to appointment procedures. As the classically liberal notions of "intellectual excellence," "freedom of the mind," the "quest for truth," etc. slipped from view, it became possible to promote candidates on the basis of very little, when judged in the light of earlier criteria – "publications," "international reputation," etc. All that was required was that people knew how to "sell" themselves. Slowly it dawned upon me that it was time to leave, but this time not to another marginalized academy, but back to center, now armed with the intellectual tools that I had refined over the years. And thus it was that I moved to the State University of New York at Stony Brook.

I went on ahead of my family, to establish a kind of advance base. Of course, Long Island was not to be compared with Jamaica, and posed nothing like the same material problems, as I was the first to appreciate as I took up residence in a pleasant house in a wooded area not far from the University. But there were settling-in problems nevertheless. As the Chair of a relatively large department, I was overwhelmed by the unfamiliar practices of the North-American academy, organized along totally different lines from the one to which I was accustomed. What were "qualifying exams," "comprehensive exams," "practica," etc.? Predictably, misunderstandings occurred on a daily basis. For example, I could not quite understand why the Department was consumed with panic when, after several weeks, I called a "staff meeting," until, that is, I realized that what I intended to call was a "faculty meeting." The bewildered professional faculty clearly thought that this closet Marxist was intending to have the secretaries and even cleaning staff participate in debate. Some days, in a state of stunned bewilderment, I would abandon the Department to wander round the campus, enjoying the late Autumn sunshine and waiting for my pulse rate to return to normal.

Eagerly, I awaited the arrival of my family. How I remember now the joyful faces of my three boys when they appeared at the airport exit! I watched anxiously as their own settling-in process began. Things seemed to go as smoothly as could be expected. Friends and colleagues were extremely supportive and there was much that was new and exciting for every member of the family. Take the weather, for instance. Neither my children nor my wife had really experienced snow before, and by chance the winter of 1993 was a brutally cold. As soon as the first flakes began to fall, they were outside with their cameras. I gently suggested that they should wait for an hour or two. That evening, by which time the snow was deep on the ground and the children were safely in bed, my wife and I went out into the street and played at rolling down the hill. It was one of those carefree moments the memory of which I continue to treasure.

Naturally, each family member experienced settling-in problems of some kind, and my wife was ominously critical of every aspect of North-American life. North-American culture can be hard and abrasive to anyone accustomed to a more organic, community life-style. I recall on one occasion, quite early on, going to pick up one of my sons from school, to save him the trip home by bus. In his confusion, he had stood in the wrong bus queue and, at the moment of my arrival, was being confronted by one of the teachers, who was abusing him in the manner of the proverbial German fishwife. From a distance, I could sense that he was completely overwhelmed and terrified. The teacher, on catching sight of me, lowered her voice immediately, and blushed deeply. I asked her if, even as an adult, she had ever been lost in a foreign culture, and if so, could she possibly imagine what it must feel like for a child. She laughed nervously, seeming not to understand the question.

If I sympathized with my son, it was because I continued to experience problems of my own. Things would have been easier had my arrival in New York not coincided with a budget blow-out and corresponding cuts at university level, which meant that I was sucked into the whole game of academic politics and the defense of turf. In such a situation, it became very difficult to sustain an on-going research programme. At first, I was not particularly perturbed. My initiation into American academic politics would, I guessed, be one way of overcoming the marginalization that I had experienced in New Zealand. But this marginalization, I discovered, ran deeper than I realized, in that it was bound up with a habitus that pervaded every aspect of my being. The truth is that I remained, at heart, a working-class boy, who feared being "shown up" in public. This same fear explains why, even after its embourgeoisement, my family still found dining out in a restaurant something of an ordeal. Always the obsession with "how to go on." Over the years, this layer of my being has been obscured by a certain sophistication, just as my northern English accent, while easily discernible to an English ear, has been softened and smoothed over, with only the hard vowels remaining. But a basic uncertainty and timidity, even vulnerability, remained, and never more so than at the "Chairs meetings" that I was obliged to attend on a regular basis.

Fortunately, in North America I was afforded a measure of protection by the very cultural barriers that I was otherwise engaged in overcoming. "Oh, I so like your English accent!", I would be told repeatedly over the phone. And gleefully I would enter into the spirit of the masquerade. But this American blindness to indices of class status has its drawbacks, as was brought home to me recently on the occasion of a university meeting, called in connection with "equality of opportunity." (The policy of the Administration is routinely to monitor departments in which appointments are pending, with an aim to maintaining proper ratios.) Impishly, I raised the question of class-based inequalities. Such meetings, I well knew, focus only on issues of race and gender, which are the only ones that speak to the condition of middle-class American feminists and Afro-Americans, and I was scarcely surprised to receive looks of blank incomprehension from the other committee members. But feeling in a stubborn frame of mind, I proceeded to press my claims. Other things being equal, should decision procedures in appointments be slanted in favor of a middle-class woman or a working-class male? When you think about it, the question cries out for serious discussion. Why the preoccupation with gender if the students to be taught are Hispanic kids from the back-streets of New York, and within a public institution to boot? Why the preference, in such circumstances, for a Latina of a privileged class and the product of private education? Is she not bound to feel a natural antipathy towards the very Latino students for whom she is supposed to function as some kind of role model?

Nor does the relevance of such issues cease at the tertiary level. I have discovered, for example, that graduate students from Latin America are more disposed to enter into the discussion of gender and race, as opposed to class, and for very obvious reasons. After all, such students have come to the North-American academy basically to carve out academic careers for themselves, and in the mad scramble for academic positions, their interests are best served by the foregrounding of gender and ethnicity. There is no comparable tactical leverage to be derived from the focus upon class, an area which finds them already relatively privileged. To some extent, this logic operates unconsciously: students do not see class as an issue because they are not disadvantaged at this point in their everyday lives. But conscious opportunism is a factor not to be entirely discounted. The American academy, it bears reminding ourselves, is very much a market, determined by the interplay of vested interests and opportunity costs, and success goes to those who know how to play it.

And yet I have lingered in America, although alone – my family long since gave up the cultural struggle and returned to New Zealand. I will leave it to others to ponder my motives. Here as elsewhere conscious and unconscious forces doubtless enter into play. For my own part, I continue to value the lack of snobbishness that dogged me in English society, which is not to say, of course, that America is not a profoundly class-ridden society. Secondly, it has provided me with the space and freedom to do the kind of work that I would have been unable to do elsewhere. And thirdly, and most importantly, I am firmly persuaded that the future, for socialism, lies beyond America, and can only be reached, if it is possible to reach it at all, by blasting one's way through the core of American culture and society, and coming out the other side. To this extent, America is a constant reminder to me of the impossibility of ever returning to what preceded capitalism.

Of course, I am sometimes nostalgic for the working-class communities in which I was raised, for the sense of community and simple social security that they provided. While I cannot at this moment remember my car registration or telephone number or, to the intense amusement of Americans, my social security number, my old Co-op number – 1036 – is carved upon my mind. Part of such nostalgia is the regressive yearning to return, and on one or two occasions, in the grip of some obscure impulse or Freudian death drive, I have even gone as far as to solicit university Chairs in the UK. Invitations to attend for interview have followed – although significantly withheld by Bristol University – and gratefully accepted. But on such occasions old animosities have resurfaced, as university bureaucrats have eyed me suspiciously across their board-room tables, and at some key moment during the interviewing process ("Now Professor Read, about this Marxism ..."), my compulsion to self-destruct has been totally overwhelming. For, in truth, where would be the logic in "succeeding," after having come so far, when the opportunity is there to "fail," and to keep failing, until the blessed end?

Bibliography

Aguirre, J. M. 1976. "Apostillas a 'El somnambulismo de Federico García Lorca'." *BHS* 53:127-32.

Althusser, Louis. 1971. *Lenin and Philosophy and Other Essays*. Trans. Ben Brewster. New York: NLB.

Apple, Michael W. (ed.). 1982. *Cultural and Economic Reproduction in Education*. London: Routledge & Kegan Paul.

Archer, Margaret S. 1995. *Realist Social Theory: The Morphogenetic Approach*. Cambridge: Cambridge U.P.

-----. 1996. *Culture and Agency: The Place of Culture in Social Theory*, rev. ed. Cambridge: Cambridge U.P.

-----. 2000. *Being Human: The Problem of Agency*. Cambridge: Cambridge U.P.

Aricó, José. 1982. *Marx y América Latina*. 2nd ed. Lima: Alianza Editorial Mexicana.

Atkinson, William. 1923. "Why Learn Spanish?" *BHS* 1: 74-75.

Baldick, Chris. 1983. *The Social Mission of English Criticism: 1848-1932*. Oxford: Clarendon Press.

Becker, Ernest. 1973. *The Denial of Death*. New York: Macmillan.

Bell, Aubrey F.G. 1926. "An Arias Montano Pilgrimage." *BHS* 3: 170-73.

-----. 1933. "Liberty in Sixteenth-Century Spain." *BHS* 10: 164-79.

-----. 1936. "The Genius of Spain." *BHS* 13: 4-13.

-----. 1944. "Spain from Without." *BHS* 21: 73-79.

-----. 1946. Review of Allison Peers' *St. John of the Cross*. *BHS* 23: 282-85.

Benn, Caroline and Clyde Chitty. 1997. *Thirty Years On: Is Comprehensive Education Alive and Well or Struggling to Survive?* Harmondsworth: Penguin Books.

Bergmann, Emilie L., and Paul Julian Smith (eds). 1995. *¿Entiendes? Queer Readings, Hispanic Writings*. Durham: Duke U.P.

Beverley, John. 1996. "A little azúcar: una conversación sobre Estudios Culturales", *Siglo XX/20th Century* 14, 1-2:15-35.

Bhaskar, Roy. 1978. *A Realist Theory of Science*. Hemel Hempstead: Harvester Wheatsheaf.

-----. 1986. *Scientific Realism and Human Emancipation*. London: Verso.

-----. 1989 (1979). *The Possibility of Naturalism: A Philosophical Critique of the Contemporary Human Sciences*. 2nd ed. New York: Harvester Wheatsheaf

Boland, Roy. C., and Alun Kenwood. 1989. "Hispanism in Australia and New Zealand." *Monographic Review/ Revista monográfica* 5:14-23.

Borja de Riquer I Permanyer. 1995. "Social and economic change in a climate of political immobilism" in Graham and Labanyi. 259-71.

Bourdieu, Pierre. 1984. *Distinction: A Social Critique of the Judgement of Taste*. Trans. Richard Rice. Cambridge, Massachusetts: Harvard U.P.

Bowles, Samuel, and Herbert Gintis. 1977. "Capitalism and Education in the United States." See Young and Whitty. 192-227.

Brantlinger, Patrick.1990. *Crusoe's Footprints: Cultural Studies in Britain and America*. New York: Routledge.

Brown, Norman O. 1968. *Life against Death: The Psychoanalytical Meaning of History*. London: Sphere Books.

Brenan, Gerald. 1965. *The Face of Spain*. Harmondsworth: Penguin Books.

Brooker, Peter and Peter Humm. (eds). 1989. *Dialogue and Difference: English Now and For the Nineties*. London: Routledge.

Callinicos, Alex. 1987. *Making History: Agency, Structure and Change in Social Theory*. Cambridge: Polity Press.

-----. 1991. *The Revenge of History: Marxism and the East European Revolutions*. Cambridge: Polity Press.

-----. 1995. *Theories and Narratives: Reflections on the Philosophy of History*. Durham, North Carolina: Duke U.P.

-----, and Chris Harman. 1987. *The Changing Working Class: Essays on Class Structure Today*. London: Bookmarks.

Carnoy, Martin. 1982. "Education, Economy and the State." See Apple. (ed.). 79-126.

Chomsky, Noam. 1966. *Cartesian Linguistics: A Chapter in the History of Rationalist Thought*. New York: Harper & Row.

-----. 1972. *Language and Mind*. Enlarged edition. New York: Harcourt, Brace Jovanovich.

Coffey, Mary. 1998. "Spanish Cultural Studies in the undergraduate classroom." *Arizona Journal of Hispanic Cultural Studies* 3:251-67.

Creaven, Sean. 1988. *Marxism and Realism: A Materialistic Application of Realism in the Social Sciences*. London and New York: Routledge.

Cruickshank, Don. 1975. Review of Edwin Honig, *Calderón and the Seizures of Honor BHS* 52:167-68.

Dale, Roger. 1982. "Education and the Capitalist State: Contributions and Contradictions." See Apple. (ed). 127-61.

Díaz, Elías. 1995. "The Left and the legacy of Francoism: political culture in opposition and transition" in Graham and Labanyi. 283-91.

Diworkin, Dennis. 1997. *Cultural Studies in Postwar Britain: History, the New Left, and the Origins of Cultural Studies*. Durham, North Carolina: Duke U.P.

Dunn, Peter N. 1990. "A Post-Modern Approach to the Spanish Renaissance: Paul Julian Smith on Literature and Literary Theory of the Golden Age." *BHS* 67: 165-75.

During, Simon (ed.). 1993. *The Cultural Studies Reader*. London and New York: Routledge.

Edwards, Gwynne. 1975. Review of P. Halkoree, *Calderón de la Barca: "El alcalde de Zalamea,"* *BHS* 52:168-69.

Evans, Peter. 1987. Review of *Hacia Calderón. Séptimo Coloquio anglogermano, BHS* 64:372-73.

-----. (ed.). 1990. *Conflicts of Discourse: Spanish Literature in the Golden Age*. Manchester: Manchester U.P.

Feal Deibe, Carlos. 1977. "García Lorca y el psicoanálisis. Apostillas a unas apostillas," *BHS* 54:311-14.

Fekete, John. 1977. *The Critical Twilight: Explorations in the Ideology of Anglo-American Literary Theory from Eliot to McLuhan*. London: Routledge & Kegan Paul.

Field, Nicola. 1995. *Over the Rainbow: Money, Class, and Homophoba*. London: Pluto Press.

Frow, John. 1986. *Marxism and Literary History*. Cambridge, Massachusetts: Harvard U.P.

Gallagher, P. 1974. Review of J. Rodríguez-Puértolas, *De la Edad Media a la edad conflictiva, BHS* 51:373-75.

Giddens, Anthony. 1973. *Class Structure of the Advanced Societies*. London: Hutchinson.

Gifford, D. J. and L. L. Brooks. 1976. "The Association of Hispanists of Great Britain and Ireland, 1955-1976," *BHS* 63:95-98.

Gorz, Andre. 1977. "Technical Intelligence and the Capitalist Division of Labour." See Young and Whitty. 131-50.

Graham, Helen and Jo Labanyi (eds). 1995. *Spanish Cultural Studies: An Introduction: A Struggle for Modernity.* Oxford: Oxford U.P.

Grant, Linda. 1996. "Lessons to be learnt." *Manchester Guardian Weekly* 154 (no. 12), 19.

Grossberg, Lawrence, Cary Nelson, Paula A. Treichler. 1992. *Cultural Studies.* New York and London: Routledge.

Hall, Stuart. 1992. "Cultural Studies and its theoretical legacies" in Grossberg, Nelson and Treicher. 277-95.

Harman, Chris. 1988. *The Fire Last Time: 1968 and After.* London: Bookmarks.

Hogan, David. 1982. "Education and Class Formation: The Peculiarities of the Americans." See Apple (ed.). 32-78.

Hoggart, Richard. 1958. *The Uses of Literacy.* Harmondsworth: Penguin.

Holly, Douglas. 1977. "Education and the Social Relations of a Capitalist Society." Young and Whitty. 172-91.

Holzinger, Walter. 1977. "Ideology, imagery and the literalization of metaphor in *A secreto agravio, secreta venganza,*" *BHS* 54:203-14.

Huarte de San Juan, Juan. 1976 [1575]. *Examen de ingenios para las ciencias.* Ed. Esteban Torre. Madrid: Editora Nacional.

Jacoby, Russell. 1987. *The Last Intellectuals: American Culture in the Age of Academe.* New York: Basic Books.

Jameson, Fredric. 1993. "On Cultural Studies," *Social Text* 34:17-52.

Jordan, Barry. 1992. Review of Abigail Lee Six, *Juan Goytisolo: The Case for Chaos, BHS* 69: 394-96.

Kelly, Gail P. and Ann S. Nihlen. 1982. "Schooling and the Reproduction of Patriarchy: Unequal Workloads, Unequal Rewards." See Apple (ed.). 162-180.

L****. 1926. "Carta de Madrid." *BHS* 3: 175-77.

-----. 1930. "Carta de Madrid." *BHS* 7: 179-81.

Lambert, A. F. 1980. "The two versions of Cervantes' *El celoso extremeño*: ideology and criticism," *BHS* 62:219-231.

Lentricchia, Frank. 1980. *After the New Criticism.* Chicago: Chicago UP.

Lerena Alesón, Carlos. 1976. *Escuela, ideología y clases sociales en España.* Barcelona: Ariel.

Leys, Colin. 1989. *Politics in Britain: From Labourism to Thatcherism,* rev. ed. (London and New York: Verso)

Lomax, Derek. 1972. Review of *"Libro de buen amor" Studies,* ed. by G. B. Gybbon-Monypenny, *BHS* 49:67-68.

Mariscal, George. 1990. "An Introduction to the Ideology of Hispanism in the US and Britain." See Evans (ed.). 1-25.

Marx, Karl. 1978. *The Marx-Engels Reader.* 2nd ed. Edited by Robert C. Tucker. New York: W. W. Norton & Company.

McGaha, Michael. 1990. "Whatever Happened to Hispanism?" *Journal of Hispanic Philology* 14: 225-30.

McKendrick, Melveena. 1985. Review of David Jonathan Hildner, *Reason and the Passions in the "Comedias" of Calderón*, BHS 62:395-96.

Millington, Mark. 1989. "The Unsung Heroine: Power and Marginality in *Crónica de una muerte anunciada*," BHS 66:73-85.

Montero, Rosa. 1995[i]. "Democracy and Cultural Change" in Graham and Labanyi. 315-20.

-----. 1995[ii]. "Gender and Sexuality" in Graham and Labanyi. 381-85.

Moore, Robert. 1987. "Education and the Ideology of Production." *British Journal of Sociology of Education* 8: 227-42.

Morley, S. Griswold and Albert E. Sloman. 1952. "William James Entwistle: Two Memoirs," BHS 29: 183-92.

Mountford, Sir J.F. 1953. "Bruce Truscot." BHS 30: 10-11.

Mulhern, Francis. 1979. *The Moment of "Scrutiny."* London: NLB.

Norris, Christopher. 1992. *Uncritical Theory: Postmodernism, Intellectuals and the Gulf War.* Amherst: Massachusetts U.P.

Ohmann, Richard. 1991. "Thoughts on Cultural Studies in the United States," *Critical Studies* 3.1: 5-15.

Parker, A.A. 1953. "Reflections on a New Definition of 'Baroque Drama'," BHS 30: 142-51.

-----. 1982. Review of Gwynne Edwards, *The Prison and the Labyrinth. Studies in Calderonian tragedy*, BHS 59:340-43.

Paterson, Alan K. G. 1983. Review of *Critical Perspectives on Calderón de la Barca*, ed. by Frederick A. de Armas, David M. Gitlitz and José A. Madrigal, BHS 60: 69-70.

-----. 1993. "Tirso de Molina and the androgyne: *El Aquilis* and *La dama del olivar*", BHS 70: 105-14.

Peers, E. Alisson. (see Truscot). 1923. "Literary Pilgrimages in Spain," BHS 1: 11-15.

-----. 1924. Review of Aubrey Bell's *A Pilgrim in Spain*, BHS 2: 54-55.

-----. 1936. "The Teaching of Spanish in Secondary Schools." (Report of the Spanish Committee of the Modern Language Association, 1935, BHS 13: 61-79.

-----. 1996. *Redbrick University Revisited: The Autobiography of "Bruce Truscot."* Edited, with introduction, commentary and notes by Ann L. Mackenzie and Adrian R. Allan. Liverpool: Liverpool U.P.

Peris, Teresa Fuentes. 1996. "Drink and Social Stability: Discourses of Power in Galdós' *Fortunata y Jacinta*," BHS 73: 63-77.

Pym, Richard J. 1998. "Tragedy and the Construct Self: Considering the Subject in Spain's Seventeenth-century *Comedia*," BHS 75: 273-92.

Read, Malcolm K. 1981. *Juan Huarte de San Juan*. Boston: Twayne.

-----. 1983. *The Birth and Death of Language: Spanish Literature and Linguistics: 1300-1700.* Madrid: José Porrúa Turanzas.

-----. 1990. *Visions in Exile: Language and the Body in Spanish Literature and Linguistics: 1500-1800.* Amsterdam and Philadelphia: John Benjamins.

-----. 1992. *Language, Text, Subject: A Critique of Hispanism.* West Lafayette, Indiana: Purdue U.P.

-----. 1993. *Jorge Luis Borges and his Predecesors or Notes towards a Materialist History of Linguistic Idealism.* Chapel Hill: North Carolina U.P.: Studies in Romance Languages and Literatures [242].

-----. 1998. *Transitional Discourses: Culture and Society in Early Modern Spain*. Ottawa: Dovehouse Editions.

Rees, J.W. 1924. "Spanish Mysticism." *BHS* 2: 95-97.

Resch, Robert Paul. 1992. *Althusser and the Renewal of Marxist Social Theory*. Berkeley: California U.P.

Robertson, Sir Malcolm A. 1935. "Argentina and Great Britain," *BHS* 12: 77-88.

Rodríguez, Juan Carlos.1990 (1974). *Teoría e historia de la producción ideológica: las primeras literaturas burguesas (siglo xvi)*, 2ⁿᵈ ed. (Madrid: Akal).

-----. 1994. *Lorca y el sentido: un inconsciente para una historia*. Madrid; Akal.

-----. 1999. *Dichos y escritos (sobre "la otra sentimentalidad" y otros textos fechados depoética)*. Madrid: Hiperión.

Round, Nicholas G. 1986. Review of Read (1983), *BHS* 63: 150-52.

-----. 1992. Review of *Hispanic Studies in Honor of Alan D. Deyermond. A North American Tribute*, ed. by John S. Miletich, *BHS* 69: 179-80.

-----. 1992-93. "The Politics of Hispanism Reconstrued," *JHR* 1. 134-47.

Ruano de la Haza, J. M. 1991. Review of Alexander A. Parker, *The Mind of Calderón: Essays on the Comedias*, *BHS* 68: 537-39.

----- 1993. Review of Catherine Larson, *Language and the "Comedias": Theory and Practice*, *BHS* 70: 462-63.

Ryan, Jake, and Charles Sackrey. 1984. *Strangers in Paradise: Academics from the Working Class*. Boston: South End Press.

Sharman, Adam. 1993. Review of Barry Jordan, *British Hispanism and the Challenge of Literary Theory*, *BHS* 70: 283-84.

Sloman, Albert E. (1982) "Foreword," *BHS* 59: 189-90.

Smith, Paul Julian. 1987. *Quevedo on Parnassus: Allusion and Theory in the Love Lyric*. London: Modern Humanities Research Association.

-----. 1988[i] "Review of *Literature Among Discourses: The Spanish Golden Age*, ed. by Wlad Godzich and Nicholas Spadaccini, *BHS* 65: 294-95.

-----. 1988 [ii]. *Writing in the Margin: Spanish Literature of the Golden Age*. Oxford: Oxford U.P.

-----. 1989. *The Body Hispanic: Gender and Sexuality in Spanish and Spanish American Literature*. Oxford: Clarendon.

-----. 1991. Review of James A. Parr, *Don Quixote: An Anatomy of Subversive Discourse*, *BHS* 78: 330-31.

-----. 1992. *Laws of Desire: Questions of Homosexuality in Spanish Writing and Film, 1960-1990*. Oxford: Clarendon Press.

-----. 1994. *Desire Unlimited. The Cinema of Pedro Almodóvar*. London: Verso.

-----. 1995. *García Lorca/Almodóvar: Gender, Nationality, and the Limits of the Visible*. Cambridge: Cambridge U.P.

-----. 1996. *Vision Machines: Cinema, Literature, and Sexuality in Spain and Cuba, 1983-93*. London: Verso.

-----. 1997. Review of *Spanish Cultural Studies*, see Graham and Labanyi (eds), *BHS* 74: 528-29.

-----. 2000. *The Moderns: Time, Space and Subjectivity in Contemporary Spanish Culture*. Oxford and New York: Oxford U.P.

Sprinker, Michael. 1997. "We lost it at the movies," *MLN* 112.3.385-99

Swanson, Philip. 1996. Review of Pamela Bacarisse, *Impossible Choices: the Implications of Cultural References in the Novels of Manuel Puig*, BHS 73.222.

Truscot, Bruce. 1945. *Redbrick and these Vital Days*. London: Faber and Faber.

-----. 1946. *First Year at the University: A Freshman's Guide*. London: Faber and Faber.

-----. 1951 [1943]. *Red Brick University*. Harmondsworth: Penguin.

Turner, Graeme. 1990. *British Cultural Studies: An Introduction, Media and Popular Culture* 7. Boston: Unwin Hyman.

Walters, Gareth. 1990. Review of Paul Julian Smith, *Quevedo on Parnassus*, *BHS* 67: 188-89.

Whinnom, Keith. 1975. Review of Stephen Gilman, *The Spain of Fernando de Rojas: The Intellectual and Social Landscape of "La* Celestina," BHS 52: 158-61.

-----. 1980. "The problem of the 'best seller' in Spanish Golden-Age literature," *BHS* 57: 189-97.

Widdowson, Peter. (ed.). 1982. *Re-reading English*. London: Methuen.

Williams, Raymond. 1963. *Culture and Society: 1780-1950*. Reprinted with a postscript. Harmondsworth: Penguin.

-----. 1983. *Towards 2000*. London: Chatto & Windus, The Hogarth Press.

Wilson, E.M. 1975. "A Defence of the 'British Critics' of the 'comedia'," *Hispania* 58: 481-82.

Wilson, Margaret. 1966. *Spanish Drama of the Golden Age*. Oxford: Pergamon Press.

-----. 1992. Review of Melveena McKendrick, *Theatre in Spain, 1490-1700*, BHS 69: 193-94.

Wolfenstein, Eugene Victor. 1993. *Psychoanalytic-Marxism: Groundwork*. New York, London: The Guilford Press.

Wood, Ellen Meiksins. 1986. *The Retreat from Class: A New "True" Socialism*. London: Verso.

Young, Michael, and Geoff Whitty. 1977. *Society, State and Schooling: Readings on the Possibilities for Radical Education*. Ringmer: The Falmer Press.

About the author

Malcolm Read was born in Derby, England, in 1945. Educated at the Derby and District College of Technology (1960-64) and at Bristol University (1964-68), he graduated with a First Class Honours degree in Spanish. He gained his PhD at the University of Wales Aberystwyth (1976), where he lectured in Spanish from 1968 to 1980. He was lecturer and senior lecturer at Auckland University, New Zealand, from 1980 to 1993, during which time he held a visiting professorship at the University of the West Indies in Jamaica (1987). He moved to the USA in 1993 to become Chair of the Department of Hispanic Languages at the State University of New York at Stony Brook, where he continues to teach. Professor Read is the author of numerous books and articles in major journals on Spanish linguistics, the history of ideas, literary theory and the sociology of literature.